Escape to
PROVENCE

Escape to PROVENCE

The story of Elisabeth Starr and Winifred Fortescue
and the making of the Colline des Anglais

MAUREEN EMERSON

CHAPTER AND VERSE
SUSSEX

Published by
Chapter and Verse
King's House, 8 Church Street, Cuckfield, West Sussex RH17 5JZ, UK
First published 2008

ISBN 978-0-9558321-0-9
Copyright © Maureen Emerson, 2008

British Library Cataloguing in Publication Data
A catalogue record for this book is available from the British Library

Set in Adobe Garamond
Design by 'talkingdesign", Worthing
Printed in the UK by Alden Press Ltd

To Christina, Gavin and David

The Houses and their Occupants on the
Rue de la Fontaine Opio

Le Castello
Elisabeth Starr
An American from Philadelphia

La Bastide
Polly Cotton
Cousin to the Marquess of Anglesey

Fort Escu
Winifred Fortescue (Peggy)
Author and widow of Sir John Fortescue

San Peyre
Charles, 6th Marquess of Anglesey

Contents ❧

Part 2 ALL CHANGE

List of Illustrations

Cover: Elisabeth Starr in the courtyard of the Castello, 1934. Photograph by Lady Caroline Paget. Reproduced by permission of Mr Charles Duff.

Between pages 44 and 45

Dr Louis Starr
Mary Parrish Starr as a young woman
Louis Starr Jr
Dillwyn Parrish Starr as 2nd Lieutenant, Coldstream Guards
Elisabeth Starr as a teenager
Mary Parrish Starr
Corinne Roosevelt Robinson
Caroline Paget
Peggy Fortescue as an actress

Between 92 and 93

Elisabeth Starr in the early 1920s
Stewart Roosevelt Robinson. Portrait by Ellen Emmet Rand
Dorothea Watts in her *CARD* uniform
Dorothea and Bertie Landsberg at Villa Malcontenta
Tribute to Caroline by Rex Whistler
The Swimming Pool at the Castello, Opio, by Augustus John

ACKNOWLEDGEMENTS

By gracious permission of Her Majesty Queen Elizabeth II I have been allowed to reproduce the letter from King George V to John Fortescue, for which Her Majesty holds the copyright.

I am grateful to the following for their very special help with this book:
Henry, the 7th Marquess of Anglesey, without whom this book could not have been written, for allowing me to copy invaluable family letters and use photographs from his personal scrapbooks. Above all, for reading the entire text and giving his literary advice, coupled with unflagging encouragement over the years it took me to write this book.
The Marchioness of Anglesey, for her kind hospitality on the occasions I visited her home to work, and for her guidance and suggestions as the book progressed.
Mrs Faith Grattan, for allowing me to quote freely from her aunt's books and for her friendship, a constant flow of information, encouragement and unfailing faith that this book would see the light of day.
Mrs Fay Starr Todd of New Jersey, for her kindness in encouraging this book and lending me all she could find about Elisabeth and the Starr family, including family photographs, and for allowing me to draw freely on *The War Story of Dillwyn Parrish Starr* by Dr Louis Starr.
Mr Charles Duff, for giving me permission to copy from his precious scrapbooks and quote from family letters, including those from his father to Cecil Beaton, for reading the text, and for his friendship, advice and unfailing support for this project
Mrs Katherine Urquhart Ohno, for letting me sit under the apple trees in her garden to read and allowing me to use the fascinating correspondence of her Parrish ancestors.
Mr and Mrs Michael M. Starr, for discovering and allowing me to use illuminating papers on Elisabeth Starr and her family.
Mr Claude Marcus, for permission to translate and reproduce his article on his escape from Opio to Spain in 1943.
Mr Frank Mauran, for valuable information about Dorothea Mauran Watts Landsberg and permission to use her letters and the copy of her portrait.
Miss Elizabeth Winthrop, for fascinating conversations on the Roosevelt and Alsop sides of her family, her support, and permission to quote from the Alsop papers.
The Society of Authors as the Literary Representative of the Estate of Lady Fortescue.
To Winifred Fortescue herself, whose extracts from her books light up the pages of this biography.

And to others whose memories, guidance and permissions have been invaluable:
Mrs Patricia Alsop – Dorothy Kelleher's letter to Winifred Fortescue; Madame Arnando, cook for Elisabeth Starr and Winifred Fortescue – information on the households on the hill; Madame Andrée Bachemont and the Staff of the Municipal Archives at Cannes; Madame Danielle Baudot Laksine – introductions to people in Opio; Lady Barbara Bossom – her diaries of the months spent at the Monkey Club in Opio; Mrs Ailsa Bowker – her quotation as a guest at Opio and memories of her time there; Ms Martha Burns, The Plympton Historical Society, Mass. – research concerning Elisabeth Starr, Lucy Upton and Plympton; Mrs Dorothy Chamaide – memories of the Riviera and its wartime history, as described in *The Hideout*; Mr

Richard Chapman – Dr Dallas Pratt's papers on Elisabeth Starr and memories of
visits to the Castello; Monsieur and Madame Pierre de Courcel – their friendship
and generous hospitality; Mr Jeremy Crow of The Society of Authors – guidance
and patience in dealing with the issue of copyright; Mr Wallace Dailey, The Curator,
The Roosevelt Collection, Houghton Library, Harvard College – constant help in
sourcing reams of Roosevelt correspondence over the years; Amanda Davies – details
of the founding of the St Christope clinic; Monsieur Gilbert Etiemble – interesting
conversations about Dr Dallas Pratt; Mr Julian Fellowes – for an important
introduction; Messrs Dale Fishburn and Dudley Fishburn – letters from Winifred
Fortescue to their father; Mr Nigel Foxall – introduction to the village of Amberley;
Mrs Christine Fremantle – information about her stepfather, Charles Gouveneur
Paulding, and permission to refer to his diaries; Madame Gilosi, housekeeper to
Elisabeth Starr – memories of life at the Castello; Mr Anthony Harrington – help with
cover and portrait design; the staff of Haywards Heath Library, Sussex – patiently
tracing countless obscure books; Mr Bevis Hillier – allowing me to quote from his
biography *Young Betjeman*, reading the typescript and providing invaluable guidance;
Mr Geoffrey M.T. Jones of New York – the invasion landings and subsequent civil
duties of the Liberation Force in the south of France; Dr Valerie Langfield – history of
the Villa Malcontenta and Bertie Langford plus sound advice; Mrs Carolyn McGinnis
– reading and commenting on the typescript; the Staff of the Mediathéque of Cannes;
Monsieur Roger Michel, past Mayor of Opio, and his family – details of life in Opio
and permission to quote his father's speech; Monsieur Jean Panicacci, President of
the Museum of the Résistance at Nice; Mrs Denise Patterson, 'Denise' to whom
Richard Hillary dedicated *The Last Enemy* – valuable guidance on the chapter on
Richard Hillary; Miss Susan Perkins, Herkimer Historical Society, NY– information
on Corinne Roosevelt Robinson and her son Stewart; Miss Eve Pell – information
on Isabel Pell; Lord Phillimore – permission to use Albert C. Landsberg's poem *The
Stone*; Mr Julian Potter – help in editing this book; Mrs Jean Prest – for the interest
she and her husband have shown in the book and memories of her aunt; Ms Niki
Riley – translation of Mayor Michel's eulogy, Opio, 1951; Mr Peter Riley – much
good advice and including the book on his *Perfume from Provence* website; Mr David
Ross – technical advice and permission to draw on his biography *Richard Hillary*;
Lord Sackville – letter from Edward Sackville West to Raymond Mortimer; Sir John
and Lady Sainty – reading the typescript, meticulous corrections and sound advice;
Mr Henry D. Sharpe – information on Dorothea and Bertie Landsberg and the Villa
Malcontenta; Monsieur Marc Streitz, olive farmer *extraordinaire* – advice on the
flora and fauna of Provence; Sir Hugh Stuckley of Hartland Abbey – for information
on Winifred Fortescue's stay at Hartland and for his and his family's memories of
her time there; Mrs Rosemary Transenster, who 'knew everyone' on this part of the
Riviera – her friendship, endless fount of knowledge and valuable introductions;
Monsieur and Madame Joseph Vasselo – who taught me so much about Provençal life;
Mr Hugo Vickers – for much guidance and his fathomless knowledge of the social
scene of France and Britain; Ms Diane Winkleby – for her tactful, and vital, shaping
of the manuscript.

And last, but certainly not least:
The present owners of the Castello, San Peyre and the Bastide, who have welcomed me
into their homes and always shown patient interest during the long process of writing
this book; Philip, my husband (and unpaid business manager), who rapidly conquered
the intricacies of design and printing and read and re-read the text many times;
Christina and Mike, who were always there with sound advice; Gavin, who struggled
manfully over the years with my technical incompetence onthe laptop; David, who
made important recommendations on how to lighten and relax the style of the text
and my daughter-in-law, Philippa Baker, who, with her professional editorial expertise,
saved the day.

My thanks go to the following for photographs and illustrations:
Mrs Fay Starr Todd – Dr Louis Starr; the two photographs of Mary Parrish Starr;
Louis Starr Jr; Dillwyn Parrish Starr as a Coldstream Guards officer; Elisabeth Starr as
a teenager; portrait of Elisabeth as young woman.
Ms Ellen Rand, Mrs Mary Culver, Ms Elizabeth Winthrop – Stewart Robinson,
portrait by Ellen Emmet Rand.
Theodore Roosevelt Collection, Harvard College Library. By permission of the
Houghton Library, Harvard University (*87M-102) – Corinne Roosevelt Robinson.
Mr Frank Mauran – Doreathea Watts in her *CARD* uniform, portrait by Ruth
Thomas.
Mr Henry Sharpe – Doreathea and Bertie Landsberg at Villa Malcontenta.
Mr Charles Duff – Polly Cotton with her dog Babs; Elisabeth painting in her studio;
Elisabeth in the doorway of the Bastide; Caroline Paget and Rex Whistler in Austria;
cover photograph.
The National Portrait Gallery – Peggy as an actress by Alexander Bassano; Sir John
Fortescue by William Strang.
Mrs Faith Grattan – E.H Shepard with his daughter Mary; Peggy Fortescue at Fort
Escu; back garden of Fort Escu; salon at Fort Escu; Peggy on an English beach; Many
Waters; Peggy and The Ark on Exmoor; Peggy and Dominie in 1943.
Curtis Brown Group Ltd. By permission of the Estate of E.H. Shepard assuming there
is no other copyright holder for this illustration – Frontispiece to *Sunset House.*
Henry, 7th Marquess of Anglesey – Caroline Paget; Charles 6th Marquess of Anglesey
in court dress; Charles Anglesey at San Peyre; Caroline entering the gate of the
Castello; Caroline in the garden of the Castello.
© Estate of Rex Whistler/DACS 2007 – *Tribute to Caroline* by Rex Whistler.
Mr David Ross from the David Ross Collection – Richard Hillary in RAF uniform.
Lady Barbara Bossom – Students of the Monkey Club picking grapes.
Bridgeman Artists Copyright Service. © Estate of Augustus John; Christie's Images;
Mr and Mrs Hugh Geddes – *The Swimming Pool at the Castello* by Augustus John.

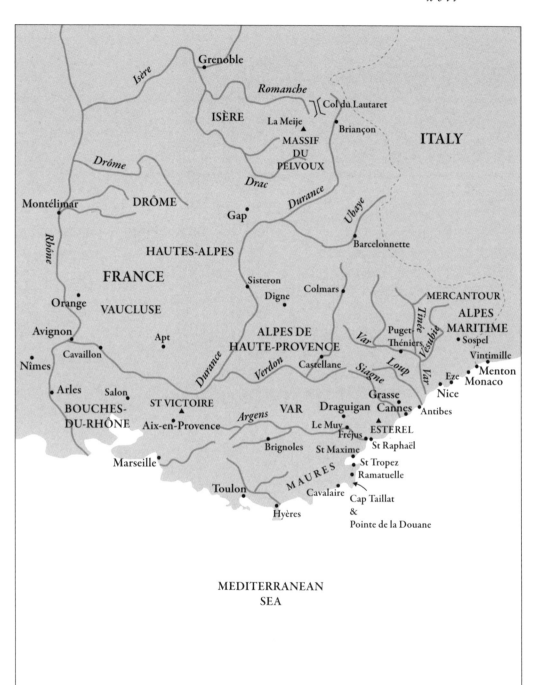

MAP OF THE RIVIERA AND
ITS HINTERLAND

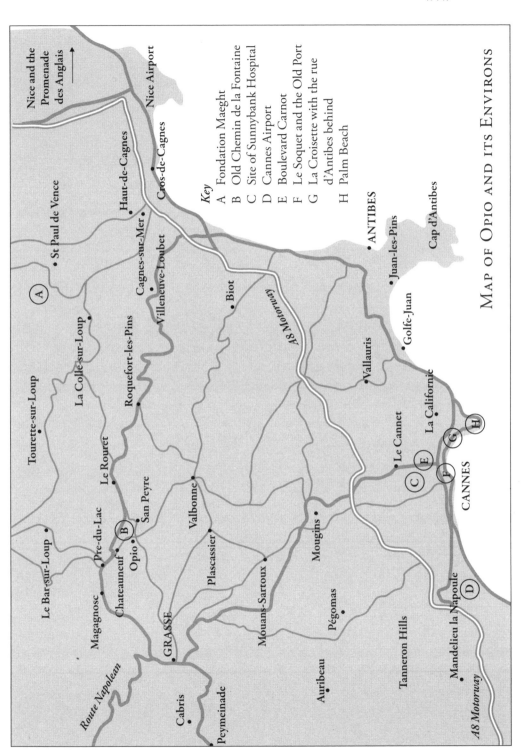

MAP OF OPIO AND ITS ENVIRONS

Key

A Fondation Maeght
B Old Chemin de la Fontaine
C Site of Sunnybank Hospital
D Cannes Airport
E Boulevard Carnot
F Le Soquet and the Old Port
G La Croisette with the rue
   d'Antibes behind
H Palm Beach

Nice and the Promenade des Anglais

Nice Airport

Cros-de-Cagnes

Haut-de-Cagnes

St Paul de Vence

Cagnes-sur-Mer

Villeneuve-Loubet

Biot

A8 Motorway

ANTIBES

Juan-les-Pins

Cap d'Antibes

Tourette-sur-Loup

La Colle-sur-Loup

Roquefort-les-Pins

Golfe-Juan

Vallauris

Le Cannet

La Californie

Le Rouret

San Peyre

Valbonne

CANNES

Le Bar-sur-Loup

Pre-du-Lac

Opio

Chateauneuf

Magagnosc

Plascassier

Mougins

GRASSE

Mouans-Sartoux

Pégomas

Auribeau

Tanneron Hills

Mandelieu la Napoule

Route Napolean

Cabris

Peymeinade

A8 Motorway

INTRODUCTION ❦

I began to research this book in the year 2000, shortly after leaving France. Now, eight years later, my children have begun to take it seriously. I feel this is an accomplishment in its own right. When I began, we had no grandchildren, now we have four. After living in the south of France for twenty-two years, we moved our home from a small farmhouse in the Alpes Maritimes to a village house in Sussex and learnt how to live in England once again. Researching and writing wove their way through these events, driven by a determination I did not realise I was capable of. But two very resolute and unusual women were behind me all the way, and I was never allowed to slacken off for long.

Almost opposites in character, Elisabeth Starr and Winifred Fortescue (known to her friends as Peggy, the name I have used in this book) were, between them, enigmatic, dramatic, obstinate and courageous – and this is their story.

Elisabeth, from Philadelphia, and Winifred, from England, left their respective countries for quite different reasons. Elisabeth turned her back on her Philadelphian family after an unhappy childhood followed by personal tragedy. The First World War, towards which she was drawn with a sense of purpose, even relief, brought exhausting and dangerous aid work on the Western Front, followed by the decision to abandon America and make her home in France. She chose the village of Opio, in the hills above Cannes.

Winifred, with her husband Sir John Fortescue, the historian of the British Army, sought in Provence an elegance of life they could neither aspire to nor afford in England. After John's death Peggy became famous, publishing her best-seller of the 1930s, *Perfume from Provence*, followed over the years by five other autobiographical books.

The two women were brought together by a mutual desire for a close and understanding friendship and the need to keep loneliness at bay. Peggy, no longer able to live in her married home with her 'beloved ghost' found her second home on Elisabeth's hillside in Opio. They had both chosen the hills above the coast, among wild flowers, vines and animals. Here, during the years of uneasy peace between the wars, they combined caring for their properties with spells of rustic living in the mountains of the High Alps or in remote coves by the sea – until the threat of war changed their lives for ever.

The history of the south of France is that of a succession of civilisations. Bordered by the Alps to the north and east and the Rhone to the west, Provence has been inhabited since prehistoric times. First came the Ligurians, followed by Greeks, Phoenicians and Romans. After the fall of Rome, Visigoths, Franks and Moors invaded this land where every Mediterranean race has left its footprint – not forgetting the marauding feet of barbarous pirates.

But in the nineteenth century came an invasion with a lighter touch, when the coastal region's winter warmth and beauty were discovered by the rich and noble of Britain, Russia and America. With them came the artists, attracted by the brilliant light and glowing colours, to which they did so much justice. From then on, apart from the clouds of war, there was no going back. The allure of that long stretch of coastline, gently lapped by the Mediterranean and protected by the mountain ranges of the Alpes Maritimes, still endures in spite of great change. The English call the entire coast, from Marseilles to Genoa, the Riviera, but the French prefer to call their portion the Côte d'Azur. The hills inland from the coast are the *arrière-pays* – and this is where 'Provence' begins its wide sweep across the south of France.

In spite of the new fashion for summer sunbathing before the Second World War, most visitors still went to their Riviera villas for several months in the winter season. These were holiday homes, often rented out to others. But for some the south of France became their only home and for them it was not the same.

Those few expatriates who made their permanent homes among the thyme-scented terraces and olive groves of the hills rather than the bougainvillea and citrus fruits of the coast below, grew to understand and enjoy the land and its people to a far greater extent than did those who seldom ventured into the mountains. But the coastal towns, for those who had transport, were sometimes visited and it was towards lively and elegant Cannes, rather than Antibes or faraway Nice, that

Elisabeth, Peggy and their friends gravitated to shop, visit a doctor or enjoy a meal in a good restaurant.

But this is not only the story of two expatriate women who were drawn to Provence in the first part of the twentieth century. It is also about the friends they gathered around them on their hillside, the houses they all lived in and the fate of those whose lives touched theirs. It is a book of portraits of people who lived through a particularly tense period of history. The Second World War would affect them all profoundly, first with the threat of occupation, then the fall of the south of France to the Vichy regime and finally the Italian and German Occupation. And, at the end of the tunnel, in an event that military historians seem to have taken rather lightly, there was bravery and drama in the liberation of the south of France by the Americans, the Free French and the southern Resistance fighting side by side.

As well as researching in archives and mediathéques in England, Paris and the south of France I have worked indirectly with universities and archives in the United States while researching this book. I have been lucky, many of Peggy's letters were discovered in sundry places, and in the underground muniments room of a great house lay a biographer's dream – files full of information concerning the two women and their families, including important correspondence written by Elisabeth. Peggy's family were immensely supportive, from the moment they received my first tentative letter. Another letter, to America, led Elisabeth's great niece who, although she knew little of Elisabeth's life, generously to send family albums, documents and correspondence that were of great value. I spent several happy hours in a small orchard in the south-east of England reading letters found in trunks in a Sussex barn, which had been written between members of the family Elisabeth had left far behind. Contacts and friendships that have sprung from writing this book have been a wonderful and unexpected bonus.

My own home, for twenty-two years, was in a neighbouring village to Opio in the hills of southern France and, by coincidence, my home in Sussex is now in the next village to where Peggy spent the war years at Many Waters. But when I think of Elisabeth and Peggy, it is always on their quiet hillside in Provence, where so much happened and which the local people called La Colline des Anglais.

Part 1

AN AMERICAN IN PROVENCE

Chapter 1 ❧
HOME

A citation of November 1919 reads: 'To Miss Starr (Elisabeth Parrish) the *Médaille de la Reconnaissance Française* in Silver. Voluntary nurse and member of the French War Emergency Fund. Head of Reconstruction of the Civilian Section of the Somme region. She showed proof of devotion and unflagging zeal.' The medal, which is awarded to foreigners in recognition of services to France, hangs from a sand-coloured ribbon with blue stripes. On one side is a rather craggy depiction of 'Marianne', the symbol of the Republic, and on the other a sprig of oak leaves. It would seal Elisabeth's bond with her adopted country. It was decisive, for it proved that here in France, her qualities had been recognised.

After four years spent on the edge of the battlefields of the Great War her beauty was beginning to fade. At thirty-one, constant exertion and years of wartime rations had caused her to lose weight, fined down her face and made her large dark eyes seem even larger. Her slender body was weary, but she still moved with grace and her walk was swift, covering the ground with long strides. Her 'soft, slow voice' with its Transatlantic accent, was attractive. Above all, she was enigmatic, which trait found its own admirers.

She had decided that the village of Opio, in the Alpes Maritimes, would become her home. East of the perfume town of Grasse and 17 kilometres above Cannes and Antibes, the village was, by any standards, very simple. The Castello, the ancient, stone-built house she chose, was tucked under the lee of a hill, overlooking one of the loveliest views in the south of France and surrounded by 8 hectares (about 20 acres) of land, laid down to grazing, olives and vines.

It was a Provençal winter when she signed the deeds in November 1921. When it rained the countryside became monochrome and the dusk fell in a grey-green mist. The air was damp and smelt of pines, and the leaves of the olive trees on the hillsides flickered with delicate silver flashes in the breeze of a dying light. Hilltop towns and villages gave themselves up to the night as oil lamps were lit one by one in the tall, narrow houses, while above them the mountain ranges faded from grey to black. As the night drew in the thick walls and tiled floors of old buildings were often chillingly cold and dank, and then it was time to burn brushwood and seasoned olive logs in the stone fireplaces. Elisabeth was content then to be the only foreigner in the village (the Italian immigrants were scarcely foreign) but that was something she would gradually change.

Far below, on the glittering coast, lay the post-war reawakening of the Riviera. The life down there did not tempt her. Generally, at that time, the very rich stayed on the coast and those of slimmer means went to the hills. Elisabeth was comfortably off rather than rich and the countryside and its animals were what she needed. So it was possibly the rustic simplicity of the small village with its promise of peace, coupled with the rather haunting atmosphere of the Castello, that attracted. She intended the old, dim house to become a sanctuary for the rest of her days. She did not intend to return to America. It was all a very long way from Philadelphia.

Elisabeth Parrish Starr was born on 29 April 1889 at 1504 Walnut Avenue, Philadelphia, Pennsylvania. She had been christened Elizabeth with a *z* but, as one of her gestures of defiance to her family, she would change the *z* to *s* in the French fashion, and that was the spelling she would always use. She was born, as the youngest child, into a secure and accepted family in the right kind of house, in a sought-after street, in a city where social standing and family achievement were of immense importance. Perhaps she would have been more extrovert and less enigmatic in temperament if she had been better loved as a child, but this is idle speculation, as is trying to understand the depth of the problems in the Starr household that would create the rift to come.

Elisabeth's father, Louis, was the son of Isaac Starr, a banker. His mother was a French woman, Lydia Ducoing, whose family, originally from Bordeaux, had fled the island of Santo Domingo (now Haiti) during the slave uprising of 1791. The Starrs were descended from an earlier Isaac Starr, an English Quaker, who emigrated from England and settled in Delaware in 1710. At forty, Louis Starr was one of

Philadelphia's most successful doctors. One of the first to establish paediatrics as a branch of medicine in its own right, he would become internationally acclaimed in his field.

The family of Mary Parrish, Elisabeth's pretty, spirited mother, was well-to-do and active in the Society of Friends as well as many charitable causes including education, concern for the poor and the abolition of slavery. Mary's Quaker pedigree was faultless. Her grandparents owned the houses and lands of Oxmead Farm, across the Delaware River in New Jersey, and so combined wealth with a highly developed social conscience. Dr Joseph Parrish, Elisabeth's great-grandfather, had kept one of the safe houses on the 'Underground Railroad' at his home at Mulberry Street in Philadelphia, helping slaves to escape from the South. This compassionate action, along with others of a similar nature, ensured the Parrish family became known for its high moral standing. Mary's uncle, Professor Edward Parrish, a pharmacist, invented Parrish's Food, whose ruby-red bottles gleamed in chemists windows in the United States and Europe for several generations.

William, Mary's father, a handsome man 'of generous impulses' did not go to college as did his clever brothers (all doctors or pharmacists) but became involved in property development, particularly the exclusive Riverton area of country homes on the New Jersey side of the Delaware River. The enterprise was eventually a success, but William did not live long enough to profit from it or enjoy the attractive house he had built for his family on the river bank. He died in 1863 at the age of forty-eight leaving his widow, his daughter Mary and her brothers Dillwyn and Alfred without the fortune that had been hoped for. The three children would have to make their own way in the world with more difficulty than many of their peers. They would all, during the course of their lives, leave America and make their homes in England and France.

A studio photograph, taken perhaps for Mary's engagement, shows an attractive young woman with a china-doll complexion and a fan held lightly against her cheek. She wears a flounced and pleated dress of velvet and taffeta, with deep collar and cuffs of thick white lace. The photographer has allowed himself a breath of pink colouring on her cheekbones. She is unlike her future children, who would inherit her husband's dark, Latin looks.

It was in no way extraordinary that Mary Parrish and Louis Starr should meet, as both families were involved in the medical circles of the city and he was probably a good catch for a girl without a large dowry. Louis, as well as having a successful medical practice and academic work, became the author of respected medical books. One of his publications, *The Hygiene of the Nursery*, contains much common-sense advice on the care of young children, although such recommendations as, 'Every well-regulated house should be provided with two nurseries, one for occupation by day, the other by night,' and 'The third floor of a house being a better elevation for a day nursery, as such rooms are remote from the ordinary domestic disturbances', shows this was not a book intended for those of slender means. Mary Parrish could have done far worse.

In September 1882 the couple went to England, where Mary's two brothers, Alfred and Dillwyn Parrish, now had active business interests. Here they were married, not in a Quaker Meeting House, but in the Parish Church of Bickley in Kent. A marriage in England possibly avoided a large and costly Philadelphian wedding. Louis was thirty-three and Mary, at twenty-seven, a rather mature bride for her generation. The profession of each of their fathers is entered on their marriage certificate simply as 'Gentleman'.

For the socially ambitious, as Mary was, the main route to the high tables of the great families of Philadelphia and on to the East Coast was to discard the Quaker mantle and become Episcopalian, the American branch of the Anglican church. In his book *Philadelphia Gentlemen*, a study of the social history of Philadelphia, Digby Baltzell writes that such a conversion was typical of those hoping to move into the indigenous aristocratic elite of the city at the end of the nineteenth century. These leading families, known as 'Proper Philadelphians', were almost exclusively Anglican or Episcopalian, 'the congregation of wealth, fashion and position', although their own origins may well have been Quaker. The city was imbued with an 'edgy or complacent class consciousness, depending on where your family stood in the social structure of the town'. Mary felt her rightful place was among the Proper Philadelphians, but the Starr family were uneasy about her aspirations, foresaw problems and were later to accuse her of being their cause.

Three children were born to the Starrs: Louis junior; Dillwyn (after his Parrish uncle) and the youngest, Elisabeth. The family home was in Rittenhouse Square, the most fashionable residential section of the city and the home of Philadelphia's 'Victorian aristocracy'. From the very first, Mary, kittenish, rather superficial and with a touch of eccentricity that would deepen as she grew older, concentrated her love and ambitions on her two sons. Her letters show she seemed to have had little interest in her only daughter and to have singled her out for indifference. It would be a long time before Elisabeth's quiet charm and dark beauty would attract admiration and love. But not, it seems, from her mother. There is a photograph of Elisabeth as a teenager, perhaps fifteen years old. She is attractive, and wears a soft hat at a rather rakish angle, perched on dark curls held back by a Gibson Girl bow. She stares straight into the camera, arms folded across her chest, perhaps to hide her hands which, like her feet, were very long. Her look is determined rather than defiant. She seems to be a girl who knows her own mind.

While the children were growing up, Louis Starr continued to establish his reputation as a medical academic and successful doctor. He needed to do so, for Mary had determined that her two sons should follow in the footsteps of other sons of Proper Philadelphians and go to the best East Coast schools and colleges. Her choice was Groton School, founded by the illustrious Endicott Peabody, loosely related to the family on Mary's side, and then Harvard. Thus a way of life was established for the couple that would carry with it the anxiety of constant money worries. Unfortunately the scholastic achievements of the Starr boys did not live up to Mary's expectations. By 1902 it was clear that neither was academic and she was forced to admit 'certainly our boys do not shine in the field of learning'. But she refused to be deflected from the course she had mapped out for them, and declared: 'Harvard must be tried for at any price.' By dint of intense private tutoring for the entrance exam, first Louis and then Dillwyn were squeezed into that most elite of colleges.

Elisabeth visited her brothers at Harvard. And there, at nineteen, petite, with upswept hair and her compelling dark eyes, she met Stewart Robinson, nephew of the President of the United States.

Chapter 2 ❧
STEWART

Stewart Robinson's mother was President Theodore Roosevelt's youngest sister, Corinne. She was as bright, energetic and intelligent as her brother. A poet, in later life she became an acclaimed public speaker and political campaigner. Not beautiful, her face nevertheless had an expression of compassion and great sweetness, borne out in her nature.

Due to the assassination of his predecessor, President William McKinley in September 1901, Theodore Roosevelt had become, at forty-three, the twenty-sixth and youngest ever President of the United States. In her book My *Philadelphia Father*, Cordelia Biddle, a Proper Philadelphian, described both her own father and Theodore as 'Products of a rough age. Surging enthusiasms, headlong championship of causes and mania for the physical. Military amateurs of the furious type, they did everything with the throttle pulled far out, they were almost belligerently Christian and American and they both began as puny little boys suffering from asthma.' This was the uncle Stewart Robinson knew and on whose country estate he spent many happy hours with his siblings.

In 1882 (the year of Louis Starr and Mary Parrish's wedding), Corinne Roosevelt married Douglas Robinson, a property developer and banker with a rather dour, reserved personality. Six years older than Corinne and successful in business, Douglas was so frequently away from home that it was she who was chiefly responsible for bringing up the family and running the houses in Orange, New Jersey; Manhattan and Herkimer in New York State. They were an amicable but not devoted couple. Four children were born: Theodore (after his uncle), Corinne (known as Corinney to distinguish her from her mother), Monroe and, in 1889, the same year as Elisabeth's birth, Corinne's precious Stewart – her 'Beloved'.

Stewart was an enchanting child, 'tow-headed, thatched-roofed and sturdy' with an extrovert charm. The children were allowed much freedom and Stewart concocted, as his personal mode of transport, a little two-wheeled cart pulled by a Shetland pony. In this he took to the roads, roaming far and wide, escorted by his four wildly excited dogs while the son of the coachman, a boy like himself, acted as groom.

His brother Monroe had entered Harvard in 1905 and Stewart, rather young at just over seventeen but insistent on going to college as well, followed him in 1906. He overlapped Elisabeth's brother Dillwyn by two years and academically their college careers followed the same path. Dillwyn was by now a famous college football player and his social life revolved around his friends, clubs and, above all, his sporting activities. For his part Stewart, now tall and well built, threw himself whole-heartedly into hedonistic pursuits and 'was having a very good time' throughout his three years at college. He seemed quite unable to apply himself to his studies of history and economics, or to attend lectures and tutorials on anything like a regular basis. Like Dillwyn and Louis Starr Jr (who had dropped out of college after one year to go into business) he was totally un-academic, demonstrating that the tradition of shoehorning young men from good families into the top universities of the country regardless of their capabilities, caused everyone concerned – students, parents and tutors alike – anxiety and frustration. And, as with Dillwyn, admonishments for bad attendance, warnings over low marks and threats of probation followed Stewart throughout his college life. But apart from one or two low moments, he always appeared good-humoured and charming. To his sister Corinney he was tremendously lovable and the 'most delicious companion'.

It is not known exactly when Elisabeth and Stewart Robinson became engaged – certainly during his college years. Between Elisabeth and Stewart's mother, Corinne, there quickly developed a strong mother-daughter relationship. The older woman gave her the unconditional love the young girl had not received from her own mother and, always referring to herself as Elisabeth's 'Heart Mother', she became a loving substitute. There are no family records of Elisabeth's engagement to Stewart (none of her letters and few papers relating to her were kept and her photographs in the family albums are not labelled). Neither is there any remaining trace of the Starrs having met either Stewart or his parents. It seems extraordinary that Louis, and especially Mary, were not overjoyed by the engagement. This should have been the fulfilment of Mary's social dreams, opening doors to presidential family gatherings, glittering receptions and visits to Sagamore Hill – the Roosevelt home at Oyster Bay, Long Island. Perhaps the Starrs felt Stewart was immature and 'loafing' rather than working, and generally showing a lack of responsibility. Although it seems he rarely drank to excess, they may have feared he would begin to follow in the footsteps of his brother Monroe who, although clever enough eventually to graduate from Harvard, was by now drinking enough to be cautioned by the authorities. Corinne's brother Elliott Roosevelt, Stewart's uncle and the father of Eleanor Roosevelt, was known to be an alcoholic whose behaviour caused great distress to his wife and family. But there may have been other, unexplained, reasons as to why Elisabeth was embraced so whole-heartedly by Corinne while a relationship with Elisabeth's parents seems to have been non-existent. It is also strange that the Robinsons agreed to their son's engagement to a girl who was rapidly becoming estranged from her own parents – a socially awkward situation to say the least. But Elisabeth captivated Corinne and her children, as was borne out by later events – but whether Douglas Robinson was similarly smitten is unknown.

Although he became a first-class hockey player, Stewart continued to miss lectures and his marks were consistently low. Tutors were hired, summer camps attended and simple and appealing little notes promising to do better were sent to those trying to keep him on the academic straight and narrow. During February of 1908 he was withdrawn from college for low marks – later being reinstated with cautions and conditions.

In July, in a round childlike hand, he wrote to his mother from a tutorial summer camp:

Dearest Mother,
You must have thought me dead or the most undutiful of sons, but this time it has really not been my fault. [He goes on to explain that they have been cut off telegraphically for two weeks and the store had run out of envelopes] ... The last two weeks have been a constant drive of work from seven in the morning until ten at night, when we go to bed feeling as if we'd been wrung through a clothes wringer. I feel rather discouraged, for in some of the tests I have not done well. This is an absolutely useless letter and

does none of the things you ask, but I am dead tired and much
discouraged and not altogether happy to-night. Tomorrow night
I promise to write all the things you asked about my bills etc.
Goodnight, dearest Mother, there is no cause for worry.
Most affectionately,
Stewart

But there was cause for worry, for although Stewart did make an effort
to improve his work, conviviality won out over study. It was now clear
it had been a mistake to send him to university at such a young age
when he had little interest in studying. He could have been sent to
the Roosevelt ranch in Dakota, as his Uncle Theodore had been in
his youth. In such an environment he might well have matured in his
own time and been content and at ease, working with animals and
waking each morning to an open-air country life, far from tutorials
and the pressure of academia. As his brother Monroe would later write
in an account of their childhood: 'When the bleak Mohawk hills were
buried deep in snow, the maple-syrup tapping, the cider-drinking
country parties, the dashing sleigh rides over field and furrow ... were
to Freddy [Stewart] an experience of delirious joy.' But he was not,
after all, the only student who was finding the discipline of college life
irksome. Many men from elite families reacted in the same way, their
college days proving to be by no means the most successful period of
their lives.

   In October Corinne, with a mixture of hope and anxiety, replied to
one of Stewart's letters: 'Your little note to father was a comfort to me
for it sounded manly and determined and that is what I want you to
be so much. There shall not be failures this time, shall there? I feel as
if I would not stand another disappointment.' He had been home for
a brief visit and Corinne goes on to say how much she loves and needs
him when he is not with them, for then 'I always feel as if a big piece of
the sunshine of home was lacking.' His father was unwell and Corinne
was worried that her husband was overworking and on the edge of a
nervous breakdown: 'I want you and Monroe both to help him by not
giving him anxiety of any kind.'

   The events of 21 February 1909 will always remain a mystery.
According to reports at the time, after attending a Saturday night
party and at about 4 o'clock in the morning, Stewart toppled through

the open window of a Harvard bedroom and dropped six floors to the ground. An hour later a patrolling policeman found his young body sprawled on the pavement below. It seemed that death had been instantaneous. When Monroe identified the body it was so badly damaged it was decided his mother should not be allowed to see it. Stewart would shortly have celebrated his twentieth birthday.

The accepted reasoning, put forward by his father at the time, was that Stewart had spent the evening with friends at the A.D. (Alpha Delta) Club in Harvard Square. At the end of the evening he had crossed the street to Hampden Hall, one of the dormitory blocks, and gone to his brother's room on the sixth floor to say goodnight. It was 11.00 p.m. and, even at that late hour, Monroe was about to leave for New York. Stewart then went to bed in a room on the same floor. Friends in adjoining rooms said they 'left him sleeping soundly'. His father surmised that in the early morning Stewart, being a fiend for fresh air, had pushed a table to the window, which was 'five feet from the floor', climbed up to open it, and fell out while half-asleep.

But there was much speculation as to the cause of death of the President's nephew. Later the family put forward contrary reasons for the fall. In an interview, his sister Corinney said that Stewart had hit his head at a party earlier in the evening and been taken to his bedroom by friends:

> The window when he opened it was very low. It was one of those low windows. His friends thought that Stewart, who used to crawl from one window to another on the outside ledge and frighten the boy in the room next to his – had either done it again and lost his balance, or else he had just gotten dizzy opening the window and fallen out ... There had been no problem, no difficulties, no anything except he was very much in love with Elizabeth Starr – but that was all right, they were engaged.

In the 1980s, Stewart's nephew, the journalist Joe Alsop, would write in his memoir *I've Seen the Best of It* that Stewart was playing a game with fellow students that involved drinking while sitting on the edge of a high window-sill. Such a scene is described by Leo Tolstoy in his account of drunken dares taken during a gathering of young aristocrats in *War and Peace*.

Stewart had been under constant pressure to improve his performance since his first term and had become the subject of his father's lively exasperation, but his temperament was naturally sunny and he was loved by many. The Roosevelt and Robinson families never countenanced the possibility of suicide. The Dean of the College wrote to his parents on 1 March 1909: 'Stewart made good in his work. Exams satisfactory.' It was too late.

To Elisabeth, the prospect of never being able to discover exactly how and why Stewart fell from that window must have been agonising. According to a letter, written many years later by a distant cousin, in her distress she blamed her parents for his death. But, if this were the case, exactly why she would do so is a mystery. Maybe it was an excuse to leave a home where she was unhappy. Whatever the reason, she left almost immediately and eventually bid farewell to America to which, except for one brief visit, she would never return.

Louis Starr's role in all this is puzzling. He was described by one of his family as someone 'whom everybody loved'. But he seemed to show no love and support to Elisabeth, even during the difficult period after Stewart's death. Was he worn down by the tension between his wife and daughter? Did he feel there would be no point in taking the side of an unresponsive young girl? He may have tried and been rebuffed. As a brilliant paediatrician, one of the first in his field with an interest in child psychology, he would surely have worked hard to resolve his own domestic problems. But just as 'the shoemaker's children never have shoes' perhaps Louis, as other fathers sometimes do in such situations, simply stopped trying to mediate, gave up and accepted the situation, unhappy as it was.

Corinne was aware of the family problems, as is borne out in some lines from a poem she wrote to Elisabeth entitled 'Impotence – To Her'. (Of the four poems Corinne wrote for her, three are entitled To Her).

> Love is so strong and yet so sadly weak!
> When I behold the glory of your eyes
> Sad with the sorrow which they may not speak –
> Dim with the forfeit of their glad sunrise,
> I long to hold and fashion all the years
> Back to your birthright and away from tears

In 1915, when Elisabeth was twenty-six and had been gone for over five years, her father published a book on adolescence. Extremely frank for its time, it was written from both a practical and psychological perspective and entitled *The Adolescent Period, Its Features and Management*. In a section on 'Suicide' he begins by describing the poverty, the unhealthy and cheerless surroundings that are contributing factors to depression in the poor. As for the upper classes,

> The foolish rich have too great ease and luxury, and too much indulgence in exciting pastimes which overshadow and destroy pleasure in simple things and produce selfishness and premature weariness of living ... School life with its intellectual forcing, monotony, fear and uncertainty as to the results of examinations and of punishment in case of failure may sometimes be predisposing conditions.

It seems Louis may have made up his own mind on the reason for Stewart's death.

And as for Elisabeth – in a chapter headed 'Disturbed Mentality' from the *Adolescent Period* Louis writes, as if from personal experience:

> Another, very contented and loving as a child, experiences a complete reversal of disposition during adolescence, turning against her parents and devotedly attaching herself to some one else; becomes very unhappy and is possessed with the idea that she is being watched and persecuted and finally throws off all family ties and duties to be independent and support herself. These are suppressions of natural affection with a craving for some unrelated, or even imaginary, older person of the same sex on whom to lavish affection, and a desire to lead what is called 'one's own life', duty to family or to society having no place in certain schools of modern thought.

These are heartfelt statements, full of frustration and hurt and obviously about his daughter.

Corinne, naturally enough, never recovered from the loss of her son, in years to come dissolving into tears whenever she saw anyone who reminded her of him. Always a poet but without a great deal of success, the tragedy prompted an outpouring of work that would be much admired – particularly by women. Distraught, she wrote several heart-wrenching poems about her grief. One of these, 'February 21st 1909', was dedicated to Stewart, recalling the day of his death:

> This was the day I died, when all Life's sun
> Was blotted out in dark and dreadful night.
> And I, who lived and laughed and loved the light,
> In one brief moment knew my race was run;
> Knew that the glory of my days was done.

And in another poem to Elisabeth, also entitled 'To Her', she wrote:

> My child in love, the beauty of your eyes
> Holds in their ardent depths a poignant pain,
> How many sad and sacramental sighs
> Breathe through their glance and wring my heart again
> What would I give could I your burden bear
> Mingled with mine; I would not sink below
> All of your grief and all of your despair
> Could I but once again transform your woe
> Into the joy whose promise fair you knew ...

Monroe, who had always considered himself the less favoured child, now had to deal with his mother's overwhelming grief for her favourite son. In a rather sad little book, dedicated to his mother and entitled *A Little Boy's Friends*, the 'Little Boy' being himself, he describes the fat little author living in the shadow of his cavalier younger brother Freddy (Stewart). He watches admiringly as the latter rides and tumbles through his childhood to the adoration of servants and family and the indulgence of his mother. When the book was published in 1926 Monroe sent a copy to Elisabeth, at her home in France, with a written dedication: 'To Dearest Elisabeth, whose care, friendship and inspiration made this little book possible. From her devoted friend. Monroe Douglas Robinson.'

In 1911, two years after Stewart's death, Louis Starr began to suffer from an acute dilatation of the heart due to overwork – 'I am never too tired to see a sick child'. He retired from his practice and related positions in the medical world of Philadelphia, bowing out with many gestures of recognition and admiration for his 'sterling honesty of thought and speech and his loyal devotion to his friends'. In commemoration the artist Joseph DeCamp painted his portrait and the sculptor Charles Grafly created a bronze bust, both displayed in the University of Pennsylvania. His professional life had been entirely satisfactory. Although the Starrs kept the Rittenhouse Square house until at least 1917 (probably renting it out), about this time Louis and Mary began a life based in Europe. Here it was cheaper to live well than it was in America and Louis was free to indulge his hobby of painting and etching landscapes. Elisabeth inherited her father's talent, but they would never discuss or admire each other's work.

Whether the shock and abandonment of Stewart's death had made Elisabeth feel she could never completely love another man again or whether she would have become attracted to other women anyway, apart from toying with another handsome and rather wild young American male who was to cross her path, for the rest of her life her deeper emotional feelings would be directed towards her own sex.

Chapter 3 ❧
DILLWYN

By spring of 1910, Elisabeth, having left her home, was already settled with a family called Upton in Halifax, Massachusetts. Along with two Upton sisters – another Elizabeth and Lucy – she began breeding dogs. The sisters were the daughters of Edgar and Bessie Upton and it was Lucy who would become an important part of Elisabeth's life. In 1911, when she was twenty-two, Elisabeth, with Lucy, bought a house plus 8 hectares (twenty acres) at Elm Street in nearby Plympton, situated in pretty, rural countryside about 55 kilometres south of Boston. The area around the small town was true farming country in the early years of the twentieth century and it still keeps its rural traditions today, its bogginess making it ideal for the cultivation of cranberries. Here the two women founded the Plympton Green Kennels and for the next six years ran a small business breeding poultry and West Ayrshire Highland Terriers. Rearing dogs and poultry was a far cry from the social ambitions of Elisabeth's mother, but by then the influence of Mary Starr had faded well into the background. Elisabeth loved animals, so it was not such a strange occupation for her to follow – and the poultry-keeping experience would eventually be more than useful. Like her father she painted, taking up sculpture later, and perhaps took lessons here, as she would wherever the opportunity arose.

The arrangement with Lucy was not one that would have been remarked upon. At that time the concept of women living together for financial or social reasons was accepted without comment by society. Even setting up house *en amitié amoureuse*, a loving friendship, was far from being regarded as more than an arrangement of convenience. It was seen to be logical that vulnerable women, with few rights, should live in such a fashion.

Elisabeth's finances are not crystal clear. Although she was breeding and selling animals, this would not have been sufficient to support her. She would be able to buy more property, keep servants, pursue her charitable work and exist without paid employment. She lived frugally, as was her nature, but did not go without. Did her hard-pressed father, at least initially, settle money on her? It seems such an amount as he could have afforded would scarcely have been sufficient to provide for the lifestyle she would keep until almost the end of her days. There may possibly have been other family money. But the answer almost certainly lies with Corinne Robinson. There is evidence that Corinne helped her financially with the mortgage for the Plympton property and that she made transfers to Elisabeth's bank, so one can assume she ensured the fiancée of her lost son would never be in want, and would be able to live in a fashion befitting her class. Corinne's constant devotion and support was of great, probably indispensable, value. And perhaps this involvement with the young woman who had been close to Stewart helped Corinne keep his memory alive.

During the Plympton years Elisabeth also met the self-possessed Dorothea Mauran Watts from Rhode Island. Known always to her friends of that time as Dolly, she was one of those cultivated Americans who felt as much at home on the boulevards of Paris as she did in Newport. Born in France, she was cosmopolitan, while remaining unmistakably American, for she never lost her 'Yankee personality'. Practical and outgoing, she would soon become another important person in Elisabeth's life.

Now with new friends, settled with Lucy in the countryside and admired and supported by Corinne and her family, these were surely contented years during which Elisabeth could relax and plan the future. But across the Atlantic, the countries of Europe were flexing their muscles, and in 1914 her brother Dillwyn went to war.

By October of that year Germany, Austro-Hungary and Turkey were at war with Britain, France and Russia. Italy, supposedly a signatory to a pact with the Central European powers, nevertheless in 1915 signed a secret treaty with the Allies. In Britain during the summer of 1914 thousands of young men hastened to join the volunteer army. In London, Harrods Department Store offered 'Acceptable Gifts for the Man on Service'. Wives and mothers would soon be able to choose from a 'Box of Good Cheer', 'Our Soldiers' Box' and, at twelve shillings, 'For the Dardanelles'.

The Democrat President Woodrow Wilson had instructed the American people to 'think neutral'. America was not to become involved in the 'European War'. For an American to join up with a European army and swear allegiance to another flag meant the loss of American citizenship. The only exception to this was joining the Foreign Legion, which was regarded as neutral. This rule assuaged the German-American element, which was becoming energetically vocal.

By August 1914 Louis Starr Jr was a father of three children and struggling with a career in the cotton brokerage business in New York. Elisabeth was long gone, busy with her dogs and chickens in Massachusetts. The next few years would change all that. Lying on the sand at Long Beach near New York while reading the latest war reports, Dillwyn suddenly announced to his friends his intention of going to France. Charming, popular and held in great affection by everyone who knew him, Dillwyn was nevertheless unemployed. Now thirty and brought up as a 'gentleman', he did not seem to be able to settle on an appropriate career and there is no evidence that he ever seriously attempted to earn his living. He dabbled in apple farming in the west and later with a finance company on Wall Street but, indulged by his parents and accompanying them on their increasingly frequent visits to England and Northern France, he seemed to be drifting pleasantly through life, enjoying his sports and friendships without any particular achievement. Of a romantic attachment there was no trace.

Poor Dr Starr – with a heart condition, a failed relationship with his daughter, a struggling elder son and a second son who seemed to avoid permanent employment, he must have been prey to a fair number of anxieties. So it was perhaps with concern but also a sense of pride that Louis and Mary received Dillwyn's announcement during a Labor Day holiday at the end of August. Abandoning the pacific precepts of his Quaker antecedents, he determined to go to Europe and 'see the war'. As a first step he set sail from New York on the SS *Hamburg* – now bearing a large red cross on her side and carrying medical aid to France. Once in London he joined up with the American Volunteer Motor Ambulance Corps, founded by the archeologist Richard Norton. Posted to Boulogne, he immediately became aware of the wages of war, as he ferried the wounded, arriving by train and horse-van from the battlefields of Arras, to the nearby military hospitals.

The war brought Dillwyn's life into focus. From entries in his diaries and the accounts of friends and colleagues, it is evident he had at last found a role in life that suited him. He recounts even horrific events in a controlled, almost matter-of-fact manner and is invariably uncomplaining, sometimes humorous, in the face of danger. The fact that so many were dying during that summer and autumn of 1914 did not seem to disturb the balanced tone of his letters, nor deter him from his ambition of getting into a proper military uniform. The repetitious ambulance work combined with periods of idleness prompted him to move on as rapidly as possible. As his father wrote in his tribute to his son, *The War Story of Dillwyn Parrish Starr,* 'He disliked the idea of being protected by a red cross on his sleeve, while so many about him were enlisted to do soldiers' work.' His two months' experience with the wounded convinced him that the German methods of making war were brutal and he came to long 'to get at them with cold steel'. Here at last was something he, sportsman-fit and used to being a team leader, could do.

The opportunity to enlist came through a friend and by early December of 1914 Dillwyn found himself back in London at Wormwood Scrubs barracks. After training he was detailed, with the rank of Petty Officer, to a 9-tonne armoured truck that carried a 3-pound gun and six men. In March of 1915, with Squadron No. 2 of the Armoured Car Division commanded by the Duke of Westminster, he left London for the front. Although Dillwyn risked losing his American citizenship, he got round the problem quite simply. In his service records, beside the line marked 'Whether of pure European descent', is written 'Canadian' followed by 'Born in Canada' (he was, of course, born in Philadelphia). As for a birth certificate, the entry reads 'Certificate not forthcoming'. This seems to have suited everyone. In his book on his son, Louis is vehemently critical of President Wilson's attitude towards the 'European War' and writes of the withholding of sympathy for the ideals of the Allies – 'a sympathy which they are very eager for here [in England] and have been justly disappointed in not receiving officially. This withholding will always be our shame. It was so little to expect, but meant so much to those who are fighting and was all they wanted from us.' Now, from their rented apartment in London, Louis began to do relief work among wounded soldiers, especially those Americans, such as Dillwyn, who had enlisted in the British Army before their own country entered the war.

Squadron No. 2 went straight into the battle of Neuve Chapelle in the middle of March. The object was to straighten out the Allied line between Armentières and La Bassée and attempts to achieve this had already cost the lives of 8,000 men on a front of ten kilometres. Dillwyn became fascinated by the idea of trench warfare and spent his spare time walking through the dugouts as close to the firing line as possible. This is where he now longed to be.

After a short leave with his parents in London in May, he was sent with his squadron to Gallipoli. Here the Allies found themselves under siege by the Turks – a formidable enemy. Through all this there seemed to be little doubt in his mind that the virtue of the Allied cause merited the high risk of death or wounding. But he missed 'American friends' and bore the brunt of America's neutrality and its policy of not coming to the aid of the Allies: 'I am constantly in hot-water about home, as all here know I am an American. Although my commander is friendly, I sometimes get furious.'

During the following couple of months he swam every day, slept under trees in the open at night and explored the country towards the firing line on foot or on horseback. He was pragmatic about the daily realities of the stench of unburied bodies, lack of drinking water and a diet of bully beef and bacon – and always the threat from snipers and flying shrapnel. The prevailing atmosphere being now only of defeat, despair and disillusion on the part of the Allies, he was relieved when the news came that the Armoured Car Division was to be disbanded.

Louis and Mary were now almost permanently in England, staying in London hotels or with Mary's brother Alfred Parrish at Amberley in West Sussex. Meeting Dillwyn at Paddington Station as he returned on leave, Mary and Louis noticed very quickly that their son was a different man to the one they had waved off at Dover. Sunburnt and fitter than ever, he spoke little of his experiences but made no secret of his ambition to get as quickly as possible into the trenches on the Western Front. His parents made no attempt to dissuade him. With a friend, he spent a month's leave shooting and fishing on Waldorf Astor's estate in Scotland. He had made up his mind that from now on he would associate himself only with fully trained soldiers and, having made the necessary contacts, accepted a much desired commission as a 2nd Lieutenant in the Special Reserve of the Coldstream Guards.

January 1916 found Dillwyn at Victoria Barracks, Windsor. In joining the Guards he had scarcely expected the rigorous attention to minutiae in dress and carriage, drill and technical detail that ensured the perfect discipline of a Guards officer. But, once in the embrace of the system, he took to it with enthusiasm, and a photograph taken at the end of his training shows just how effective it was. From an ordinary young soldier he had turned into a confident, moustached and burnished Guards Officer. Living, working and playing sport with men of a similar background to his own, he was completely happy. Here, being an American did not give rise to insults or argument, for his fellow officers considered him honourable to have joined the Allies on his own initiative.

He saw his parents frequently, for Louis and Mary took houses at Sunningdale in Berkshire and then in Windsor itself in order to be near him. Here they entertained his friends, but there was still no sign of any romantic episode in Dillwyn's life. He seems to have been a confirmed bachelor, valuing his social life, his extended family and remaining close to his parents. In July 1916 he set off again to war, this time from Waterloo Station in a reserved compartment, 'with a lunch table daintily set'. He had achieved his ambition – he was going to the front line.

By July 1916 the first wave of battles of the Marne, the Aisne and Ypres had come and gone, resulting in stalemate. The British professional army, all but destroyed in the first two years of the war, had been virtually replaced by volunteers. Strategy along the Western Front dictated that it would be mainly the British Army that would launch the offensive of the Battle of the Somme. It was eventually decided that 1 July 1916 should be the date that the British, with support from the over-stretched French Army, would begin the attack that was intended to reclaim captured ground and push back the German line. It was into this theatre of war that Dillwyn arrived in northern France on 14 July.

He was sent to a town called Bray, where he met some of his military friends, who gave him a warm reception, and he wrote home: 'I am sure that I am going to enjoy myself!' He sent many letters to his mother. In one, he is still having 'a very interesting time', as his part of the line is very active and 'there is a tremendous roar of guns all around us'. They are told to prepare for a counter-attack and are aware the Germans have had weeks to prepare for this, bringing up more men and guns. Ever cheerful Dillwyn asks for 'a small silver star for a field cap which you can get at Smiths in Ebury Street [London] like the one in my dress cap, only smaller'.

By 9 August he is playing 'socker' [sic] against the Grenadier Guards – 'and I don't know the first thing about it' – but manages to score the equalising goal. He asks his parents to send cigarettes: 'Woodbine and Goldflake are the best. The soldiers get paid very seldom and can't buy them. I have fifty men. Don't worry about me. At least I hope you will not because I shall be all right.'

For the rest of the month his battalion marched from point to point in the Albert region engaged in constant action and by late August, for the first time, he allows a note of trepidation to creep into his letter home:

Have just been relieved from the front line and moved to the reserve trenches and only wish that I may never get it any worse than I have this time. There was one casualty this morning when a Sergeant got hit in the leg by shrapnel. It is the kind of wound that I am looking for. The reserve trenches where I am now are pretty rotten having been blown in some time ago. This makes things interesting.

Encountering French soldiers at close quarters he admires them as strong, fine-looking men and praises the 'great things' they are do-ing, and is glad he has French blood in his veins through his paternal grandmother.

In early September the order came to go to Ginchy near Lesboeufs. The battalion was detailed, along with two others, to attack and drive back the Germans at this point to straighten out the line of defence. Dillwyn was about to achieve his ambition to lead his men in a charge, for he was selected as platoon commander as 'his men would follow him anywhere'. He was poised and undaunted in the face of the task ahead and his soldiers admired and trusted him. The proposed attack, on Friday 15 September, was to go down in history for two reasons: It was to be the first time in Coldstream history that the three battalions would go into battle together and the first time tanks would be used on a battlefield. Created to counter the machine gun and barbed wire, in 1916 tanks were unstable and 'mechanically immature'. However, they were scheduled to be part of the Ginchy offensive.

The trenches to be taken stretched for several hundred metres parallel to those occupied by the Guards, and between the lines was a typically desolate scene of a shattered orchard, once full of autumn fruit and now of blackened tree stumps. To the left was a sunken road full of German machine guns, and it was along this road that a squadron of tanks was to advance, to silence these guns and cover the Allied attack. Carrying, as always, his silver-topped cane, Dillwyn spent the moonlit night of 14 September talking quietly and cheerfully to his men and trying to catch a few moments of standing sleep, for they were packed tightly and there was no room to lie down. The orders were, once in no-man's land, to advance steadily in straight-line formation towards the enemy and to take the trenches one by one.

At dawn the battalion was taut and ready, waiting only for the tanks to come up the sunken road in a surprise manoeuvre and destroy the German machine gun emplacements there. At 6.20 the Guards were to go over the top. On the dot at 5.40 the tanks were heard to start up and advance. They rolled forward a short distance and, under heavy machine-gun fire, came to a complete stop. The soldiers, in their trench and poised for attack, realised immediately their left flank would be unprotected. Asked by his sergeant what they should do now, Dillwyn replied 'We will go on without them'. When the designated time of 6.20 arrived, crying 'Come on, 12 Platoon, come on!', he put one foot in a niche and, with his silver-topped cane in one hand and his revolver in the other, jumped over the edge into a hail of machine-gun and rifle fire from the trenches in front and the unprotected road on the left. Moving always ahead of his platoon, his men falling left and right behind him, he reached the first enemy trench, leapt on to the parapet and was spun into everlasting glory.

The news of Dillwyn's death came to Louis and Mary at Almond's Hotel in London, where they had taken rooms. Mary's sister-in-law, Kate Parrish of Amberley, recorded in her diary that 'Mary was pathetic in her grief and poor Louis like a statue, so wonderfully calm and self-contained.' Stricken as they were, there was much to do in Dillwyn's memory. There were many tributes in his honour. Letters of genuine sadness and compliment poured in from fellow officers and the men who had served with him in his various units from the time he joined up with the Allies in 1914. The Porcellian Club of Harvard sent an ambulance to France in his name; a bed at the American Military Hospital in Paris was funded in his memory; a stone bench was dedicated to him at Groton School and a plaque placed on the wall of Harvard College Library. A memorial service was held at the Holy

Trinity Church in Sloane Street, London, for the twenty-five officers of the Guards who fell in September on the Somme. But the greatest tribute of all was the memorial service for Dillwyn alone at Trinity Church, Lower Manhattan, in October. Britain was represented by the Consul-General and 'The church was packed with many hundred friends and relatives.' The accolades Dillwyn had not received in life were eagerly presented to him in death.

There is a row of memorial headstones to Dillwyn and his fellow soldiers in the beautiful Guards' cemetery at Ginchy in Northern France. In this great field each soldier has his own perfect bed of spring and summer flowers. For miles around, the rolling, silent countryside is enveloped in a peace that, sadly, passes all understanding.

Chapter 4 🦋
WOMEN IN UNIFORM

By 1916 Elisabeth had not had contact with her parents for seven years. Past grievances and the independent lifestyle she had chosen meant that reconciliation had now become impossible. But perhaps it had been Dillwyn's decision to go to France that spurred her, along with Lucy Upton and their friend Dolly Watts, to join the many American women heading for Europe as nurses and ambulance drivers, although it seems they did not leave until early 1916.

Back in 1902, when Elisabeth was thirteen, a family friend and neighbour at Rittenhouse Square, Dr J. William White, had removed her appendix and written a delightful verse about the event, 'In Memoriam Appendices':

> It has gone, it has fled, its brief life is sped
> It's defunct – which is better by far
> Than to twist and to turn, and to wriggle and squirm
> Inside of Elizabeth Starr.
> It has curled up and died, and lies on its side
> On a shelf, in a little glass jar;
> And I really must say I prefer it that way
> And so does Elizabeth Starr.

Now this same surgeon was instrumental in raising money for the Philadelphia Ward at the American 'Ambulance' at Neuilly in Paris. Virulently anti-neutral and making no secret of his scorn and anger at President Wilson's policy of appeasement of German-Americans, he wrote a *Primer of the War for Americans* that expounded his theory of necessary intervention and aid to the Allies. Agnes Repplier, in her biography *J. William White MD*, quotes a letter from White's friend, the American author Henry James, now living in Rye in the south-east of England:

With passion I desire that those who surround you should range
themselves intelligently on the side of civilization and humanity against the most monstrous menace that has ever, since the
birth of time, gathered strength for an assault upon the liberties,
the decencies, the pieties and fidelities, the whole liberal, genial,
many-sided energy of our race.

It was in the American hospital, with which White had been so
much involved, that Elisabeth, Lucy and Dolly began their work
in France, donning their hospital uniform 'of snow-white, with red
crosses on their breasts and a little coif on their heads, mediaeval in
its effect'. The funding of the hospital ensured that its capabilities,
plus scrupulous cleanliness, earned it a reputation that caused some
soldiers to place a note in their pocketbooks requesting they be taken
to Neuilly if they were wounded.

In the last years of the nineteenth century and into the twentieth,
Paris was the chosen European city for the sophisticated and well-
heeled of the New World. American students at the Ecole des Beaux
Arts, for example, greatly outnumbered the few Englishmen there in
the early 1900s. Rome, Florence and Berlin each had its own particular
culture, beauty and way of life, but France had firm historical links with
the United States, was a highly civilised society and welcomed *mar-
ginales*. Prince Jean-Louis de Faucigny-Lucinge, in his autobiography
Un Gentilhomme Cosmopolite observed '*Une certaine liberté de ton et de
pensée régnait en France, comme nulle part en Europe*'. (A certain liberty
of mood and thought existed in France, as in no other part of Europe).

In a more Europhile era, the American elite felt it natural to speak
at least two languages, own a home on the Continent and spend part
of the year across the Atlantic enjoying the culture of the Old World.
And it was not irrelevant that the dollar bought an appreciable amount
of francs, ensuring a comfortable standard of living at a lower cost than
in the United States. As far as the social and private lives of individuals
were concerned, France was a non-judgemental society and American
men and women of independent means found a haven in which they
could liberate inclinations unacceptable in their own country. As the
century progressed Paris, particularly, became a base for many who,
although they did not usually break the ties with their own countries,

found a true home from home for their artistic and other leanings.

Aid to France by American citizens was not a new phenomenon in 1914. An American colony consisting of businessmen, merchants and bankers was already well installed in Paris by 1860. Their social world revolved around the American Church in the Rue Berri or the Church of the Holy Trinity in the Avenue de l'Alma. This community provided significant aid to its adopted country during the Prussian siege of Paris in 1870, creating the first so-called 'American Ambulance' – an efficient and well-equipped military hospital. This was the brainchild of Dr Thomas W. Evans, an American dentist from Philadelphia who became the most sought-after dental practitioner in France. Evans had bought up the surplus medical equipment remaining from the American Civil War and found use for it when setting up the 'Ambulance'. His charm, good looks and excellent surgery won the affection of the Emperor Louis-Napoleon and his wife Eugénie.

An American Hospital for civilians had also opened its doors in the Rue Chauveau at Neuilly-sur-Seine in 1910 and, as soon as war was declared in August 1914, a new American 'Ambulance' was created at the nearby Lycée Pasteur to care for the victims of battle. It was from the courtyard of the Lycée that the first young ambulance drivers of the American Field Service, with their donated and converted Fords and Panhards, set off for the front. In spite of the uneasy policy of neutrality in their country, a growing number of Americans became determined to help the Allies in as many ways as possible following the outbreak of hostilities. In a programme of aid unprecedented in history, socialites, bankers, merchants and young graduates of Ivy League universities came together, turned their thoughts towards Europe, formed committees and began to pour money, equipment and themselves into the Allied cause. In 1916 a meeting was held at the Sorbonne in Paris to thank the United States for its help in France's hour of need. A telegram signed by thirty Americans, including Theodore Roosevelt, was read out: 'To the citizens of our great and dear sister Republic. It was the breath of France that gave us life. It was the idealism of France that formed our minds.' It was felt a debt was being repaid for the military aid and moral support France had given America during her War of Independence. Corinne, in a poem written in the same year, proclaimed:

Ah, France, who gave us Lafayette
When we were scarred as you are now
Before your wounds we humbly bow
And bless you for our deeper debt!

In early September 1914 Paris had been saved from invasion by the courageous defence of the French troops at the Battle of the Marne, assisted valiantly by the British Expeditionary Force. Now droves of women, young and not so young, American and British, along with other Allied nationalities, walked out of their comfortable drawing rooms, took off their long, soft, beribboned dresses and changed their lives and fashions for ever. Those in the field hospitals, ambulances and dressing stations exchanged damask tablecloths for blood-soaked stretchers. The men they gazed at were no longer their healthy, well-scrubbed dancing partners but the shattered, filthy and lice-ridden bodies of exhausted soldiers. In place of well-laden dinner tables, the nurses often shared a tin beaker of tea made with doubtful water and a piece of bread they ate quickly in order not to think of its origins. For many the living, working and sleeping conditions were frequently almost intolerable. A 'vigorous body brushing' was sometimes a necessary substitute for washing when the 'cup of water' was not available. Danger and suffocating weariness were, for many, constant companions. But very few gave up and went home. Their resolution grew with the horrors they endured and their bravery, in its own way, was as remarkable as that of the young soldiers sent relentlessly into the maw of battle.

The three women, as auxiliary staff under the charge of Mrs William K. Vanderbilt 'the principal American hostess in France', had joined the ranks of well-bred nurses, some of whom were already resident in Paris. Along with other volunteers, usually young, single, and preferably with a knowledge of French, they would have been expected to supply their own uniforms, pay for their voyage and be self-supporting once in France. If they then wished to join other agencies and add ambulance work to their capabilities they were, especially at the beginning of the war, sometimes asked to supply their own vehicle – and be able to drive and maintain it.

It was at the 'Ambulance' that Elisabeth began a love affair with the *poilus* (French private soldiers) that was to remain constant for the rest of her life. The British and Americans were lavish with their praise for the courage and cheerfulness of the *poilus*, 'the most courteous and gallant gentlemen imaginable'. They had entered the war clad in the scarlet trousers, knee-length blue coats and breast armour worn in the Franco-Prussian War of 1870. The need to be less conspicuous in this new type of warfare led to the adoption of the *bleu horizon* uniforms and low-crested helmets issued in 1915.

For the auxiliaries at the 'Ambulance' the days passed busily in a well-run routine of serving meals, working in the receiving hall, rolling bandages, changing dressings for every kind of wound, assisting at operations and, the most difficult job of all, nursing in the gangrene ward. So infected were the men in this ward that 'the odour seemed a conglomeration of every foul and evil thing'. Among the maimed, the burned, the blinded and the shell-shocked, Elisabeth began to win her spurs.

In the summer of 1916 an infection in her arm required an operation. Such an infection was easily caught if, with even a slight cut, one had been working with badly wounded patients. As a result she and Dolly decided to return to America for a rest. But Elisabeth did not stay long – she had other plans.

Dolly, remaining for a while at the Watts family home in Newport, wrote to Corinne Robinson, assuring her that 'Elisabeth is always herself, the most true, dependable and real soul it is our privilege to call friend.' This assertion referred to a rift with Lucy Upton caused, it seems, by the fact that Lucy wanted them all to continue to work together in a provincial hospital, but Elisabeth had begun to make enquiries about finding her own more dangerous work nearer the front line. Feeling hurt at not being consulted, Lucy did not hesitate to make her feelings known. It seems Elisabeth had tried to mollify her, promising they would join a group together – on condition they were as near to the battlefields as possible. But the quarrel had been a serious one. As Dolly confided to Corinne: 'I cannot tell you how deeply sorry I am and only pray that it will not leave a scar for Elisabeth, she has had enough ... This wonderful opportunity of pioneer work for the English [sic] Fund for French Wounded came. They have donned uniforms and are going to Peronne [on the Somme] – isn't it splendid?' She also suggested that, if Corinne wished to send money, she could do so through the auspices of the J.P. Morgan Bank in Paris, now as involved in the war as any Allied government.

The scholarly French Ambassador to the United States, Jean-Jules Jusserand (who did much to ease the eventual entry of the United States into the war) provided Elisabeth with a letter of introduction to the *'Authorités Françaises'* asking those concerned to welcome her as she joined the 'British Fund for French Wounded', for she had been 'specially recommended by the family of ex-President Roosevelt'. Madame Jusserand was a close friend of Corinne Robinson, which fact gave rise to this useful letter.

The so-called 'British' or 'English' Fund, whose correct name was The French War Emergency Fund or FWEF (in France *L'Oeuvre Anglaise*), was probably the most aristocratic aid programme working out of Britain. From its President, the Duke of Connaught (a son of Queen Victoria), through various committees to representatives throughout the counties of Britain, titles of every order prevailed. Elisabeth and Lucy, their misunderstanding resolved, were now joined by Dolly and settled down to work with the British. But Lucy would soon move on to quite another life – an event that would create yet one more change in Elisabeth's own.

From the pristine white of the American 'Ambulance' the women now changed uniforms. The winter outfit for the Fund consisted of smart blue jackets and flared skirts of heavy wool reaching to just above the ankle, a soft cap for the head and, for overwear, a long khaki gabardine coat. On the jacket collar was pinned a badge composed of a little silver cock complete with red comb – for the French Red Cross – and the letters FWEF.

Based in Peronne, Elisabeth was near the battlefield at Ginchy where Dillwyn had met his death. It is not known whether brother and sister ever met in France, for Elisabeth's name is not mentioned in their father's book *The War Story of Dillwyn Parrish Starr*, nor in Dillwyn's letters to his family. However, in the 1920s her mother's family published a small booklet, *The Parrish Family – A Reunion*, in which it seems everyone (including Elisabeth) is mentioned but Dillwyn is forgotten. In pencil, in her firm hand, Elisabeth has written angrily in her copy, 'Why isn't Dillwyn Parrish Starr in this?' So it seems he, at least, was still dear to her.

The war, tortuously, began to change course. After a period of calm on the high seas, in January 1917 Germany announced to the United

States government its decision to renew its policy of submarine warfare, causing the Americans to break off diplomatic relations. A subsequent approach by the Germans to the Mexican government to form an alliance against the United States was the last straw. President Wilson, who had been re-elected in 1916 with a greater share of the popular vote, did an about-turn and on 2 April 1917 Congress declared war on Germany. However, Wilson insisted that the United States was to be regarded not as an 'Ally' but an 'Associate'. The first regiments of the untried American Expeditionary Force, under the command of General John Pershing, crossed the Atlantic throughout the summer of 1917 and into 1918.

Among the first of those to enlist voluntarily was Louis Starr Jr. Life had not gone well for Louis. In 1912 he had founded, with a colleague, his own cotton commission merchants, Starr, Watkins and Co. While Dillwyn, deeply mourned as a hero by his parents, was spoken of with reverence, Louis was caught in a failing marriage and a falling cotton market. The opportunity to enlist in 1917 was perhaps a welcome relief. Joining as a private with the Railway Engineers, he ended the war as a 1st Lieutenant in the 6th Balloon Company. He saw continuous active service in almost every American battle, from the skirmishes on the Somme in 1917 to the second battle of the Marne in 1918, the St Mihiel salient – vigorously fought over and won by American troops – and the Meuse-Argonne offensive – the final Franco-American battle of the war. Floating high in a basket under his gas-filled balloon, swinging over the battlefields and prey to aircraft and high-flying shells, he was as brave as Dillwyn had been and as praiseworthy. But his courage would go unsung. Whether this brother and Elisabeth ever met on the war-torn stretches of the Western Front is not recorded.

In the FWEF Elisabeth began to carve out the sort of role she had longed for. As well as ambulance work, the Fund's remit was to support military hospitals, fighting men and stricken local families in every way possible and to equip emergency medical stations on the front lines. She spent the next eighteen months on the shattered, shell-cratered roads of the Western Front, always within the reach of booming guns. Under teeming rain, spring sunshine and bursting shells she transported wounded soldiers to dressing stations and field hospitals and endlessly delivered supplies, visiting far-flung and neglected medical posts, ruined villages and tiny, hopeless hospitals – anywhere wounded soldiers had been taken and where help was sorely needed. She drove along roads between wastelands where each blasted tree was like a monument to a dead soldier and where the value of life now seemed to have no meaning.

Travelling in such conditions in overworked vehicles was hazardous and exhausting. Whether ambulance or supply drivers, women were supposed to work in pairs, but if someone was sick or had been unable to report for duty, an ambulance or truck would often go out containing one slight figure, frequently driving at night and sometimes forced to do so without lights if she found herself too near the front line. All women drivers knew how to maintain their vehicles, but it could not have been easy to change a huge, unwieldy tyre, slippery with churned-up mud, and perhaps in darkness. During one of her field missions on the northern edge of her area, Elisabeth discovered a bronze cross, almost buried in the mud. She rescued and kept it for many years until one day she found for it a place of rest.

In 1917 Elisabeth was appointed Head of Reconstruction, with Dolly in the Distribution Bureau. July found her in Nesle, one of the 'rubbish heap' villages under her care. Here, with other female aid workers, two masons and a carpenter, she spent several weeks building makeshift wooden huts with cement floors and roofs covered with roofing paper, in order to encourage the peasants back to their destroyed villages. Special appeals were made to add *foyers* – properly equipped social rooms – to French military hospitals and convalescent homes where none had been before, so spartan was the lot of the French *poilu*. The only steady comfort they could rely on was the government issue of *Tabac de Troupe*, for tobacco and cigarettes were a basic need for soldiers of every army. The *foyers* project was one to which Elisabeth became particularly committed.

In March 1918 everything changed, for from then into July, Germany threw everything into one last push towards the west. Five major offensives against the Allied troops (in most of which Louis Starr Jr was involved) began with the battle of Picardy in the middle of Elisabeth's zone and turned 'Areas of Reconstruction' into battlegrounds again and everyone there into refugees once more. The field members of the Fund were evacuated along with the rest and the emphasis for aid changed from reconstruction to helping evacuees. Often under shell fire, among thousands of troops marching to and from the front, they went west while the battles raged at their heels.

A little further to the south, under the guidance of the American heiress Anne Morgan (daughter of the banker J. P. Morgan) and her partner, the lovely Anne Murray-Dike, the American Committee for the Devastated Regions of France was rapidly and efficiently evacuating itself and the people in its care. Known (from its French acronym) as *CARD*, this small organisation devoted itself to helping the people of their area in every practical way. It was based at the Château of Blérancourt in the Aisne, a château in name only. Destroyed in the French Revolution, only the grand entrance and two elegant guard houses were left. The sturdy *barraques* or wooden huts from which *CARD* ran its operation now filled the former gardens.

It was to Blérancourt that Elisabeth came, with Dolly but without Lucy, when the French War Emergency Fund began to wind down. Here she worked as a chauffeur and Dolly as a nurse. And it was here that she met two English nurses, Clare Hedley-Peek, of the Peek Frean biscuit family, and Clare's life-long companion, Winifred Morris. They would play an important role in one of Elisabeth's future projects.

A year later, back in Rhode Island, Dolly sat for a portrait drawn by the American artist Ruth Thomas. She is wearing her *CARD* nurse's uniform: a headdress with a white scarf underneath a darker one and a pointed-collared blouse. On the side of the headdress is a small rosette in the colours of the French *drapeau tricolore*.

In November 1918, to a land gripped by sadness and weariness, peace came at last. It was estimated that by 1919 the people of the United States had donated three billion dollars to France in cash and materials, not counting the funds given for the final work of reconstruction. Elisabeth Marbury, the American impresario and friend of Anne Morgan, remarked drily: 'The French did not ask for charity. France's friends did the asking while she was worshipped for her grace in receiving.' The world settled to an uneasy peace and post-war politics now ensured the love affair between France and America would begin to lose its ardour.

In Paris in 1917, Lucy Upton met E. Petrie Hoyle. Born in 1861, British by birth but now an American citizen, Hoyle was fifty-six. A strikingly handsome, powerfully built man, he was a leading member of the international homeopathic community and would be decorated three times by the French government for his work in military hospitals.

He and Lucy married quickly, towards the end of the year, embarking on what seems like a long and happy relationship. This included Lucy taking on a handful of Petrie's children in Charleston, South Carolina, and ended with his death at their second home in Mallorca, Spain, in 1955, aged ninety-four.

Charming though all this was, it would change Elisabeth's life once again, leaving her alone with 8 hectares (20 acres) and the house in Plympton, Massachusetts. Lucy had gone, and there now seemed little reason for Elisabeth to try to remake a home in America once the war was over. In 1921 she bought out Lucy's share of the land and house of Plympton Green Kennels, and this exercise must have been distressing in its finality. But the transactions were done by lawyers, for Elisabeth was by then far away in the scented hills of southern France. The settlement of the Plympton Green affairs would continue over several years, the last piece of land not being disposed of until 1930. Perhaps she felt she should not burn all her bridges too rapidly.

That she stayed in touch and visited Lucy and her family is indicated by a conversation she had many years later, in which she asked a shopkeeper in Cannes whether his oranges came from Mallorca, where the Petries had their second home. She told how she knew and loved the island and how much she missed the delicious little red sausages she had eaten there.

Chapter 5 ❧

THE CASTELLO

Europe had been ablaze and the fires had gone out. The soldiers of the world had gone back to their countries and the continent began to haul itself very shakily to its feet. For better or for worse France would now always be home for Elisabeth – after all, her grandmother had been French.

Dolly having disappeared from the scene for a spell, Elisabeth joined up with Evelyn Wyld, an English architect and designer who had been Secretary of the French War Emergency Fund. They travelled to Grasse in the south to help with the resettlement of refugees who had fled from the battlefields of the north. This was a programme carried out in conjunction with the French Red Cross and Quakers of the Allied countries. Evelyn Wyld would also make the south her home, turning to rug design and, with her friend Elizabeth Eyre de Lanux (an architect and associate of Le Corbusier), opening a shop called 'Deco' in Cannes, which failed during the Depression.

The Castello, Elisabeth's new home, had formerly sheltered eight peasant families and their animals. According to local lore it had in the past served as one of the grand summer dwellings of the monks of a local monastery, possibly the rich and powerful Benedictines of the Île St Honorat off the coast of Cannes (an order now replaced by Cistercians).

Opio had been one of the poorest villages in a remote area, the land around it annexed over the centuries by its more aggressive neighbours, leaving it struggling for survival. It was not until the boundaries were redrawn in 1865 that it was granted the land that would ensure its identity as a commune. The two villages of Opio and its loftier neighbour Châteauneuf de Grasse are perched on their respective limestone outcrops in the hills above the Mediterranean and, at that time, were surrounded by olive groves, cultivated fields and vineyards. Horses pulled ploughs between rows of truncated vines, and cows, sheep and goats grazed on the short, tough grass of the fields and *restanques,* or terraces. The soil was not good for growing cereal crops so only a small proportion of the land was laid down to wheat, and this was already giving way to the almighty vine.

From the end of the eighteenth century jasmine, *roses de Mai*, violets and tuberoses were planted on the land around Grasse to supply the growing perfume industry that would make the town world-famous. In the summer months, when the heat seemed to throb in time to the rasping of the cicadas and the warm scent of the maquis or scrubland drifted down from the hills, there were times when the very air seemed infused with perfume.

To the south-west of Opio, in the distance, lie the red volcanic rocks of the Esterel mountains, and further away still rise the Massif des Maures with their wooded heights of maritime pines and cork oaks. Here is the real, harsher Provence, whose countryside is prey to the wild mistral winds which lose their violence as they blow eastwards towards Italy. To the north-east the limestone hills grow steadily higher and more rugged until they reach the snow-capped mountains of the High Alps. The landscape is punctuated by tiny villages perched on their rocky promontories above plunging ravines. Everywhere the maquis is dotted with wild thyme, lavender and myrtle, home to scuttling lizards, small black scorpions and darting adders.

But the landscape around Grasse is less dramatic. This was the fiefdom of the Comte de Grasse, who took ship to fight the English in the American War of Independence and became a hero on that continent. Here too was born the painter Jean-Honoré Fragonard, whose round-cheeked maidens swung their lace-frilled legs on swings draped with swags of full-blown roses, and it was to here he returned to escape the violence of the French Revolution, which had put an end to the patronage of the court. Over a century later, royalty, in no danger, visited Grasse when a small dumpy figure in black took her afternoon airing down the length of the soon-to-be-named Avenue Victoria.

Surely intriguing the people of Opio as an unusual being in their midst, this is where Elisabeth settled. Now repudiating fashion, except when it brought her comfort, she adopted the long bob she would favour for the rest of her days – either with a fringe or pinned to one side. Make-up of any sort was disregarded. Her hands had rather bony, sensitive fingers and her feet were so long and slim she found it difficult to find shoes to fit and had her Greek-style sandals made specially for her by a shoemaker at St Tropez. Just as soon as trousers became more or less acceptable for women she never wore anything else, unless forced to do so for town or social occasions. She smoked cigarettes and enjoyed her own wine. Preferring climbing mountains to walking, she relaxed by expressing herself in carpentry, painting and sculpture. She was also a talented amateur architect and designer – skills she would put to good use on her hillside. Although there was always a cook at the Castello, she cooked well herself, on the close-to-nature expeditions she valued so much. These escapes to a simpler life became increasingly important as the years went by.

Her friend Peggy Fortescue described her:

> That little sleek dark head, that sweet, unlined oval face which sometimes seemed all eyes, so large they were, belonged to a girl, though the soul to be seen in those eyes was that of a woman who had struggled and suffered much. Shy as a fawn yourself, except with those who knew and loved you; refusing fiercely to exploit your beauty, your talents and your charm; the perfect child of Nature, happiest in hours of wild freedom in the mountains or by the sea, when you became part of your surroundings.

Above all, she hated fuss, and swung between needing affection and the need to be in control. That nothing frightened her is certain, and taking hair-raising risks seemed to placate her soul – even if it did little for those with her at the time.

The Castello was in the part of Opio called Opio St Peyre, on a hillside to the east of the main village and separated from it by a valley. From a crossroads on the valley floor, where six narrow roads meet, one route climbs, via two steep hair-pin bends, to the neighbouring village of Châteauneuf de Grasse and eventually on to the town of Grasse itself. Another narrow country lane to Opio, the village proper, rises past a small cemetery and swirls up and around the restored remains of an ancient fortressed château next to the town hall or *mairie*. From the terrace of the thirteenth-century church of Saint Trophime, looking south, the view stretches from the Italian Alps in the east to the Esterel in the west. Wound around the top of this hill are some simple old village houses. It is quiet and peaceful.

Elisabeth would have driven, in one of the very few cars in the neighbourhood, up yet another lane, rising north-east from the cross-roads, past olive groves, a couple of large farmhouses, some cottages and small shops. At the St Peyre *lavoir*, where the village women gathered to scrub and pound their clothes, she would have turned sharp left up a steep, narrow road, bordered by terraces and olive groves on which were dotted maritime pines and the odd Mediterranean oak. A sharp climb in low gear and another swing to the left would have brought the car on to a well-worn stony track that followed the contour of the hill. She was now on her own land, leading to her new home. The name of the road from which the track branched has changed from time to time over the years but then it was called the rue de la Fontaine, for a natural spring ran down under it to the *lavoir* below.

To the south of the narrow, stony track leading to the house were terraces of olive trees, where goats and ragged Provençal sheep grazed between dry-stone walls that swept down in rigid waves towards pine woods far below, then on to market gardens and eventually the glittering coastline and the town of Antibes. On the right, a steep bank bordered the track, flattening out as it approached the entrance to the Castello. On top of the bank, spaced well apart, were two old buildings, one large, the other small, the former being home to as many peasant families as it could hold, the latter, nearest to the Castello, occupied by Elisabeth's gardener. At the end of the track, a rough stone wall was inset with great wooden entrance gates, rarely closed in Elisabeth's lifetime. Outside and to the right of the gates a tiny and very ancient chapel, with an apsidal east end and tiny bell tower, had been used for many years as a stable or cart-shed and would become her garage.

The wooden gates gave on to a courtyard of thick, uneven paving stones. To the left of this rose the front of the tall, rather stern, house with vertical slit windows and a heavy wooden front door, inset with a metal grille. On the right a high wall ran up against the side of a two-storey cottage. Facing the main gates and enclosing the courtyard on the fourth side was another wall with, set into it, a small warped door. The whole gave an impression of rugged protectiveness. But once the warped door was manoeuvred open, another world presented itself and must surely have been one of the reasons Elisabeth chose the property. A terrace that had served as an animal enclosure was suspended in a breathtaking panorama. Ahead rose the two villages of Opio and

Châteauneuf, perched on their respective promontories. The higher, Châteauneuf, was crowned by its church tower topped by a delicate iron cage. Opio lay below, its few houses clustered around its own solid little church. In the middle distance the town of Grasse spread itself out along a fold in the mountain, and beyond rolled away the hills of the Low Alps. Further towards the south-west, with the Esterel mountains as a distant backdrop, were the hills of Tanneron where mimosa trees grew like weeds and puffed their evocative scent from their fluffy yellow flowers into the cool air of late winter. And far below the waves of descending terraces, punctuated by dark fingers of slender cypresses, was a glimpse of the sea.

The property cost Elisabeth thirty-five thousand francs, possibly paid for by Corinne until the Plympton leases were sold, and perhaps with some help from Dolly, for she had now moved in too but was not involved with the restoration, which was Elisabeth's project alone. She did two things straight away. She renamed the house, (which was cited in the deeds as 'Le Château de St Peyre') 'Mère Castello', or Mother Castle – but this soon became simply 'Le Castello'. Using the word 'mother', she wished from the very beginning to show that she and her home would be 'open to every lost, unhappy or unfortunate being'. This wish would, in years to come, be put to the test.

Two old masons were hired to begin the gruelling task of restoring and modernising. The house had suffered badly over the years. The outside was shabby and uncared for, with broken shutters punctuating the façade. Inside, the walls were smoke-blackened and many of the floors were of rough earth. In the lower rooms this was topped by a layer of ground-in manure provided by the animals that had been stabled there during the winter months. But there was one important small, tiled room on the ground floor, for this is where the peasants' babies had been born. The masons lived in servants' rooms in the house for almost two years – and by the time they were finished Elisabeth had her new home. The roof was repaired with traditional red Roman tiles. Walls were pointed, plastered, and limewashed, hall and salon floors tiled in black and white and new shutters hung at the many windows around the house. In each one of these was cut Elisabeth's own symbol – a seven-pointed star. This star is sometimes seen as a symbol of the elements and as one of the emblems of the Cherokee Indians, but she almost certainly used it to echo the points on the crown of the Statue

Dr Louis Starr

Mary Parrish Starr as a young woman

Louis Starr Jr

Dillwyn Parrish Starr as a 2nd Lieutenant, Coldstream Guards

Elisabeth Starr as a teenager

Mary Parrish Starr

Corinne Roosevelt Robinson

Caroline Paget in 1931

Peggy Fortescue as a young actress. Photograph by Alexander Bassano.
The National Portrait Gallery.

of Liberty – pointing to the 7 continents and 7 seas of the world.

The monks' former kitchen opposite the front door became the salon, the beams restored, its tall elegant windows gazing down across the terraces to the plain below. Here the furnishings were simple, with Elisabeth's own paintings on the walls, fireside chairs and a chaise longue. The cavernous fireplace, with half-moon apertures for long-ago saucepans, was restored. Its capacious chimney would one day be put to a use that had little to do with saucepans. A small room at the side of the salon became Elisabeth's library. Her books, including George Borrow's *Lavengro* (about the life of gypsies) and Charles Erskine Scott Wood's *A Poet in the Desert* (a Christmas gift from Corinne in 1915), show an affinity with those who aspired to a life of freedom. Such was the life of the Indian philosopher Rabindranath Tagore, whose *Poems* included such lines as 'The waterfall sings: I find my song, when I find my freedom,' which would have suited her down to the ground. Virtually all she had left of her life in America, her books were important and they said much about her. Manuals on poultry keeping, car maintenance, anatomy and drawing and her medical dictionary from the Great War sat alongside *Birds of the Riviera* and *All the Dogs of my Life* by Elizabeth von Arnim (who had a house in the nearby hills) and novels by John Buchan, John Galsworthy and Virginia Woolf. And one member of Elisabeth's family had not turned her back on her, for an inscription in a novel reads: 'Darling Liz. Love from E.W'. The author Edith Wharton, a distant relative by marriage, had done sterling work herself in the Great War.

But it is Corinne's books that are of the greatest interest in establishing the importance of the Roosevelt family in Elisabeth's life. She sent many, both her own and those of other authors, each with a loving dedication, usually ending with 'H.M.' for 'Heart Mother'. In *From One Woman to Another And Other Poems* of 1914: 'For my Elisabeth from one who loves and understands her.' In another, *Service and Sacrifice* published in 1919: 'For my beloved Elisabeth whose "Service and Sacrifice" in the Great War has been ardent and selfless beyond belief, and of whom no-one is quite so proud as her devoted "H.M.".' And in a copy of *Roosevelt As the Poets Saw Him* by Charles Hanson Towne, she writes: 'For my darling Elisabeth Starr for whom my brother Theodore Roosevelt had love and admiration, from her devoted H.M., 23 February 1923.' The Robinson family were loving and admiring, but they were a very long way away and perhaps, in the end, this was right for everyone.

On the same floor as the salon and to the left of the entrance door was Elisabeth's bedroom. Here she had the floor tiled pitch black and the furniture was made of zinc metal edged with broad black bands. Bedhead surrounds, cupboards, tables all matched, and the fireplace was surrounded in black stone. Madame Gilosi, her housekeeper of later years, heartily disliked working in there and pronounced it *mortuaire*. But it was, in its time, the latest thing in Art Deco, being in the style of Norman Bel Geddes, the American industrial designer who branched out into metal furniture of just this kind. The maternity room became Elisabeth's bathroom, the water being sourced from a great cistern that stood on level ground high above the house. Her taste was eclectic, for here she installed a tank bath with swans'-head taps, a touch of the *belle époque*, which caused stunned amazement to those peasants who later returned to see the room where they had been born.

One of the most striking features of the Castello was its staircase, swirling down from the first floor to ground level and on to the dining room and the kitchen below, the main flight seeming airily unsupported. It is grand and evokes a former residence designed to be grand. The dining room on the lower level, with its stone-built corner fireplace, was furnished traditionally in a no-nonsense Provençal style of dark wooden table, chairs and dresser. But set into the wooden floor of this room was a large trapdoor which, once hauled up, revealed stone steps leading down to a room that was in marked contrast to the rural solidity above. On this floor of the house, which gave on to a lower terrace, were the ancient stables – and these Elisabeth converted into her sensuous 'Arabian Room'. Two dim, cool spaces were lit by a stained-glass hanging lantern and mother-of-pearl-shaded corner lamps. In the larger, outer space, a single-jet fountain played from an old stone trough, and the walls were painted stark white and decorated with long Arab rifles. Curtains of Eastern silk hung in front of shallow arches, giving the impression of other rooms beyond. Rugs of rich colours were thrown on the floor, upon which stood mother-of-pearl-inlaid tables and chairs. In the small inner room, separated by a pierced wood partition, brightly coloured cushions were strewn on stone ledges, and on the floor a large feather mattress was covered in a sheath of colourful silk.

Outside, where the paved terrace was hung with vines, the thick entrance door was decorated with heavy North African-style ironwork and studding. Here it was always cool, and here Elisabeth and her friends relaxed and smoked opium – at least the villagers, who knew the house, always maintain that the Arabian Room was an opium *fumoir*. Opium was a sophisticated drug for bohemian Europeans at that time. If Elisabeth did indulge there is no sign it had any adverse effect on her.

A studio was indispensable. In the two-storey cottage on the opposite side of the courtyard, a flight of stairs led to a long room with a large window. Here she established her easel, her painting equipment, sculpting tools and her right to privacy. The French windows at the end of the room opened on to a narrow terrace that ran along to her little chapel-garage by the main gates. This was where, she told her close friends, she would eventually like to be buried – 'so cosy' as she put it.

The estate had to earn its keep. There were servants and gardeners to pay and the house and land to maintain. There was no jasmine crop but many vines and olive trees. The usual arrangements were made with local people who would care for these in return for a proportion of the produce. The *potager*, to which Elisabeth always attached great importance, had to be maintained to a high standard. Chickens, ducklings and rabbits were bought and the successful production or hatching of eggs became an important part of the life of the smallholding. Flocks of neighbours' sheep grazed the terraces, providing rental. In some of this she was already experienced from her years at Plympton, although there was now no Lucy to work alongside her. From now on the progress or otherwise of her livestock, along with the olive and grape harvests, wove itself into her daily life. Fortunately the Castello wine, which she appreciated, had the reputation of being extremely good. Dolly does not seem to have been deeply involved in this new life as a smallholder, but the initial rough living conditions at the Castello were to be an excellent training ground for her own future.

By 1923 Elisabeth's home was complete. Her thirty-four years had not been tranquil ones. Childhood, marked by her mother's coldness, had been followed by the tragedy of Stewart's death and the cutting of all ties with her family. She had been through the danger of warfare and had welcomed the chance of putting her life at risk in order to help its victims. Now, at last, she had found a haven. Apart from its charm there were plainly other reasons why she had chosen the Castello. This was a retreat where she would nevertheless be in a position of influence. In this small and simple rural village she would occupy one of the largest houses and have the ability and means to be respected, consulted and, most importantly, bountiful – and therefore needed. That this would fulfil her need to be wanted, even loved, there is no doubt. But it would not always be quite enough.

Corinne visited the Castello. This was almost certainly when she embarked on an arduous official tour of France in 1921, visiting cemeteries and attending ceremonies and services at war memorials, for she does not seem to have visited the country again. The house was still in the throes of restoration, but Corinne liked what she saw. In the poem 'From My Window – The Castello' she described her impressions and the view from her bedroom window as she gazed out at the village of Châteauneuf on the hillside opposite:

> 'Oh! Little town of dreams and deep sweet bells
> That clings against a line of lilac light
> What mystery within of beauty swells
> Enriching all my being as I gaze
> Knowing, no matter what may come of night
> I shall possess thee now; for all my days
>
> Elisabeth, the beauty that you are
> Has made this fair creation all your own
> For you and beauty stand as one, alone
> Just as the glory of the evening star
> Envelopes all the sky and shines afar
> Embracing heaven, being with heaven one
> The seeds of beauty, where you move are sown
> And blossom, rooted in an earthen jar.

Chapter 6 ❧

LIGHTS AND MUSIC

Now the Riviera, far below Opio, slowly began to return to a semblance of its former self. During the Great War the area had become a vast hospital for the wounded. But gradually the old life of catering to privileged visitors returned, although in an increasingly different form. By the 1920s the towns along the coast were alive with the *atmosphère excitante d'après-guerre*. As the decade advanced so did the pleasure of travelling there by train. The Golden Arrow to Dover became the Flèche d'Or at Calais, which raced on to Paris. At the Gare de Lyon one could board the PLM (Paris-Lyon-Méditerranée) Pullman Express or its overnight partner the Train Bleu – the first of its kind with metal carriages, manufactured by the Leeds Forge Company of Birmingham. This luxurious, first-class-only train sped through the night, its restaurant and wagons-lits decorated with exquisite Art Nouveau marquetry by K. Morisson and René Prou. The paintwork, blue with a gold trim, heralded its destination – the blue waters and skies of the Mediterranean. This train, headed for the sun, was the inspiration for the ballet *Le Train Bleu* of 1924, for which Jean Cocteau wrote the text, Darius Milhaud the music, with costumes designed by Coco Chanel and stage curtain painted by Pablo Picasso. And in the early 1930s Cannes would be the first town on the Côte d'Azur to have its own airport.

Although Nice was already a winter resort for the British and Russian aristocracy by the end of the eighteenth century, Cannes, which the writer Stéphan Liégard felt 'can boast a sun forged especially for duchesses', was not discovered by the international *beau monde* until the 1830s. Curving around its wide bay, the beach is blessed with sand rather than the pebbles of Nice and has a gentler climate, protected as it is by its amphitheatre of hills. At the western end is the old port, flanked by the Quai St Pierre, overlooked by the original village, Le Suquet, perched on an outcrop of rock. Believed to have been built on the site of the Ligurian town of Aegitna and owned by the Benedictine Abbey on the offshore Île St Honorat for eight centuries, during most of its history Cannes was no more than a simple fishing village. Discovery of its charms in the mid-nineteenth century by Lord Henry Brougham, an ex-Chancellor of the Exchequer of the British government, transformed it into one of the most elegant and sought-after resorts in the world. By the end of the 1880s Guy de Maupassant would write laconically of the town: '*Des princes, des princes, partout des princes.*'

In the early 1920s the small port was still filled with the wooden fishing boats and spread nets of the fishermen who frequented the bars on the quay above. Nearby, the pretty white Casino Municipal of 1907 was the gate-lodge for the palm-lined Croisette. This elegant promenade, flanked by its famous hotels, runs for around 2 kilometres along the shoreline to the eastern point. Here, in April 1929, the 'Summer Casino' – the kitsch oriental Palm Beach – was built and began its reign of costume balls, dances and receptions.

Behind the hotels, and running parallel to the Croisette, is the rue d'Antibes, always the smart shopping street of Cannes. Between these thoroughfares Napoléon Bonaparte set up overnight camp on his return from Elba in March 1815 before marching north through Grasse, destination Paris, on what would become known as the Route Napoléon. Behind the town the Boulevard Carnot gently begins the long climb into the hills, flanked on the east by the heights of La Californie, with its grand villas and stupendous views of the sea below and, on the west, the mountains of the Esterel.

But now, among the palm trees, oleander and bougainvillea, the Riviera was undergoing a change. The *belle époque* was over. As a result of the Bolshevik revolution the Russian nobility had either transformed themselves into hotel managers, receptionists or servants or simply disappeared from the coast, leaving their beautiful onion-domed churches as proof of passage. Their great villas were converted into hotels or taken over by other wealthy expatriates of both old and new money.

As the trauma of the First World War faded, the crowds of international socialites returned for the winter season. Such visits were an opportunity for glamour, sophisticated entertainment and the chance to meet old friends and make new ones. Enjoyment was enhanced by starlit nights beside the rippling Mediterranean and the frisson of a

Latin environment. It was not for nothing the couturier Jeanne Lanvin named her perfumes, created in Grasse, My Sin, Scandale, Rumeur and Prétexte. At cocktail hour on the Croisette (which began life as the 'Path of the Little Cross') the lounges of the Carlton, the Grand Hotel and the flower-decked galleries of the Hotel Gray et Albion were filled with well-bred voices of diverse nationalities. These included *le gratin*, the royalty and aristocrats of Europe, who chattered to the accompaniment of the clinking of ice in newly created cocktails, and the tinkling of Irving Berlin or Jerome Kern tunes on a baby grand. Later in the evening there would be dinners in private houses or at fashionable restaurants. The women chose their *garçonne*-look, drop-waisted gowns from Poiret, Molyneux or Vionnet, worn over silver hose and, to keep off the chill of a Riviera winter evening, cloak-coats edged with fur. For the young, and sometimes not-so-young, it was mandatory to spend the rest of the evening dancing the two-step, charleston or tango in one of the newest creations of the 1920s – the nightclub, 'the fever of the age'. How better, if one had the means, to try to forget, even for a moment, those lost forever?

For many decades the hotels had closed their doors firmly from early spring until the beginning of the winter season, for it would have been unthinkable to visit the coast during the scorching summer months. But now a new, younger set, *La Bohème Chic*, began to realise there was much pleasure to be had in lying in the sun on a beach by a warm, clear sea. In 1924, on the Cap d'Antibes, Scott Fitzgerald's *Tender is the Night* was born when he and his tempestuous Zelda, with their friends the Murphys, set the astonishing trend for summers in the sun. To the west, at Juan-les-Pins, the jazz scene on the Cote d'Azur was born. It was here that beach pyjamas were first worn, to the despair of the old guard of nearby Cannes, and Jean Patou invented the first sun cream – Huile de Chaldée.

But the summer season was slow to take off. The financial crash in 1929 kept all but the richest Americans away and the subsequent collapse of sterling had the same effect on the British. Happily for the coast, soon the French themselves realised they did not have to take a chance on the weather in northern resorts such as Deauville and Le Touquet and, with the growing acceptance of a golden skin, turned their faces to the south. The vogue for sunbathing and outdoor exercise became firmly established. In 1931 the most important hotels of the region held a meeting during which a collective decision was made to open for the entire year. So the city-dwelling middle-classes began to take their summer holidays in the south of France and changed the ambiance of the Riviera for ever.

As the 1920s passed into the 1930s fashion became more sober, as did the general mood. The straight, low-waisted dresses, fringes and long, swinging necklaces of the past decade gave way to less racy pleated skirts, worn with sailor blouses or jumpers and lace-up shoes for informal wear, all more appropriate in the Depression years. Breasts reappeared and well-fitting suits with slim skirts made their appearance. Hats were still important, now often perched on the top of the head or brimmed and tilted fetchingly over one eye, more flattering than the tight cloche of past years. Trousers for women began to creep into some sort of acceptability.

The contrast between the coast and the hills was never more marked than at this point in time, and there were those in the hills who did not go down to the coast during their lifetime. While the towns below sparkled with electric light, running water and gleaming bathrooms, a short motor ride to a hill village would reveal lighting by paraffin lamps and, for many households, the only water had to be fetched from the village pump. Clothes washing was still done in the communal washing trough and flush lavatories did not appear, in some cases, until the early 1960s. In what was then intensely rural, even primitive countryside, the peasants still took their animals into the lower rooms of their homes in winter, as they would for many more years. Conditions of life were as frugal as they had been over the past few centuries. Even if she had been rich rather than comfortably-off, the hills were where Elisabeth preferred to be and where she was happy. An aura of monastic seclusion suited her and she made no secret of the fact that she heartily disliked the life of the smart set. Although she took her visitors to the sophisticated places they yearned to see when they visited the south, it was an obligation and not a pleasure.

For Dolly, however, *La Bohème Chic* was not spurned when the time came.

Chapter 7 🦋

CHARLES GOUVENEUR PAULDING

'Gouvie dear,' wrote Dolly in November 1923, 'I've just come back from a long rainy afternoon at La Rourée, the partridge were delicious for lunch and Papa was glad of your letter. I wish you were here because I wish awfully we could all dance. Though it would be rather hard on you if, with the wish, I could not produce a *partenaire*.' Elisabeth and Dolly had just bid goodbye to their winter visitors, and Dolly's parents had taken, for the season, the elegant eighteenth-century Château de La Rourée, a short drive away from the Castello.

Elisabeth had not quite finished with men. Charles Gouveneur Paulding, an international American, schooled in France and the United States, badly wanted to marry her and, to this end, made several rather highly charged visits to Opio in the early 1920s. Known affectionately as Gouvie, Paulding was from Cold Springs, New York, and distantly related to Dolly. Members of his family included a mayor of New York, an admiral and the writer James Kirke Paulding, reputed to have been the originator of 'Peter Piper picked a peck of pickled peppers'. Seven years younger than Elisabeth, he had left his Harvard studies to become Private Secretary to the Director of the Rockefeller War Relief Commission to Europe during the Great War. They had possibly met in France during the war as he always called her 'Starr' – her wartime name.

With the war over and no college degree, like some of the other men who had passed through Elisabeth's life, Gouvie seemed unable to settle on any sort of career. In early 1922 he was leading a tormented existence of drunken brawls – in Paris throwing a stool through the door of Maurice's Bar: 'They rush out like ants' – and frequent liaisons with girls of various nationalities. Handsome in a 1920s fashion and over 1.8 metres (6 feet) tall, he had no problem in attracting a stream of young women with whom he fell in and out of love with ease.

August of 1923 found Gouvie in Opio, visiting the Monte Carlo casino with Elisabeth and Dolly and pressing his case. Feeling that the calm, controlled Elisabeth might well be his salvation and give his life ballast and substance, he persuaded her, initially successfully, that they could have a future together. What Elisabeth's reasoning was in all this is unclear. As well as being drawn romantically to women she also seems to have been attracted by wild, good-looking young men. She may have felt that Gouvie was basically sound raw material and that he had potential, if hidden under a seemingly feckless demeanour. Perhaps he was simply large and attractive and it might not be bad to have such a person in her life. Above all, she may have been drawn to him by the temptation to have a child (for she would say how she regretted this had never happened) – a child with whom she would not have made the same mistakes as her parents had with her. So by the autumn of 1923 it was a 'maybe' on Elisabeth's part.

Gouvie's abandoned diary and papers were found many years later in the attic of the Castello. In the diary is an account of his life when he returned to the United States in the winter of that year. He was in Boston, disorientated and, as well as finding it difficult to get started as a writer and translator, quickly discovered yet another alluring girl. Clinging to the thought of Elisabeth and stability, he wrote: 'I read what I wrote about Evangeline. I don't even bother to go back to Sylvia, Jane, Olivia, Milly, Peggy, Lizok – and how can I trust this latest business? Well, there must be no new name this winter.'

True to his word, he determined it would be Elisabeth he would concentrate on, and to this end began to send her letters containing plans for their future together and his proposed return to France the following summer. She replied, irregularly, both coolly and warmly, which only served to increase his keenness. In his diary he agonised: 'I must see Elisabeth and must marry if only she could possibly want to. It would be unbelievable but I would do my best never to fail her. Dearest Elisabeth, if you can only care for me and forgive my littleness and weakness. It is only in certain directions. In others I am strong.' But not so strong. The properties at Plympton, where Elisabeth and Lucy had happily raised their dogs and chickens for six years before the war, still needed attention and Elisabeth asked Gouvie to help her with this as he was on the spot – a request he found 'a fearful nuisance' and so did nothing about. By the end of the year he received a curt telegram from faraway Opio: 'Doing Plympton Green myself.' But by then he had managed to find a job translating, from French into English, a book on the Great War by Jean de Pierrefeu. This provided funds, so Christmas and New Year became a perfect excuse for social-ising in New York. After a dinner party at which he met yet another beguiling girl he wrote: 'I am perfectly aware of the danger to Opio all through the evening – I feel the dissolution and can do nothing about it ... My God, it endangers Opio and everything else. I have not the faintest trace of will power.' The year ended with frequent visits to The Eagle, a nightclub on 57th Street: 'A frightful New Year's racket but the industrial equivalent of the church bells across the valley at Opio.'

Nevertheless, by October 1924 he had managed to get back to Provence, full of uneasy hope. His mother wrote to him there, from Annecy in the French Savoy: 'Darling Boy, Longing for news that you are good and happy – that Elisabeth is improving [perhaps she had succumbed to one of her many chills] and more nearly yours, since you want her. No bottles!'

The two 'lovers' made a trip to Aix-en-Provence together and, in a truly terrible poem he called 'Fever in Aix', Gouvie describes lying in bed in the room below Elisabeth's and trying to sleep:

> And does this system speed the hours,
> Which grow no faster than do flowers,
> So better to face the room above,
> Where fever fights it out with love.

If Elisabeth was indeed suffering from a chill, she may have found this a rather useful excuse for warding off Gouvie's ardent advances.

But the romance was over. For Elisabeth the attraction was no longer there and Gouvie was not worth the risk and the sacrifice. A friend of them all and an occasional visitor to the Castello was Howard Morley Robertson, a young American-British architect destined to become President of the Royal Institute of British Architects and to receive a knighthood. A letter of his, which probably served to dash Gouvie's hopes permanently, survives among the latter's papers: 'Gouvie, in the last year or so I have had my suspicions confirmed. I have the soul of a *petit bourgeois*!' He refers to the relationship between Elisabeth and

Dolly. He had also discovered Elisabeth's true age.

Although they remained friends, Elisabeth would never again contemplate the possibility of marriage. Gouvie eventually became a respected journalist, was widowed and then married Virgilia Peterson, critic, translator and literary programme host on early television. When, many years later, copies of his discovered diary were sent to him in America, he replied to the sender: 'I spent an evening of considerable embarrassment.'

As for Dolly, according to the letter she sent to Gouvie after one of his visits to Opio, she seems to have regarded the whole episode with amusement.

Chapter 8 ❧

St Christophe

In April 1921 the gentle Louis Starr Jr, for whom life had been fraught with difficulties, had died in London. Beset with financial problems, he had left America after being demobbed. Settling into a lonely existence in Upper Hornsey Rise in Islington, divorced from his wife Margaret and far from his three children, his new life was far removed from the one his mother had wished for him. One spring day, in his lodgings, he collapsed suddenly from a cerebral haemorrhage. He was thirty-eight. His parents, staying in Dinard in Britanny, were visited by Mary's brother Alfred Parrish as soon as news of the death reached the family. Alfred wrote to his wife, Kate:

> I went in to see Louis Starr yesterday and he seems to be tak-
> ing the death of his son very calmly and philosophically. I fear
> sister Mary is having the worst time, because it seems likely that
> there will have to be a coroner's inquest to investigate the cause
> of death. I hope Mary keeps out of it all but I fear that is not
> her way. I rather gather that Dillwyn Starr, the soldier of the
> Coldstream Guards, had all the love and interest of the Starrs'.

But Elisabeth would later name Louis's son, her nephew, as her Stateside executor.

From then on, into old age and living on the north coast of France, on the same land mass as their daughter, as far as they were concerned Louis and Mary were childless. Four years later, in September 1925, Elisabeth's father died in the Villa Castlemar in Dinard. He was seventy-six. Family life had failed him (or he had failed his family, one will never know which) except for the single-minded devotion of Mary. But his last years were rendered more pleasant by the acclaim given to his etchings of scenes of the French countryside, which were shown at various exhibitions in London and Philadelphia. At his death, tributes and condolences poured in from America and England. His small estate, which included their Dark Harbor holiday house in Maine, was left exclusively to Mary. Elisabeth was not mentioned in his will.

Mary's tendency to a certain scattiness became total distress. Writing from Dinard to her family in Amberley she was: 'Made more unhappy by the countless papers and the FLOWERS!!! I just can't talk about it much less face it. I can't get on without "dear uncle" for months as the others do.' Knowing she should leave what had become their home in Dinard to settle back in the States, half wishing to remain in France, uncertain as to whether to try to lend her French servants out in order not to lose them completely, dreading the journey back to America, all caused the months after Louis's death to be a period of total confusion. 'I could cry,' she wrote in despair, in the midst of all these muddled plans, 'I wonder if HE knew how much they [his colleagues] and I too loved and appreciated him and if I couldn't in some subtle way have managed to keep him longer.'

She quickly had offers of help from her own Parrish family in America and even from a cousin of the Starrs, which family had been warily disapproving of her. So for the next few years her time was spent with relatives, at her house in Dinard (which she kept on) or with her brother Alfred and Kate Parrish in Amberley and at their villa Il Poderino near Florence. Making the best of things, she settled down to being an eccentric and amusing aunt and great-aunt. She died, at seventy-three, in New York in December 1928, three years after her husband. How did she look back on her family life and the fate of her children? It is possible that her particular mixture of targeted affec-tion and unthinking selfishness protected her from self-reproach. But, poignantly, in her will Mary left half her small estate (of which there was little left) to Elisabeth – a daughter so estranged she felt unable to get on a train and visit her mother in Northern France after her father's death. As well as small bequests to other members of her family, to Elisabeth she also left her diamond pendant and silver fox fur, to be sent care of Morgan's Bank in Paris. It is said that one grieves most over the death of a parent with whom one did not get on, for then any prospect of a reconciliation is lost for ever. Now at thirty-nine, once one of a family of five, Elisabeth was truly alone.

With no realistic chance of having a child of her own, in 1926 Elisabeth embarked, with Dolly, on a project that would go some small way towards filling this gap. They had seen only too closely the effect of malnutrition brought on by the war and the many sick and malformed children left in its wake. One of the sad products of those dark years was tuberculosis of the bone and their plan was to open a modern convalescent home for children who had undergone treatment for the disease. This needed funding. Much as she disliked the life of the *beau monde*, Elisabeth now felt herself obliged to approach and even charm them. They were indispensable for their position in society and their wealth. It must have been an agony for her to don a smart blouse and skirt and, supported by the more sophisticated Dolly, begin to beg for funds from the owners and tenants of the grandest houses in the area. But she and Dolly were not alone.

The Pagets were a family of note in this part of Provence. They had owned the Château Garibondy on the edge of the village of Mougins, about 10 kilometres above Cannes, since the end of the nineteenth century. Garibondy was a *belle époque* house with a view of the Mediterranean, surrounded by parkland and gardens in which grew an umbrella pine planted by Queen Victoria at the beginning of the 1890s. The owner of the house in the 1920s was the elderly Amy Paget, a daughter of Lord Alfred Paget, Equerry to the Royal Household and twelfth child of the one-legged 1st Marquess of Anglesey, who won fame at the battle of Waterloo. Her mother had been Lady-in-Waiting and Wardrobe Mistress to Queen Victoria. Unmarried, Amy had inherited Garibondy from her parents, made the Mougins château her permanent home and was much involved in local life in all its aspects. She was consequently one of the *grandes dames* of the expatriate community and a great asset to Elisabeth, having the ability to sail into any elegant house and cajole its inhabitants into contributing generously to 'their' little clinic.

Gradually the financing came together. A small olive mill on a south-facing site had come up for sale about ten minutes walk from the Castello, in the commune of Châteauneuf de Grasse, an ideal situation. The plans for the building of the clinic were drawn up by Elisabeth. This was a scheme she had nurtured for some time and, as soon as it was well on its way to becoming a reality, she invited over the two English nurses she had worked with at Anne Morgan's CARD organisation in the north of France at the end of the war. These were Clare Hedley-Peek and Winifred Morris – or Hedley and

Morris as they would always be called by their wartime colleagues. They came almost immediately and, in April 1926, having started off from Southampton and driven across France, arrived in Châteauneuf. Clare wrote in her driving log: 'We found Watts [Dolly] waiting for us in the sweetest little house imaginable surrounded by glorious views of the mountains stretching away on every side.'

Their nursing careers had started in the slum hospitals of the East End of London in the first years of the twentieth century, continued with caring for the wounded on a hospital barge off Dunkirk in the First World War (until this was badly damaged by bombs) then nursing with CARD in the Aisne region, helping to mop up the detritus of war. Now, among the quiet, scented terraces of Provence, they would settle for the next fourteen years – until their lives were disrupted by yet another war.

The building of the clinic block took over two years. Plain, two-storeyed, with long balconies wide enough to take beds and cots facing the sun, it was to be run on the modern principle of heliotherapy – therapeutic treatment by sunlight. The idea was that the children were to be exposed for a period each sunny day in order to strengthen weak and brittle bones. On 12 September 1928 the contract for the association of the clinic was signed. It was named St Christophe.

The project was funded principally by Bridget Guinness, an artist, through her husband, the banker Benjamin Seymour Guinness. Their Mougins home was Nôtre Dame de Vie, later to be owned by Pablo Picasso. Although it was fashionable for the rich to found and fund private hospitals (especially for children), St Christophe was on a small scale and rather tucked away. So the committee and patron list from 1930–33 is surprisingly impressive. The amiable Duke of Connaught, now a widower with a house on the Riviera, agreed to become patron. This was a great coup, for where he went others followed. One of those who did follow were the ex-Duchess of Marlborough, Consuelo Vanderbilt Balsan, now happily married to the pioneer aviator Jacques Balsan, whose family had, over many years, manufactured the *bleu horizon* uniform for the French Army. Also rounded up were the Comte de Grouchy, whose ancestor, detailed to bring reinforcements, Napoléon had looked for in vain on the battlefield of Waterloo; Lady Trent of Nottingham, wife of the founder of Boots the Chemist, whose villa, Springland, was in Cannes;

Mrs Cunliffe-Owen, wife of Hugo of the British-American Tobacco Company and founder of the Cunliffe-Owen Aircraft Corporation; Sir Henry Mallaby-Deeley, designer of the Prince's Golf Club at Sandwich Bay in Kent; Princess Gennaro de Bourbon des Deux Siciles, with Baroness Knut-Bond representing the Swedish aristocracy.

Elisabeth gradually withdrew from the actual running of the clinic, leaving the administration in many capable hands, but she kept in close touch with the children as they came and went, making sure they wanted for nothing and visiting frequently. Using her talent for carpentry she built toys for their enjoyment, including an exquisite dolls' house, fully equipped with furniture. At Christmas time she always appeared, laden with presents.

The children were always there; she could simply walk up the hill and love them.

Chapter 9 ✿

MALCONTENTA

At what stage did Dolly begin to feel it was time to move on from the bucolic, 'comfortable peasant' existence of a sunlit hillside in Provence? Already spending far less time at the Castello by the end of the 1920s, she was always able to stay in the family house in Newport, Rhode Island, or join her parents, who travelled constantly in Europe. Sometime in the 1930s she bought a home of her own in Venice. She did not abandon the St Christophe clinic, remaining vice-chairman for several years. But by 1938 she had left Opio and was being rowed in a gondola by L.P. Hartley, author of *The Go-Between,* through the water-gate that led to the Palladian Villa Malcontenta. She was going to have dinner with the man she would marry, Alberto Landsberg, in what was to become her impressive new home.

Alberto Clinton Landsberg, always known as 'Bertie', was a Brazilian of German-Jewish extraction whose father had been financial advisor to the Emperor of Brazil and whose mother was American. He was artistic, an aesthete with a well-developed sense of humour, and bisexual. An internationalist, educated at Harrow and Trinity College, Cambridge, he had friends everywhere and was at home in most of the cities of Europe.

In the early years of the century his close friend, the architect Paul Rodocanachi, built and, with Bertie, decorated a *hôtel particulier* – a grand town house set in a small park at Neuilly on the outskirts of Paris. It was from here that Bertie – discreetly in order not to offend Paul – would climb out of a window dressed in a French sailor's outfit and visit a local brothel. Such escapades he would recount to friends with great gusto in later years. In 1926 the house was sold to the Chilean collector Arturo Lopez-Willshaw. It is now the Musée des Automates, dwarfed by the apartment blocks that fill the park.

Bertie had published a book of poems called *Tumult and Order,* for which Picasso had drawn his portrait. One, 'The Stone', describes a particularly heavy hangover:

Like a stone alone, I roll in a hole
Such is life, And its strife
And rest, At its best
All champagne is vain –
All drink, Makes breath stink
In a hole, I roll
Alone, Like a stone

In 1925, Bertie, always short of funds and with the Neuilly house about to be sold, left for Italy. Catherine d'Erlanger, a French woman of good family married to the banker Baron Frédéric d'Erlanger and smitten by Bertie's particular charm, had bought him the supremely elegant but decrepit Villa Malcontenta on the Brenta Canal near Venice.

'Malcontenta' was a local name that had originated either from the outlaws or *malcontenti* who roamed the deserted marshes of the area at the time the house was built, or from the legend of a disturbed woman. This told of 'La Malcontenta', whose family decreed she should be kept in the countryside, away from the eyes of sophisticated Venetians. The real name of the house was, and is, the Villa Foscari, having been built by Andrea Palladio for two Foscari brothers in the mid-1500s. The brothers were descendants of the famous Doge Francesco Foscari, who was head of the Venetian Republic at the height of its power and prosperity.

Designed to be approached by water, Villa Malcontenta rose as a giant cube fronted by a great loggia. Level with the first floor, the loggia was approached on each side by sweeping staircases and protected by a roof held aloft by eight Ionic columns. The building had been considered one of Palladio's masterpieces.

But in 1925 Malcontenta was no longer grand. Occupied by Austrian troops during the 1848 siege of Venice, used as a military hospital in the Great War and as a granary and storehouse by local farmers, it had suffered greatly. Everything of wood had been stripped out and the frescoes, its great treasures, whitewashed over. The French writer Paul Morand, describing the enormous project Bertie was taking on, felt that 'one lifetime wouldn't be long enough'. In his book *Venises* he tells how, after a dinner eaten off assorted china while seated on wooden boxes and 'straw chairs', guests were asked to keep their knives in order to set to and scrape the whitewash from the surrounding walls. Underneath frescoes by Giovanni Battista Zelotti and Battista Franco were gradually exposed. Among the famous guests who participated in this 'restoration' were Sergei Diaghilev and the dancer Serge Lifar. The ancient, delicately coloured wall paintings, both graceful and powerful, filled the walls in the great salon under the soaring vaulted ceiling. In the Room of the Giants immense Baroque titans lay prone among the bases of columns, struck down by one of Jupiter's thunderbolts. Such dramatic surprises were gradually revealed throughout the house.

Bertie planted trees in the grounds for protection and to dispel the rather desolate feel of the surrounding marshlands. An avenue of poplars added to the elegance and a grove of willows became the haunt of nightingales. The restoration became his passion. Never really finished, rustic rather than *soignée*, Villa Malcontenta was nevertheless a magical place and loved by Dolly who accepted it as it was. Here, according to an architectural magazine of the time, 'The beautifully weathered brown and orange sails of barges plying between Venice and Padua are seen all day long beyond these perfect columns that are tarnished silver in colour.'

This was the very different world Dorothea, never again to be called 'Dolly', exchanged for Opio. Malcontenta was open house to international celebrities – the dancers, writers and artists of the period – which suited her very well. So when one day Bertie said 'You are fifty, I'm fifty. Our ages total one hundred. Let's get married,' she was in total agreement. Theirs was an exceptionally contented arrangement. She brought her New World practicality to bear on their lives and bossed and cherished Bertie to his entire satisfaction. During the Second World War they lived in America, then post-war between Malcontenta, Rhode Island and eventually Sintra in Portugal, where Bertie, true to form, found an ancient farmhouse to restore and turn into a distinctive home for them both. Summers were spent at Malcontenta until the time came when it was too much to handle, at which point it was bequeathed to the British architect Claud Phillimore.

In the 1950s Bertie wrote: 'Happy and lucky as I am in my marriage, I sometimes feel old.' He died in 1965, sitting in his chair at Sintra and, fittingly, reading a book on architecture. Dolly followed him eight years later in 1973, aged eighty-four. They are buried together in the British cemetery in Lisbon.

Dolly had gone out of Elisabeth's life many years before and those who knew her say she spoke not at all of her early life and Opio.

Chapter 10 ❧

THE BASTIDE

Now quite alone, as far as her immediate family were concerned, on her fortieth birthday, 29 April 1929, Elisabeth gave herself a present – she took French citizenship. Her *Médaille de la Reconnaissance Française* was cited in favour of her application to the French government and the acceptance letter describes her as an artist and orphan and states: 'The results of investigations into her conduct and morality are very favourable, she is highly regarded by the local people and her naturalisation will be well received.' She had no regrets.

The stone cottage situated on the slope above the path leading to the Castello, just beyond Elisabeth's little chapel-garage, had been her gardener's home for several years, until, that is, she met Polly Stapleton-Cotton, the first of those she would draw around her on the hill. Tempted to move to France, as were so many others, by economy and the opportunity to live as she wished without censure, Polly had received her own medal for work in the Great War with the YMCA in northern France in 1916. She had also served, for a spell, as a deputy administrator in the Women's Royal Air Force. It is possible that Elisabeth, had met her through Amy Paget, who was Polly's distant relative. Christened Pauline but always known simply as Polly, she was the daughter of Colonel Robert Stapleton-Cotton who had been one of the founders of the Women's Institute in Great Britain. The family were related to the 6th Marquess of Anglesey.

The former gardener's cottage was restored, extended and turned into a charming small house, and by 1927 Polly was tucked up there. Decoration was kept to a minimum, but comfortable armchairs and sofas were a must, for few Englishmen or women are able to live without them. It was named, rather grandly, 'La Bastide', but to the people of Opio it would become the 'Maison Cotton'. It now sheltered someone who could share Elisabeth's desire to live tranquilly and who could fill the role of travelling companion, one who was unlikely to be tempted by a proposal of marriage. So, in a way, Polly replaced Dolly.

The relationship between Elisabeth and Polly was almost certainly one of supportive friendship rather than romance. Polly at this stage was in her late forties, with the demeanour of a comfortable, middle-aged lady, and her demands were few. Plump, round-faced, with short greying hair topped by an old beret or straw hat, usually wearing an open-necked shirt and sailor's trousers finished off with heavy shoes, she required only reasonably good meals, a few glasses of local wine and an endless supply of books to ensure her calm happiness. But she was scarcely alone in the world, for her blend of warmth, ironic wit and open-mindedness ensured she was a much-loved aunt and cousin to a large and interesting family, the members of which she visited in the summer time in their elegant country houses around Britain.

Life at the Castello was settling into a routine. Between the wars there was still an ample supply of servants, and few expatriate houses were without sufficient staff to help run them smoothly. These were usually friendly, lively Italians, or the dignified natives of Provence, who needed to be handled carefully and with tact, and sometimes Elisabeth's *penchant* – White Russians. Victims of the Russian Revolution, dispossessed White Russians took work wherever it was offered. Many went to the Côte d'Azur because of its tradition as a Russian holiday resort, and the expatriates there were sensitive to their plight. Some were given parcels of land, as happened near the hill town of Vence, scraping a living as smallholders.

Elisabeth, loving their music and drawn to their tragic aura, often had one or two White Russians in her entourage. In 1923 a Monsieur Garkorevno who, with his wife, looked after the running of the Castello, wrote to Charles Gouveneur Paulding thanking him for the gift of a pullover. He explained that he had mended Gouvie's bike but was rushed off his feet for he was now, all at the same time, mason, gardener and cook:

But my wife and I are not discouraged [although] the Bolsheviks would surely be very happy to know that a student who has studied for nine years at different colleges, devoting himself to intellectual pursuits, has given himself up to labouring work. I would certainly have preferred not to delight the Bolsheviks and to have been born a century earlier. But what good does it do to think of all that – it's too late. What has happened, has happened.

It must have been difficult to have had one's life changed so radically, and Elisabeth does seem to have worked him hard.

About this time she began to suffer too easily from bouts of influenza and so began her obstinate battle with the frailty the war years had wrought. But this she did her best to ignore and, with the Castello restored and her smallholding running smoothly, she could now indulge in what she came to enjoy more than anything else – 'nesting'. This entailed turning a barren, preferably remote space into a welcoming abode of simple comfort, soft lights, warm fires and sheaves of fresh flowers. It would become a passion. She seemed compelled to effect this transformation on small cottages by the sea, mountain huts overshadowed by glaciers and other bolt-holes she could escape to. She did this well, for she was a gifted home-maker and nesting seemed to help fill the void of loneliness with which she struggled constantly. Above all, there must always be someone with whom to share the experience. At the end of the next decade this need to create warmth and welcome was to develop in a way she could not have imagined in those quiet years.

In this period, when German National Socialism was gaining a grip on that furious and beleaguered country and fear and hatred of the Communist movement grew among the bourgeoisie of Europe, Elisabeth and Polly, relatively removed from seething politics, periodically loaded the necessities of life into Elisabeth's Peugeot and headed for a mountain plateau or remote bay. In the mountains their destination of choice was the Col de Lauteret in the High Alps. With their beloved dogs, Sophie, Polly's curly-haired Kerry Blue, and Babs, Elisabeth's little dock-tailed Provençal sheepdog, they would stay in the local hotel or camp in flower-filled Alpine meadows with a view of Mont Blanc. At other times they followed the coast to Les Douaniers – a terrace of rented abandoned coastguard cottages at the Pointe de la Douane at Cap Taillat, on an almost inaccessible cove west of St Tropez. The ability to move from one to another of her chosen places placated Elisabeth's 'bogeys' as she called them and assuaged her restlessness.

Living with the rhythm of the seasons – a Provençal spring jewelled with wild flowers and fruit blossom; the long, hot, thyme-scented summer throbbing with the chant of the cicadas; the gathering of grapes in late summer and olives in the sparklingly clear days of winter, meant time slipped by quietly and pleasantly. There was always involvement, on Elisabeth's part, with the daily life of the villagers. Visitors occasionally came and went and members of Polly's family arrived to inspect her new home.

Eddy Sackville-West, later the 5th Baron Sackville, writer, critic and musician, stayed at the Castello in the early 1930s, although how Elisabeth knew him is a mystery. Eddy visited the coastguard cottages at Cap Taillat and wrote of them to his friend, the writer and critic Raymond Mortimer:

> This is a heavenly place. A little bay with a spit of land off it and a beacon on top. A row of coastguard cottages owned [sic] by Elizabeth [sic] Starr. There is a row of white pillars in front of it, which I have whitewashed and painted blue on the capitals. So pretty. The rooms have little galleries and ladders and fiercely crumbling lezarded [cracked] walls: a *décor de grand guignol* which is most romantic to live in. The water in the bay is as clear as glass and buoyant as a balloon. I live in brick-coloured shorts and shirt, with mauve belt and a tiny knitted skull-cap on the back of my head. Elizabeth wears the same. The life is delicious – bathing and reading and picking up things on the beach for Elizabeth to make into pictures, and fishing from the boat and putting down lobster pots. I wake in the early dawn and see straight from my bed out into a pale pillar against the shell-like sky. We shall be here till the end of the month, then Opio again.

At the end of the 1920s new neighbours had moved to the outskirts of Opio. John Holroyd Reece, an 'urbane and picturesque international', was a controversial publisher of art books and later made his fortune as the founder of the Albatross Continental Library (the forerunner of Penguin paperbacks), a successful competitor to the Tauchnitz paperback books. Like Tauchnitz, Albatross printed books in English for sale solely outside Britain. Reece would run through five wives before he died 'burnt out' in 1969, but now he had bought a house and land in the south of France with his Belgian wife Jeanne and her daughter

Diane van Dommelen. The mystery of Reece's private life makes it difficult to know what number wife Jeanne was, but this was her second marriage, having been abandoned by her first husband, Isadore van Dommelen, a dashing Dutchman who, taking the name Lou Tellegan, became a well-known stage and screen actor and lover of the actress Sarah Bernhardt. His embellished autobiography, *Women Have Been Kind,* is a rollicking read. In 1934 Tellegan would kill himself, spectacularly, in his Hollywood apartment by committing hari-kari on a pair of golden scissors, toppling to a floor spread with his press cuttings of many years. But at this time Diane van Dommelen was in her early twenties and living quietly with her mother and stepfather. A decade later she would become someone with whom several people would have to deal very carefully.

It is not known how the stock market crash of 1929, leading to the Great Depression, affected Elisabeth. There is little sign that it did. Perhaps the *laissez-faire* exchange rate in France at that time favoured her circumstances. She had never been extravagant, bought the bare minimum of clothes (which held no interest for her) and was largely self-sufficient regarding food. Besides her Tropezian hand-made sandals and an extra skirt or two to be donned when she needed to visit town, most of her money went on the upkeep of the Castello and the wages of her servants. And there was always a *billet de mille* (a thousand-franc note) left on the kitchen table for the needy of the village when they came to share their problems. Christmas presents were provided for the local children and those at the St Christophe clinic. She did not jettison any of her rented bolt-holes and indeed added another in the 1930s. But admonitions to economise crept in, coupled with concern that no more money should be spent on escapades than was strictly necessary but, as always with such economies, servants would be the last luxury to be dispensed with.

In February of 1933 Corinne Robinson, after a period of ill health, died of pneumonia. She was just over seventy. She had loved Elisabeth unconditionally. In her will she left her $5,000, a sapphire-and-diamond ring, a pendant that Elisabeth had once given her and a bar pin of pearls, 'in the back of which is hair'. That these were precious objects is illustrated by the fact that, if Elisabeth were to pre-decease her, the jewellery was to go to Corinne's own daughter and granddaughter. In her will she called Elisabeth simply 'My friend' and left it at that. She had been a vital part of Elisabeth's life for twenty-four years. She was laid to rest next to her husband and her son Stewart in the Robinson cemetery in the quiet woods of their Herkimer estate in New York State. Her headstone reads, fittingly, 'She Loved Much'. Elisabeth must have felt the loss of this love keenly, for Corinne had been far more than a friend.

The end of June of that year brought intense heat and great excitement when a strong and extrovert young girl fled to take sanctuary in Polly's Bastide. Penelope Chetwode, torn between her attraction to the young poet John Betjeman and a desire to return to study in the India of her childhood, was in a state of indecision and confusion. She was twenty-three to Betjeman's twenty-seven and had suddenly broken off her tenuous engagement to him and taken refuge with the 'eccentric and all understanding' Polly, whom she described as 'absolutely divine, a maiden aunt, and we all adored her'. Penelope's father had been Commander-in-Chief in India and her mother, Lady Hester Chetwode, was Polly's sister. Lady Hester and her husband were totally opposed to their daughter's attachment to a dishevelled young writer with bad teeth who had produced only one small volume of poems to date and had a reputation for flitting from girl to girl. John Betjeman himself, in an equal state of indecision coupled with despair, was advised by the author Nancy Mitford to 'go after her and get her, don't let it go like that. You must go to the south of France and win her back.' So in July he set off hotfoot to Opio and was firmly sent to stay with Elisabeth at the Castello.

It was the right time of the year – there were nightingales. The perfumed evenings first soothed and then dispersed indecision. In his biography *Young Betjeman*, Bevis Hillier describes these fraught and romantic days and quotes a letter Penelope wrote to John once he had returned to England, in the particular language they used with each other: 'The moon was nearly full and the fireflies was fillin' the olives with dancing lights.' She decided 'No, I am too young to think of giving up love just yet.' Her mind made up, she did a little touring with Polly and Elisabeth and then followed Betjeman home. They were married quietly at the end of July and Polly became aunt-by-marriage to John Betjeman, future Poet Laureate of England.

Remembering her hospitality, in later years John would send Elisabeth an edition of his poems *Old Lights for New Chancels* with the inscription: 'With love from John, the cultivated and talented author of these verses. April 1940.' It just got in under the wire.

Calm returned to the hillside and the peaceful life that Polly and Elisabeth shared continued uninterrupted for another year. Their common dislike of the sophistication and brittleness of the expatriate life of the Riviera below and contentment with their serene existence particularly suited Polly, now over fifty and happy to drift into an uneventful maturity.

Chapter 11 ❧

CAROLINE

> To more than one admirer – and who did not admire? – her
> symbol was a beautiful black cat that sometimes purred, but
> quite unreliably. Laurence Whistler, *The Laughter and the Urn*

Spring comes swiftly to Provence. It is both joyful and disturbing in its vigour. In April of 1934 the terraces were filled with wild scarlet tulips, bee orchids, tiny irises, anemones and myriad clusters of the miniature, perfumed wild narcissi that grew in pale yellow clumps under the olive trees. Peach, apple and pear blossom unfurled and frothed along their dark branches and the beads of pale green fruit, sprouting among the slender leaves of the olive trees gave promise of pleasure and security.

The warm weather was beginning. At the Castello, the door in the stone wall of the former animal enclosure now opened to a transformation. The muddy terrace had been levelled, grass seed sown and, in the centre, a small oblong swimming pool dug out of the earth and rock. Bulbs of moon lilies were planted around the edges and from here one could float lazily and gaze at the surrounding hills. Flower beds were created along the base of the high terrace wall by the pool and these were planted with flowering climbers that would come to smother the walls and drape themselves over the monks' bread oven. The enclosure became a 'secret garden', to be loved by many over the years. Much later, in appreciation of it all, the artist Augustus John would paint, in oils, *The Swimming Pool at the Castello, Opio*.

That spring was to bring a change into Elisabeth's life that she had not anticipated. In the year the German Reich created their first three Panzer tank divisions and the dancer Margot Fonteyn was making her debut as a snowflake in *The Nutcracker*, another young girl visited the hillside. A cousin to Polly, Lady Caroline Paget was the eldest daughter of Charles, 6th Marquess of Anglesey. She was already, along with her sister Elizabeth (Liz), one of the slightly rebellious beauties of the

1930s. She was the eldest of six children – five girls (Liz being next to her in age) and Henry, the son and heir, youngest of the family along with his twin sister, Rose. Caroline was in her twenty-first year. With dark, curly hair, a perfectly formed face, translucent skin and a mouth that had a tendency to pout, she was described as having 'a moonlight beauty'. Attracting devotion in spite of herself, her mixture of bestowed warmth, vivacity and enigmatic aloofness was to fascinate those who loved but could not fully possess her. She had been promised to Anthony Knebworth, son of the Earl of Lytton, captivated by her since she was twelve years old. A dashing athletic pilot of the heroic mould, Anthony had been killed when his fighter plane crashed during a display at Hendon aerodrome the previous year. Caroline was distressed but not prostrated by his death and she and Liz – 'each more beautiful than the other' – were much sought after, never lacking a stream of invitations to the endless social events that filled the years of the *jeunesse dorée* between the wars.

Yet the two girls inclined towards the rather marginal set of their cousin David Herbert of Wilton House in Wiltshire. This included the poet Siegfried Sassoon, the terminally aesthetic Stephen Tennant, the writer Osbert Sitwell and the theatrical designers Oliver Messel and Cecil Beaton, who was becoming increasingly famous as a photographer for fashion magazines and of film stars and royalty. They preferred the world of wild escapades, spirited theatricals and the light, sardonic touch of the artistically talented to that of country sportsmen, aspiring young army officers and politicians. Their younger sister Rose would lead an even more Bohemian life, in her youth becoming part of the Soho set that revolved around the Colony Club and Francis Bacon, before retiring to a country life in Wales.

The main homes of the Anglesey family were Plas Newydd on the Isle of Anglesey and Beaudesert in Staffordshire. Plas Newydd had evolved over the centuries, its final form and decoration designed chiefly by James Wyatt in the late eighteenth century, with Humphry Repton as consultant on landscaping. The house has an unforgettable setting, combining drama and tranquillity, standing as it does overlooking the flickering waters of the Menai Strait as they glide into the Irish Sea and surrounded by vast sloping lawns and acres of light woodland. Here was a much-loved home, where the children grew up in an atmosphere of appreciation of music and art, combined with generous hospitality.

This was the family with whom Polly often spent the summer.

Caroline came from an impeccable aristocratic background. One of her ancestors was Henry William Paget, Earl of Uxbridge, the brilliant second-in-command to Wellington at the Battle of Waterloo who lost his leg with sangfroid and elegance when it was smashed by grapeshot as he rode off the battlefield with the duke. The exchange between them is said to have gone: 'By God, sir, I've lost my leg!', followed by, 'By God, sir, so you have!', the Iron Duke then turning back to survey his great victory. After the amputation Henry had mused with a smile, 'I have had a pretty long run, I have been a beau these forty-seven years and it would not be fair to cut the young men out any longer.' He was created 1st Marquess of Anglesey by the Prince Regent and became an elder statesman, fathering a total of eighteen children – who in turn produced seventy-three grandchildren, the first-born son always called Henry. The Paget family had a long history of service to the royal family. On Queen Victoria's accession in 1837 there were thirteen Paget family members at court. Caroline's own father, Charles, was, for twenty-two years, Lord Chamberlain to Queen Mary, wife of George V.

Polly Cotton's loyalty and love was bestowed on very few people. Those who received it were Elisabeth, her own Anglesey cousins and above all Charles, to whom she was devoted. Known as Charley to those close to him, he was charming and elegant. In 1912 he had married Lady Marjorie Manners, daughter of the 8th Duke of Rutland and one of a family of beautiful women. Marjorie, like her mother before her, was an artist who painted and sculpted with an exquisite and delicate touch, using her children and other members of her family as models. She was also a gifted mezzo-soprano and music played an important part in her own family's life. Her sister Diana, aunt to Caroline, became internationally famous playing the Virgin Mary in *The Miracle*, a mime play with music, that toured Britain and America in the 1920s and 1930s. Renowned for her grace and classical loveliness, Diana married Duff Cooper, later Viscount Norwich, who, as First Lord of the Admiralty, resigned from Neville Chamberlain's government in 1938 in protest against his policy of appeasement. During the Second World War he would become British Representative to the French Committee of Liberation in the diplomatic melting pot of Algiers. After the war he was appointed British Ambassador to France – a post in which he was popular with the French and in which he practised the *entente cordiale* with enthusiasm.

This was Caroline Paget's family – a touch bohemian, artistic and far from boring.

It was late spring when she arrived in Opio. Baby rabbits, ducklings and chickens had shaken and trembled their way into the world at the Castello and were now developing into leggy adolescents. In the gardens, arum lilies and roses were blooming vigorously and nightingales continued to sing night and day in the woodland and olive groves of the hillside. Far from the society world she was now so much a part of, Caroline responded to the pleasures of expatriate life in the hills. In spite of her beauty, she was unsure of herself and lacked a fundamental feeling of self-worth. But here with Polly, her much-loved cousin, and a charming and sympathetic neighbour in the form of Elisabeth, she could relax and allow herself to be happy.

There was much to please. The two older women were surrounded by animals, plants and the rhythms of the earth – yet they were not peasants. They grew their own vegetables, grapes and fruit but there would always be someone else to plant, gather, cook and serve them. If the crops were eaten by pests or spoilt by the weather, there would be no hunger, for there was money to buy more. And, although the daily garb might be simple and worn, a quick trip to town in the motor sufficed to replace it. The women wore short-sleeved blouses and wide trousers, and in the heat of the day Caroline changed into shorts and sun tops. Meals were eaten on the terrace. Here Polly read and drank her wine while Caroline's dark head bent over her diary or sketch pad and Elisabeth, cigarette between her lips, looked at the girl half her age and perhaps wished she had not come to disturb her tranquillity.

She had already met Caroline and her family when they had previously visited Polly. Caroline was then scarcely out of childhood. Now she was an independent young woman and to be treated as such. As well as teaching her to draw, Elisabeth began to paint her portrait. She made sure Caroline was introduced to and knew the stories of the animals and birds, taught her the names of flowers and the gossip about their few neighbours. The young woman brought freshness and her particular form of gaiety to the Castello, and Elisabeth fell under her spell. Deeply in love she began gently to tempt Caroline to share her existence.

The visit lasted several sunlit weeks. There was much sketching and swimming in the pool, over which the unfurling white lilies reflected their perfumed heads. In the quiet evenings they listened to records, the favourites being the American 'Wagon Wheels', from the just-released Randolph Scott film of the same name, and, true to form for Elisabeth, the Russian gypsy song 'Black Eyes'. They had long conversations about their perceptions of themselves and Elisabeth assured Caroline she would help her fight against the loneliness and fears that sometimes engulfed her, so familiar was she with these chill companions herself.

It is interesting to reflect on Polly's feelings about the growing affection between her young cousin and her friend of many years, for it is plain she found it totally natural. As for Elisabeth, this brief emotional encounter was something from which she would never really free herself. Several photographs of her were taken by Caroline at this time. In one she stands in the doorway of Polly's Bastide. A cigarette, about to be lit, hangs between her lips, and her dark hair is in a straight, rather careless, bob. She has lost her beauty and seems not to care, but her face is strong and striking and her figure slim and energetic. In her studio in the courtyard cottage of the Castello she worked on the portrait of Caroline. Later she would ask for a lock of her hair to get the colour right – but the portrait has been lost.

As for Caroline, she had come to Opio simply for a holiday, and no amount of wild flowers and ducklings would captivate a young woman who had a coterie of sparkling friends awaiting her return to England. So in the middle of May she left, as she had always intended to, but touched by her relationship with Elisabeth. Though this would become distant, it would have a consequence that Caroline had not anticipated. As the train steamed towards Calais and England she was returning home to the life to which she belonged – and to another meeting.

Left behind on her May hillside, Elisabeth found the pain of Caroline's absence opened old wounds. Usually disciplined and controlled, she was dismayed to find herself so lonely and vulnerable. On 16 May, the day Caroline left on the train from Cannes, she wrote:

A dab of rouge and powder on an empty table and, to make them look less lost, a red handkerchief with white spots. A very old black rose – was it two days ago at breakfast that it was picked?

A luxurious bottle of Coty looking rather superior (thank you very much) and, alas, your black glasses to wait for you. [And two days later:] You seem to be here, at the Castello, in the pool, up a tree and coming in suddenly at a door or almost asleep in the studio. I worked there all day and even Polly says the portrait is like you. It is midnight so I shall say my prayers now as you taught me.

Although she normally found letter-writing a torment (though her letters are eminently readable) Elisabeth wrote every night, holding on to Caroline's promise that she would return to the Castello at the end of June. She made plans for them to take an apartment in the hill town of Cagnes between Nice and Cannes, where 'one can rent a big studio which used to be attics and cowsheds, in very quaint old houses'. (They would take it for the following winter and have lessons from the Russian painter Boris Grigorieff.) And: 'Do you remember the little room with the tiny window on the pool garden next to the studio where the rabbit food was kept? I want so terribly to make it into a working room for you. I am so longing to do it and I should be so happy if you nodded your head over it. That would be enough.'

The passing of the days did nothing to soothe the sense of loss, and ten days after Caroline's departure Elisabeth wanted, more than ever, to share every experience with her:

What do you think has happened? Do you remember the round stone table in the pool garden and near it the white (smelling of musk) flowers, and then a huge ugly geranium? I suddenly had a frenzy to work and clean up the border and started there when a nightingale flew away from just beside me and then I saw a nest, with five tiny olive green eggs hidden in the geranium, almost on the ground, with a nicotine plant hanging over it. And she didn't seem to mind my being there and came back again – and that's that.

Caroline, now in her other world, wrote in return, although her letters no longer exist. It seems, from Elisabeth's replies, as if she was some-times depressed and unhappy. But here Elisabeth could feel involved:

Don't you know that you can't make a multitude happy – or what you call 'those you love'? Don't fool yourself about that. It's an absolute waste of time. You would have to be a multitude of different Carolines to suit a multitude of different people, and could one do that? It would be impossible. We have all got despicable characters, I quite agree with you but don't ever, ever tell me again you are unworthy of anything because that's so utterly wrong ... Be yourself, I know you have the courage to be. You will do it by degrees and then be strong enough to face yourself ultimately. Don't be afraid of yourself. Oneself is such a terrifying thing in its demands.

The longing and loneliness of the older woman must have become a burden, and Caroline wrote to say she would not be able to return at the end of June – but perhaps in July. Elisabeth was understanding about this, feeling sure she would come later: 'Perhaps I could send you a firefly.'

Caroline also sent presents – books for Polly and records for Elisabeth. Polly replied:

Oh darling, what wonderful books, it's a library, how angelic of you – and the discs are wonderful too, Elisabeth is writing about them. It's been a horrid day, mistral blowing. We've been left two coal black puppies, Sophy [her dog] is terrified of them and Babs [Elisabeth's] hates them. There is also a baby duck living in the house. I have fed the puppies and the duck, poured some stuff into Sophy's ear, looked at the books again, played the discs and now this. I've been busy haven't I?

She also hoped Caroline would return soon.

Caroline's twenty-first birthday was the 15 June and Elisabeth had written to make an appointment to telephone her in London between 11.00 and midnight to wish her 'Happy Birthday' – rather strangely assuming Caroline would be home on such a night. As she had no telephone, she would drive over to the publisher John Holroyd Reece. In a letter headed '2.00 in the morning', she wrote:

Have just come back from John's. The number 3227 didn't

answer, neither did you. So it was foolish to try and yet I am not convinced but wonder if you got my letter in time. Your birthday is over. It has been on my mind all day, in fact incapacitated me but made me realise I must start a quite new life to-morrow for myself. *Sauve qui peut.* You see I have a tiny imaginary box with a key and occasionally in life I have opened it. How many times have I opened it? I think this is the third time. And on top of the things that are already there I will fold very carefully some things of you and then I will know, after I have been able to turn the key again, they are quite safe always to come back to. I mean when I have the courage to look in the little box again. Somehow I feel the box won't be able to shut and then I am done, but I shall sit on it hard and with Babs extra weight. Please try very hard to understand all this and forgive me if you disapprove. But perhaps you will say – which would be wonderful – not to open the little box at all.

What was already in the little box? Certainly the tragedy of Stewart Robinson, probably the death of Elisabeth's brothers, perhaps the pain of the failed relationship with her parents. She would now certainly add 'some things' of Caroline, who would not return to the Castello for a very long time, and then in very different circumstances.

Elisabeth's letters grew fewer and more distant but always loving and courteous – and Caroline kept them all, in particular one:

This is supposed to reach you when you wake up on your 21st birthday. I have appealed to Josephine [Caroline's maid] to get the roses and I do hope they smell good and have short stems and aren't out of a greenhouse. Anyway, they bring you all my wishes. The only thing of mine which I can't send with them is the Castello, but it is yours now – only unfortunately for the moment I have to be thrown in with it. God bless you. E.

She had left Caroline her great old house and all that went with it.

Caroline had her coming-out ball in the Double Cube Room at Wilton House, 'looking like an angel in shell colour'. Back in the social whirl, the weeks spent with Elisabeth must have seemed part of another world. Described by Clarissa Eden in her *Memoir* as having 'devastating charm and sex appeal', during the summer Caroline was introduced in London by her cousin David Herbert to the actress Tallulah Bankhead and her friend and travelling companion, Audry Carten. Wayward daughter of a United States senator from the Deep South, Tallulah was a dedicated professional on stage and screen, and notorious for her reckless performances in public. 'Tallulah', said Mrs Patrick Campbell, 'is always skating on thin ice. Everyone wants to be there when it breaks.' Actively promiscuous with anyone of beauty, gaining extra notoriety by amusing herself one summer entertaining boys from Eton College in a cottage on the Thames, Tallulah's husky voice, charm and generosity nevertheless ensured her popularity, and in 1934 she was famous on two continents.

But it was Audry Carten who would, as time went by, become an important figure in Caroline's life. A failed English actress, she was now an aspiring playwright. She had just been involved in her one and only film, a British musical called *Gay Love*, starring Sophie Tucker, for which Audrey was credited, along with her sister Waveney, as 'the source'. The sisters had more success as playwrights, their best known play being *Fame*, about a violinist who had lost the use of his hands, with Gerald du Maurier in the main role.

Later in what was, for her, a significant year, Caroline also met the artist Rex Whistler – yet another who would fall in love with her. Rex, who was for Diana Cooper, 'of his generation my most loved' was a young man of exceptional talent. At the Slade School of Fine Art he was considered one of the best young artists of his time. But he was not in the 'modern' mould: his work was firmly representational and frequently wildly romantic. Painter, illustrator, theatrical designer and muralist, his love for the classical Rococo would delight some and irritate others. To those whom he irritated he was 'not of his age', but those who were delighted by his work and personality would draw him into their circle and request commissions for their London apartments and grand houses. For Diana Cooper, he decorated her London drawing room with *trompe-l'oeil* panels. His highly developed sense of humour and penchant for the wittily grotesque are illustrated to perfection in his drawings for the 1934 edition of *Gulliver's Travels*. He became well known for his enchanting set designs and costumes for various plays and productions at the Opera House and Sadler's Wells Ballet.

But it is as a portrait painter that Rex could possibly have won the serious critical acclaim that eluded him, had he lived long enough to develop this talent to the full. The portraits of those he loved and admired are of great merit. If he had learnt to discipline himself and his various talents (for he could turn his hand to almost anything), he would perhaps now be as well known as that other Whistler who invariably first springs to mind. Deeply influenced by the work of the painters Claude Lorrain and Nicolas Poussin, Rex's designs and murals often depict Arcadian scenes of lawns, woodland and hills with classical buildings and bridges in the distance. Roses, cowslips and tulips abound. Harvest fields full of stooks of hay recede towards soft slopes and, as a border, sheaves of heavy-headed corn interlace with scythe and hook. Unafraid to work over large areas, he created murals that are much admired today: in the Tate Gallery restaurant (*The Pursuit of Rare Meats*, painted shortly after he left the Slade), in the drawing room of Mottisfont Abbey near Romsey in Hampshire, and in the Tent Room at Port Lympne in Kent, among others.

But his masterpiece is considered to be the mural he would create on the 18-metre-long wall in the dining room of Caroline's home at Plas Newydd. Painted while in 'an agony of unfulfilled desire' due to her caprices, it was nevertheless a happy commission and through it grew an affectionate friendship between Rex and Caroline's family as a whole. Here he depicted a wide bay, full of symbolism, sheltering under mountains and 'bristling with spires, domes and columns'. A mixture of Baroque and classical buildings overlooks rippling waters to a fishing village clustered around an onion-domed church. Boats of sail and steam travel across the bay passing a fortress island, jetties and lighthouses. In the foreground is a gondola complete with gondolier and, sailing away at the helm of a red-sailed boat, is Caroline herself. Fishing nets, baskets and anchors hang over the ornate harbour walls and the whole panorama resonates with the real-life drama of the mountains of Snowdonia and the wide waters of the Menai Strait, seen through the high windows in the opposite wall of the dining room. On the left return wall, dressed as a gardener's boy holding a broom, self-effacing and gazing out at the observer, is Rex.

In photographs, with his trim figure and strong bone structure, Rex gives the impression of dark-haired masculinity. A broken nose caused by a wild game at school enhances his 'romantic profile'. Yet he was, as a young man, drawn more to David Herbert's world. At ease with

artistic homosexuals, his close friends were Siegfried Sassoon, Stephen
Tennant and, rather less so, Cecil Beaton. His travels abroad were taken
with these or other friends from the same extended circle. In his late
twenties, however, his emotions turned, intensely, towards beautiful
society women. In 1934, at twenty-nine and in the frustrated midst of
one such infatuation he had (according to his brother Laurence) with
the spirited Tallulah Bankhead, his first satisfactory experience with a
woman.

On first meeting Liz and Caroline, Rex was charmed by both. But
soon it was Caroline with her 'rich magnolia skin' and 'dreaming,
aloof character without enthusiasm or ardour' to whom he turned,
attracted by her beauty and aura of the unattainable. At Christmas
time the following year he painted her as *The Girl With a Red Rose*. She
is glancing downwards and into a looking-glass. With her left hand she
places a red Etoile d'Hollande rose against the top of a yellow bodice
and, with the other, holds back a sweep of black hair. One white arm
is bare. The other, raised, is clothed by a long black glove. It was meant
to be a provocative picture, and was controversial in its time, but found
favour with Caroline's family. Later Rex would paint a lovely nude – a
reclining, dark-haired girl – but this painting has no title.

Chapter 12 ❧
PEGGY

Back in 1929, and nearer to Grasse, someone else had set up a new home – someone whose reaction to love, danger, beauty, friendship and almost any other element in life was instant and dramatic and whose personality attracted attention at any gathering. Tactile and demonstrative, she was tall, elegant and, infinitely preferring tea gowns to sailor's trousers, was different in every possible way from Polly Cotton, which ensured they would never be close friends.

Winifred, Lady Fortescue (Peggy to her friends and in this book), first met Elisabeth in 1933 when the former was still living in what was to become her famous house and garden at Magagnosc – the setting for her best-selling book of the 1930s and 1940s, *Perfume from Provence*. Devastated by the recent loss of her adored husband John Fortescue, Peggy was finding it intensely troubling to live in the house they had shared, and Elisabeth had invited her to take over a room at the Castello to which she could escape when it all became too much. It was to become a friendship of two lonely women who met at the right time for them both.

Born Winifred Beech in 1888 (and therefore a year older than Elisabeth), Peggy was the third child of the Reverend Howard Beech, rector of Great Bealings in Suffolk, and his wife Henrietta Godden. Childhood for the children in the rambling rectory, with its 1.5 hectares (4 acres) of garden and surrounding woodland leading down to the little country church, was one of freedom and invention. Apart from the discipline of attending their father's services, Peggy and her brothers and sister were left, even encouraged, to create their own adventurous amusements. Their loving, gentle father and equally loving, sensitive mother, encouraged confidence and strength of character, which traits emerged particularly in Winifred and her elder brother Mervyn.

Handsome and determined, Mervyn became a member of the Colonial Service and, on one of his leaves, fell violently in love with

Stella, the daughter of the actress Mrs Patrick Campbell and herself an actress. He carried her off to Africa and a life far removed from the London stage. After the birth of a baby boy, Stella returned to England, leaving her heart-broken husband alone. Conversant with fourteen native dialects and 'adored by the Africans he had devoted his life to', he died in Kenya several years later. Peggy's other brother, Guy, and younger sister, Marjory, led more conventional lives. Guy became a clergyman like his father and Marjory married a widower – the colonel of a Gurkha regiment from the Arbuthnot family of Sussex.

As for Peggy, after attending two small schools and being taught at home, she won a scholarship in 1904 to the Old Cedar House School in Slough. She studied hard and did well but, after leaving 'planed and chiselled', was at a loss as to how to earn her living – which she had to do as her parents were not able to support her indefinitely. It was at this point in her life that her father was asked to fill, temporarily, the position of private chaplain to the Duke of Marlborough, and it was at Blenheim Palace that Peggy met his Duchess, the American-born Consuelo Vanderbilt.

The pliable young heiress had been pressured by her mother into what quickly became a famously unhappy marriage with the 9th Duke. A delicate beauty, philanthropic, and with a growing tendency to organise, Consuelo was prompted to take Peggy lightly under her wing. This was a meeting that was to set her life on a course never contemplated by herself or her family, for Consuelo, rather surprisingly, suggested Peggy should become an actress. Consuelo undertook to 'keep an eye on her' from her home at Sunderland House, when Peggy began her drama studies in London. This marble-floored palace off Piccadilly had been built for the Marlboroughs by Consuelo's father, William K. Vanderbilt – and most sensibly put in her name alone. Although living in a very different world, Consuelo was as good as her word. For many years to come, beautiful scarcely used clothes, introductions, advice and quiet lunches would be bestowed on Peggy by her 'Fairy Godmother'.

But this benevolence did not mean Peggy, based in her Shepherd's Market lodgings in Mayfair, would not have to look after herself in the small theatres and grim provincial boarding houses of Britain. She worked hard and was moderately successful during the six years of her theatrical life, being accepted into Sir Herbert Tree's group of actors and finishing her career with a starring part in a touring performance of Jerome K. Jerome's *The Passing of the Third Floor Back*.

Being an actress was socially tricky. It was perhaps the wives of the late nineteenth and early twentieth century who decreed such creatures should not be accepted in society. Often beautiful and generally enticing, they could only be regarded as tiresome, even dangerous, competition in ballroom and salon. This was an attitude Peggy had to endure and it cannot have been easy for a warm, outgoing young woman to be excluded from social occasions where, if things had been different, she might possibly have been a guest. So it was fortunate that one day she was taken by friends to a tea party in Dorset at the modern, red-brick home of the writer Thomas Hardy. It would turn out to be a day unlike any other, but not because of the brief encounter with the venerable author. Gazing across a crowded garden she saw, sitting by himself, the man she had always known she would marry. It was not even love at first sight for, in her dramatic way, she had seen his face in dreams and this was simply a dream come true. Every detail was as she had imagined it, even down to his name, 'John', and 'that arrogant pose of the small head on its long neck; that high brow, that clean-cut sensitive face, that curiously beautiful mouth, that air of bored, impatient superiority'.

Born in 1860, John Fortescue was the fifth son and ninth child of Hugh, 3rd Earl Fortescue, one of thirteen children and therefore without fortune. The family home was Castle Hill near Barnstaple in north Devon, and it was here that John developed a passion for every aspect of country life. The house stood on a hillside between the moors of Exmoor and the sea, backed by tall beeches, which swayed and moaned in the winds sweeping in from the Atlantic. The trees were colonised by rooks and, as an old man, he would write from far away 'The noise of their cawing is now constant in my deaf ears.'

A delicate child with bad eyesight, John had found it hard to keep up with his strapping older brothers and, because of the expense of following two of these siblings into the army, a longed-for military career was denied to him. Leaving Cambridge without a degree and rather at a loss, he went as private secretary to the governor of first the Windward Islands and then New Zealand. Although unable to join the army, he began, in his spare time, to write its history, which eventually led to a commission by the publishers Macmillan to produce the official *History of the British Army*. The task would take him thirty-six years. For light relief, he also wrote charming children's books, the most famous being *The Story of a Red Deer*, which told of the respect and reverence felt by a hunter towards an animal he was dedicated to stalking to its death.

John was living on slender means in spartan rooms in London's Brook Street when help came at last, in 1905, in the form of King Edward VII, who appointed him King's Librarian at Windsor Castle. It was the perfect job. Leaving the diplomatic service and now with a suite in the Round Tower at the Castle, he was completely happy, having a free hand to create order from the chaos of years while working with some of the most priceless items of history. Most importantly, the post also enabled him to continue his work on the British Army. When Edward VII died, King George V and Queen Mary asked him to remain in the job and he settled down at Windsor for almost twenty-five years.

An expert on bookbinding, he began the process of designing bindings for works that had scarcely seen the light of day since their production. He was also responsible for purchasing historic works for the Royal Collection. In 1909 the Prince of Wales (the future King George V) had written from Sandringham:

> Dear Fortescue,
> I am sorry to hear from your letter of 26th that after very careful examination with Dr Warne you have both come to the conclusion that the binding of Henry VIII's book you showed us at Windsor is not genuine, and therefore you are not going to purchase it. It is lucky you found it out now before you bought it. Do you remember my asking you in chaff if you were certain that the arms had not been stuck on? Are you going to inform the dealer that it is a forgery or send it back and allow Pierpont Morgan to give some fabulous sum for it? Both the Princess and I will always be ready to help you if you find something which ought to be in the Library and you are short of money.
> Believe me,
> Very sincerely yours,
> GEORGE.

But there was the odd mistake. Some priceless volumes of seventeenth-century drawings of fruit and flowers assembled by the Italian Cassiano dal Pozzo had found their way into the Royal Library. John, pronouncing them to be 'unimportant', sold fifteen of the volumes to London dealers after the First World War. They were consequently broken up and the drawings dispersed. It was not until the 1950s that their significance was realised, and it was Anthony Blunt, Surveyor of the Queen's Pictures and later revealed as a spy for Soviet Russia, who set about tracking down those of the drawings that had ended up in private hands.

In his personal habits John was so fastidious that he changed every item of clothing twice a day and for the Dehli Durbar in India in 1911, which celebrated the coronation of George V, he packed no less than 96 vests.

On that summer day, also in 1911, when John Fortescue drew Peggy away from the other guests to sit with him on a bench at the end of a leafy arbour, her future was sealed, although nothing was said. They parted at the end of the afternoon and Peggy left with her slightly disgruntled friends – for she had scarcely circulated – and with an invitation to visit the Royal Library. But the romance was not to be easy. John was twenty-eight years her senior and worried about the difference in age. If and when he announced an engagement he would have to inform both his Fortescue family (who would never really accept Peggy) and the Royal Family (who were eventually far more inclined to do so) of her profession as an actress.

When, three years later, at the outbreak of war, they did at last get married it was a muted, hurried affair held in a side chapel of Holy Trinity, Sloane Street, London, with John slinking in by a side door. He wanted 'dispatch' – no flowers or music – and Peggy wore a simple 'little blue picture-frock'. The service was over in seven and a half minutes with only eleven people present. Consuelo (who was a witness) had given a small dinner party for the couple the night before and hosted a family luncheon at Sunderland House after the wedding. For their honeymoon John and Peggy caught the train for north Devon, to Castle Hill. This was the first time Peggy had visited John's childhood home, but the meeting with his family was a dubious success. From there they continued further west along the Devon coast and on to another family home, Hartland Abbey. Many years later she would get to know the Abbey well and in very different circumstances.

Married life in London was not what she had expected. Obliged at first to live by herself during the week in the little house they had taken in Brompton Square while John was in attendance at Windsor, Peggy felt very alone. But, after what seems to have been a period of acclimatising as far as John was concerned, an apartment in Edward III's Gatehouse at the Castle was extended to accommodate a married couple. The King and Queen visited them there, Peggy being greeted graciously and allowed to spend a little more time at Windsor. It was the outbreak of the Great War that allowed her to live more permanently in the relative safety of the Castle, away from the threat of bombs over London. During the course of the war, the rule that excluded those engaged in commerce and the theatrical profession from being publicly received by their sovereign was swept away by the King, and Peggy was presented formally at a Buckingham Palace Garden Party, along with the actress Ellen Terry.

She engaged in the war work expected of ladies of leisure, taking blind servicemen for walks in London, visiting hospitals and packing comforts for the troops. Soon after her marriage, and possibly brought on by anxiety due to her separation from Windsor and John, Peggy contracted what she would always, from then on, call her 'poison'. It was a condition that was to be with her for the rest of her days. Many years later she would tell friends she had been scratched by a cat, but her symptoms were closer to a form of lupus than the shorter-lived cat-scratch fever. There are various forms of lupus, frequently linked to an autoimmune disease. Peggy's periodically attacked her whole body and, above all, her skin. She was prone to fevers, throat infections and painful joints as well as eruptions across her brow and cheeks. Over the years this skin condition became hardened and permanent, necessitating, each morning, long treatments that involved peeling and creaming her face, using the dainty towels embroidered for this purpose by her niece, Fay Arbuthnot. Experimental medical treatments would last throughout her life, often more painful than the condition itself. Combined with endless hit-and-miss prescriptions, treatments and injections, these attempts at a cure would leave her frequently debilitated and exhausted. From specialists in London to consultants she saw on her regular visits to the Institut Pasteur in Paris – and indeed to any doctor who promised her relief – no one was ever able to rid her of the condition. These were the days before corticosteroids and antibiotics, which would have helped so much. Although disguised with heavy make-up, her skin condition was striking and impossible to ignore. But her personality was such that, in spite of this, she would be described by people who knew her as *une femme belle*. Like Elisabeth Starr's, it was a personality that carried all before it.

In 1916 John and Peggy, looking for a permanent base in London, found and rented Admiral's House in The Grove in Hampstead and, from then on, never lived apart for any length of time. Here Peggy created the first of her three gardens, planting 'a myriad rose trees and foxgloves in the beds of the sunk paved garden and some thousands of bulbs in the grass and under the trees'. Happy, and proud of his new home, John now travelled to and from the Castle Library at Windsor while, in every spare moment, continuing to write his *History of the British Army*. But post-war taxation soon began to cause the money problems that would, from then on, never loosen their grip and he had to face the prospect that he might not now be able to afford the luxury of spending so many hours of low-paid work on the rest of his *History*. In the preface to volume nine he explained that this might be the last in the series. Peggy, beginning to show the determination that would become so vital in her future life, resolved that he must, at all costs, carry on and that she would be the one to enable him to do so.

John's health was beginning to be a concern. He suffered from recurring trouble with his eyesight and twice fell victim to the dreaded influenza. So, with the proceeds of the insurance money on a gold cigarette case, lost on the tube by Peggy, they set off for Sintra in Portugal for a short holiday. Here, with John's health improving, Peggy, inspired by the fabrics and craftsmanship of the Portuguese, decided to become an interior decorator. When they returned to England they were closely followed by pieces of antique furniture, lengths of ancient brocades and elaborate trimmings.

In rented rooms in Knightsbridge her company, which she called 'Cintra', was born. She had no staff at all to begin with and the physical work of hauling furniture and bales of material was as tiring as the long hours she needed to put into the business. Just as it was all beginning to be successful, a hard blow was delivered in the discovery of serious dry rot in Admiral's House. Life was destined never to be easy for the Fortescues. As they had a full repairing lease on the building they were liable for all costs, which eventually came to the then enormous sum of £3,000. Undaunted, Peggy determined to economise by moving her business from Knightsbridge to Hampstead in order to work from home. Now she included dress designing, for which she was showing a talent. Furthermore, they would throw their all into buying, rather than renting, the damaged house.

That winter, living in 'a cloud of musty brick and cement dust in an icy house half open to the sky', John continued to write his *History* on the second floor, while brocades, silks, velvets and satins were worked upon on the top floor and the drawing room became the Cintra showroom. When not working on his book, John, himself an expert in *petit point* embroidery, delighted in making necklaces of Venetian glass to enhance the clothes. He helped to choose the colours and materials for the tulle and chiffon tea gowns that were to become Cintra's trademark and also composed charming verses to be printed on the invitations for the first fashion show held in the gardens of Admiral's House. Clad in 'my magnolia-tinted georgette draperies with a trail of red roses slung from my waist', Peggy's first collection was well attended and received with enthusiasm.

The fashion side of the business was growing and, in spite of John's objections that it would all put too much strain on her health, Peggy decided she must move to 'Lower London' in order to tempt the 'lazy ladies who found Hampstead too far for them to come for fittings'. A second-floor apartment was found near Piccadilly and the new salon became an immediate success. Society and royalty flocked to her stylish premises for their tea gowns, evening dresses and cloaks. John composed a seven-verse poem, a mixture of business flier and Christmas greeting, for one of her shows held in December, entitled 'Cintra at Olympus'. It tells of a reporter sent to Mount Olympus 'on a special aeroplane' to interview the goddesses for their views on fashion:

Then next came smiling Venus: 'When I rose up from the sea
No bathing dress had been supplied for pretty little me'
But Vulcan didn't mind it; and a certain God of War
Said: 'Clothing, Venus! Nonsense! You look better as you are.'
And – well you know the scandal; it has reached your earthly flats,
For Olympus hums with gossip, and all goddesses are cats!
Still, I think the undraped business has been overdone of late,
So I'm off to Cintra, Sackville Street, at Number Twenty-Eight.

In spite of John's way with words and Cintra's popularity, costs were high and the books could not be made to balance, a situation

aggravated by the occasional non-payment of bills. Peggy was crea-
tive and artistic but no businesswoman. In addition to this worry, the
'mysterious poison', which had now become such an unwelcome part
of her life and was always made worse by stress, flared up again.

After an operation to cure 'new and strange microbes with long legs
and whiskers living in the recesses of my throat' Peggy succumbed with
enormous reluctance to pressure from both John and her doctor to give
up her work. Towards the end of a long, depressing convalescence and
devastated by the thought she could no longer help John financially
with his work on the British Army, she began to do what would come
so easily to her: she sat down to write. Her first articles met with
instant success and soon she was writing for *Punch* magazine, whose
editor Evoe Knox had once asked her to marry him and been refused
– which decision he seems to have received with some sort of relief.
Others were accepted by *The Evening News*, *The Daily Chronicle* and,
for *The Times*, her opinions on 'London Fashions'. Her most lucrative
work came as a regular contributor with control over a new Women's
Page for an Empire paper, *The Morning Post*. From now on writing
would be her profession. It began as, and remained, a necessity for
economic reasons, but her perceptive and amusing articles and books
would bring pleasure to devoted readers over the years to come.

One spring day at Windsor in 1926, John Fortescue, poised for
retirement, was summoned in his dusty walking clothes and rather
casually knighted by King George V, using a sword borrowed from an
officer on guard. Now a K.C.V.O. (Knight Commander of the Royal
Victorian Order), he was bidden to dine with the King that evening,
without the presence of Peggy, and thus ended his many years of service
to the Royal Household. But, in later years, there would be gestures of
kindness from George V to Peggy.

Retrenchment in the face of retirement meant that, with great
regret, Admiral's House would have to be sold and a smaller house,
'Little Orchards', rented in Hertfordshire. Here, succumbing once
again to an attack of her 'poison' and suddenly unable to write, Peggy
struggled to regain her health. And it was here, in the midst of orchards
and pastures, that John announced one morning 'I believe the d.....d
thing's done!' Thirty-six years of toil, producing thirteen volumes, were
over. The *History of the British Army* begins with Cromwell's Standing
Army of 1645 and ends in 1879. It was dedicated to Winifred: 'And

there is she, nearest of all to me, who, in defiance of pain and sickness, has fought incessantly to win me the leisure for completion of my task, and by sheer courage and resolution has prevailed.'

The recompense was small. The set of volumes was expensive and, in the post-war era, sales were lower than anticipated. The completion of the work did not, as was hoped, solve their money problems, but acclaim from historians, military academies and soldiers from all over the world was immensely gratifying. The scope of his research and wealth of documentation gained John the title 'Historian of the British Army' as well as the Chesney Gold Medal, given to those who had made a lifelong distinguished contribution in the field of defence of the realm.

But the constant money worries, coupled perhaps with the fact that they had a less than significant social life in England (though partly by choice), gradually convinced John and Peggy they would be better off abroad. Consuelo Vanderbilt, now married to Jacques Balsan, had a home, Lou Seuil, in the south of France, near the perched village of Eze, between Nice and Monte Carlo. Once again Peggy sought her advice, as she had done so often in the past. Consuelo recommended the region of Grasse, a good 50 kilometres to the west, for its more reasonable prices and healthy climate – and perhaps for not being *too* near Eze. In spite of the Depression the pound was strong and bought a pleasing number of francs, so in 1930 the decision was made to search for a dream home in the sun, where a comfortable, even elegant, lifestyle could be enjoyed for appreciably less than in England.

The house Peggy and John found at Magagnosc, in the countryside near Grasse, has passed into the history of the popular literature of the 1930s and 1940s. It, and the life around it, are described in Peggy's humourously extravagant yet poignant style, in her autobiography *There's Rosemary, There's Rue* and above all in *Perfume from Provence*, books that made her famous throughout Britain and its colonies.

The Domaine Fortescue, as they would call it (rather grandly for its size), was a simple house set on steep terraces of exceptionally fertile and well-cultivated soil, gazing out across a valley onto two rounded hills. Bathed in sunlight for the greater part of the day, peach and other fruit trees grew abundantly, healthy vines filled the property and, above all, there were fireflies – for Peggy a prerequisite of any home in Provence.

As a good omen, on either side of the gate to the Domaine were two tall cypresses signifying Peace and Prosperity. There were few Provençal

Elisabeth Starr as a young woman – early 1920s

Stewart Robinson. Portrait by Ellen Rand

*Dorothea Watts
in her CARD
uniform. Portrait
by Ruth Thomas*

*Dorothea and
Bertie Landsberg
in front of the
mural of La
Malcontenta at the
Villa Malcontenta,
Venice*

Tribute to Caroline
by Rex Whistler

The Swimming
Pool at the
Castello, Opio
1946
by Augustus John

Bridgeman Artists
Copyright Service. ©
Estate of Augustus John;
Christie's Images; Mr and
Mrs Hugh Geddes

farms or estates without these sentinels of hope at the entrance to their property, but it was said that Peace was always smaller then Prosperity, for there is never any peace in the world.

Was it wise to take on a house that clearly would need restoration and substantial extension? To suit their needs it would require, in addition, 'a library-dining room and two large bedrooms over it', involving much building work and expense – and John was sixty-nine years old. But he was entranced by the idea and, with 124 francs to the pound, 'we should do it easily and we can write a few articles to pay for extras'. So the house was bought from its owner, a Belgian count, and contracts signed for the whole project.

In 1931 Britain suddenly came off the Gold Standard and the value of sterling plummeted. The number of francs to the pound dropped with it and, for many permanent expatriates, life became suddenly and unexpectedly worrying. For John and Peggy, with contracts signed, it was too late to turn back. All this meant, agonisingly, that lack of money would return to haunt them. Above all, instead of the tranquil retirement so richly deserved, John would have to sit again for long hours at his writing desk and earn by his pen. Around him builders clattered and banged and filled the air with choking dust, as they had at Admiral's House. In the present depressed climate, articles about the social scene on the Riviera had lost their allure in Britain, and Peggy felt useless and guilty about her inability to earn, as she had hoped, by recording the antics of the rich and famous. Finally, one day, John had the idea she should write stories about their own rather different lifestyle in the hills and send them to her former publisher, *Blackwood's Magazine*. They were accepted immediately, to their great relief.

In spite of continual financial worries and the disastrous removal, from England to Nice, of their delicate furniture, various pieces of which were damaged, involving yet more unwanted expense, they were happy at the Domaine. Lucky in their servants, they were well and amusingly cared for. Felix, their old French gardener with a 'Rabelaisian sense of humour', and Lucie, Italian, plump and tiny, became devoted to the Fortescues, and in addition there was always a housemaid of one or other nationality to do the extra work. The rhythm of the sunlit spring days in their now completed home filled them with delight. Peggy, blessed with green fingers, planted and sowed vigorously, creating an 'English garden' in the long piece of land leading to the house and a well-stocked rose garden at the back. Photos taken a couple of years later show the sturdy terraced walls swathed in great clumps of cascading aubretia, not a usual sight in Provence in those days. When not writing, John tended his vines and fruit trees and oversaw the progress of the vegetable garden for, under Felix's care, they were self-sufficient in vegetables. In fact the crop was so abundant they were more than happy to sell the surplus to a hotel in Grasse. Hens and rabbits, installed in cages on a lower terrace, added to the food supply. The nocturnal mating call of frogs echoing from the water storage tanks all over the hills and valley, followed later by the soaring beauty of the song of the nightingales from the branches of fruit and olive trees, filled the nights with Provençal, if noisy, charm.

In winter the new salon came into its own:

A great fire of olive logs was crackling in the open fireplace at the apsidal end, and our round table, standing upon its circular green carpet, was laid with white napery, glass and silver. I had arranged a bowl of floating red roses in the centre, lit invisibly by the radiance of the hidden lights within the three arched mirror-lined niches above it, in which my collection of glass was displayed. Tall standard lamps with apricot silk shades cast a glow upon old bindings of books at the other end of the room, and shone upon the faces of his [John's] 'Gallant Company' portrayed above them. They looked very fine against their background of buffy-cream wall.

The 'Gallant Company' were prints of some of the soldiers to whose stories John had devoted most of his life. Peggy was a consummate homemaker and they had found that 'in Provence it was possible to be poor with dignity'.

But in the summer of 1932 John 'became suddenly and terrifyingly ill'. It was almost certainly a stroke, for he fell into a coma. He was cared for in this, and subsequent illness, by the respected Dr Brès, whose wife was on the committee of Elisabeth's small clinic, St Christophe – which is perhaps how Peggy and Elisabeth met. Dr Brès is remembered still as having been exceptionally gifted, treating his patients psychologically as well as medically. The illness meant that from now on John, although recovered, would always be fragile, but this didn't prevent him, in convalescence, from 'writing, writing, writing', so badly did they need to balance their budget. It was during this period that he produced the gentle autobiography of his literary life, *Author and Curator*.

After six months of a quiet regime, which seemed to suit him well, December of 1932 brought another distressing setback. Walking around on the cold tiled floors of a Provençal winter night in order to locate a banging shutter, John succumbed to a chill that quickly turned to pneumonia. Once again he managed to recover and his health improved during the following months. A trip to England in the summer of 1933, away from the *grand chaleur* of the south, was a happy interlude. They stayed with Christine Knowles, an ex-client of Cintra, at her house Spilshill Court near Staplehurst in Kent and saw members of their respective families and old friends. But part of every day was always, for both of them, put aside for writing.

With John much refreshed and looking forward to being back at the Domaine and his precious garden, they left England towards the end of September. Five contented days were spent together in the warmth of a late Provençal summer as the sun grew mellow and their grapes ripened on the vines. On the sixth John suddenly began to suffer from severe abdominal pains. After a series of misdiagnoses by several doctors, his trusted Dr Brès being absent, he was eventually taken to Sunny Bank, the Anglo-American hospital in Cannes. There, on 22 September, he died from peritonitis after an operation for appendicitis, performed too late. He had lived just over two years in his Provençal home.

The simple funeral service was held in the tiny Sunny Bank chapel-room during a sunlit break after several storm-tossed days. The coffin was covered with the Union Jack and, obedient to his wishes, Peggy did not follow him to the crematorium from where his ashes were to be sent to England, to be scattered on his beloved Devon moorland. Instead, once the hearse had left, she went into the garden of the little hospital and looked across the valley to the road beyond:

As I looked, suddenly a glorious rainbow shone forth, completely spanning it, and, under this radiant bridge, rushed a great car. I saw a flash of colour – red, white and blue ...

Then the storm broke and thunder roared a last salute.

Chapter 13 🦋

FORT ESCU

After John's death Peggy entered into a period of intense loneliness. She missed him terribly. With Lucie, her faithful housekeeper and Felix, her gardener, she struggled on at the Domaine, surrounded by memories. John's 'Gallant Company' of soldiers looked down on her from the walls of the gallery. The shelves of books on military matters, the unused writing desk, were all a constant reminder of his presence. Only her discipline and strong will prevented her from slipping into deep depression. She had to work, she had to earn her keep and to do this she must write. John had left her what little he had but this would not be enough to live on for any length of time. The following months were spent in negotiation with Blackwood's, her publishers, as to the best means of publishing her writings. It was decided she should compile, and add to, the articles she had already written on her life in Magagnosc and produce a book that would describe the years from their arrival up to the time John died. This became *Perfume from Provence* and would be her greatest success, bringing her recognition as a writer and selling 31,500 copies by the mid-1940s. A great sadness was that she accomplished this after, and not before, John's death, when the rewards would have solved some of their money problems.

It was during this bleak period that Peggy met Elisabeth, 'the woman friend John would have wanted me to have'. Although so different in character and demeanour, they were linked by a mutual need for sympathy and understanding, with Elisabeth perhaps now wishing for a more active companion than the tranquil Polly. Peggy did not share Elisabeth's preference for other women, finding far too much pleasure in the company of handsome and charming men, but she was always ready to be affectionate and her admiration for Elisabeth's style, originality and sense of adventure grew into a true *amitié amoureuse*. Also, her background in the theatre had taught her to be broad-minded. Proclaiming 'I always love or hate at first sight', she was a fiercely loyal friend, all-forgiving towards those she loved. The fact that Elisabeth was estranged from her family touched her heart. But although Peggy, in her books, maintained that Elisabeth was 'quite alone in the world' letters and photographs show that descendants of the Roosevelt Robinson family knew of the Castello and visited Elisabeth there. Although they may have become tenuous, links were never broken with her 'adopted' family.

When sadness overwhelmed Peggy, alone at the Domaine at Magagnosc, the little green room in the Castello, where Corinne Robinson had written her poem 'From My Window – The Castello', was always ready for her. Elisabeth furnished the room next to it as a study and here, from time to time, Peggy could take a short break from her 'beloved ghost'.

On 16 June 1934, the day Elisabeth willed her home to Caroline, a quiet gentleman, a different kind of artist to Rex Whistler, stepped from his hot *wagon-lit* on to the platform at Cannes station. Ernest Shepard, the illustrator of A.A. Milne's Winnie-the-Pooh and Christopher Robin books, had arrived with his pretty daughter Mary to spend ten days with Peggy at the Domaine. He had been asked by the publishers Blackwood's to take on the task of illustrating *Perfume from Provence* and, although much sought-after, had agreed to do so. During his short stay he prepared sketches for the wrapper and thirty-nine drawings of a charm and humour that matched Peggy's style of writing to perfection and must have contributed greatly to the success of the book.

But it was not all work for Ernest. He and Mary toured the coast and hills and, with Peggy, shared a beach picnic with Elizabeth von Arnim, an Australian who had married into the Prussian aristocracy and was the author of *Elizabeth and Her German Garden*. This Elizabeth was now living a contented single life at the Mas des Roses in nearby Mougins, after a brief but disastrous second marriage to Francis Russell, brother of the philospher Bertrand Russell. She was coolly disapproving of Mary eating lunch clad only in her one-piece swimsuit, while permitting her butler to serve their picnic clad in the briefest *cache-sexe* swimming trunks, all much to Peggy's amusement. The Shepards' short stay must have cheered her, for she was a considerate hostess and this was pleasure and constructive business combined.

It was in that year, during one of Peggy's respites at the Castello, after Caroline had left, that Peggy noticed, for the first time, a dilapidated cottage. She describes the event in *Sunset House*: 'In restless mood I was wandering one summer evening along the side of one of our loveliest mountains, through thickets of wild lavender, magenta gladioli, myrtle, thyme, and trailing sweet peas, when suddenly I came upon a little stone house perched upon a terrace overlooking a wide expanse of mountain ranges, valleys and olive groves.' Tucked under the crest of the hill, above and to the north-west of the Castello, it had even better views, for it was higher and hung directly over the wide plain below. Before it lay a stupendous panorama, backed by the mountains which swept in a great curve from the north and seawards to the south. As from the Castello, in the foreground the two villages of Châteauneuf and Opio were perched on their spurs, one above the other. The clocks in the towers of those villages have never told the hour at the same time. First one chimes across the valley and terraces and then the other. It is not an accident: it is done out of courtesy – and to avoid confusion.

With the willpower that was rarely lacking when needed, after the watershed of Caroline's twenty-first birthday, when she forced herself to accept that Caroline would never feel as she did, Elisabeth concentrated on the work of her smallholding and the well-being of 'her' villagers. She made plans to explore, widen her horizons and take on new challenges. So when Peggy felt, 'quite suddenly, with a certainty, that I must leave the beloved Domaine that *Monsieur* and I had made together, if I were ever to make anything of what remained to me of life', and announced she would sell her old home and buy the crumbling cottage above the Castello, it was as if Elisabeth had been given a gift. With the prospect of Peggy as a new neighbour and the conversion of a primitive dwelling into a comfortable sanctuary to occupy her talents as an amateur architect, the future seemed less of a void. Peggy, ten years younger than Polly and with an always willing and generous spirit, would be a livelier companion in any new adventure. Elisabeth, in turn, would be able to offer what Peggy now needed most of all: an 'understanding heart'.

The purchase of the small house, with its olive groves and jasmine terraces (all of which happened to be owned by Elisabeth's laundry woman), and its transformation into a comfortable home, was not rapid. The cliff-hanging negotiations over the purchase price were complicated by wildly humorous horse-trading with a wily neighbour, in order to purchase a right of passage down the hillside to the Castello, a few minutes scramble away. All this, combined with the vagaries of building work, took almost two years. At the time of purchase the house was tenanted by a young Italian family who lived there with their animals in primitive fashion. Slow to move, their departure was hastened, with scarcely suppressed impatience, by the two women keen to take possession. One must feel more than a little sorry for the hopeless household, despatched to a new hovel elsewhere to continue scratching a living.

Even though Polly might have felt she was slowly being replaced as a companion, her affection for Elisabeth never wavered. In contrast, her attitude towards Peggy was one of permanent irritation combined with resentment for the loss of the tranquillity that had formerly blessed their hillside. Polly was settled comfortably in the Bastide and life had been calm and uneventful. Her most beloved companion was now her over-indulged dog, Sophy, who, when not sleeping on her bed, ate everything edible within reach, including butter from the table and the grapes from Elisabeth's vines. So her reactions to Peggy's often rapturous view of events were invariably acerbic and, in letters to her family, she was scathing, if not cruel, when referring to this new arrival. Peggy herself would always be delicately courteous about Polly in her books, calling her 'The Reader' or 'Our Dear Neighbour', although in private she knew 'I was nothing to Poll'.

When, several months later, Peggy finally sold the Domaine Fortescue at Magagnosc and was settled firmly in the green room at the Castello, the better to supervise progress on her new home, there was no escaping the fact that she was there to stay. With her extrovert personality, her strong and vibrant actress's voice and her place as Elisabeth's new and more energetic friend, the women's lives on their hillside entered a new era.

The many months without a home of her own to run were not to prove particularly relaxing for Peggy. Elisabeth now launched herself into a period of constant activity, planning successive, sometimes exhausting, trips for the two of them. These expeditions, whether to shore or mountain, always began with the making of long lists, followed by the collection of supplies and loading up of one of the cars to capacity, with various dogs squeezed into odd corners. Whatever adventure they set out on involved, at some point or other, hair-raising journeys either along the narrow tops of cliffs or up rough mountain roads with abundant hairpin bends, where two vehicles could scarcely pass. Precipices were frequently involved. Whether Elisabeth was driving her small Peugeot estate car or Peggy her much-loved Desirée, a garnet-red Fiat saloon, such dangerous moments brought terror to Peggy and a sparkle to Elisabeth's eye.

Such an expedition was made in September of 1934, when they left for the coastguard cottages at Cap Taillat, near St Tropez, where Eddy Sackville-West had enjoyed himself so much. The cottages, with water drawn from a well on the shore, candles and lanterns for lighting, a chair, store-box and camp bed in each room and nails and ladder rungs to hang clothes, were the perfect canvas for the simple life. Fires of pine cones and driftwood were built on the beach for cooking fish brought in from the sea by local fishermen. Every sun-soaked day ended with supper eaten under the stars to the music of Elisabeth's collection of Negro spirituals played on a wind-up gramophone. Here Elisabeth painted, Peggy wrote and Polly, who joined them later, read. Work alternated with bathing in the warm sea of their secluded bay. All was calm and amicable.

After their return to Opio to supervise the work on Peggy's cottage and to deal with the many tasks awaiting Elisabeth at the Castello, it was not until November that the two women left again, without Polly, for another of Elisabeth's bolt-holes – this time her maisonette in a fisherman's house at St Tropez. The purpose of the trip was to search for furniture for Peggy's new home and for an altar and benches for the little chapel that was to be created in a cave (the former pigsty of the Italian family) underneath the cottage.

St Tropez was then in the last years of its existence as a simple fishing village. Peggy recorded a visit there in the early 1930s:

> Someone had taken me to one of the restaurants (once a mere cave where fishermen had housed their boats, nets and barrels of wine) bordering the port. We had arrived at the aperitif hour, when semi-nude modernity in all its forms invaded the place to drink cocktails. Its arrival was heralded by a chorus of shrieking klaxons, as great cars came snorting into the town, covered by those curious creatures (seen only in the south of France, and they must be seen to be believed). They overflowed the seats

inside, squatted on the bonnets, and balanced themselves on the running-boards. They assaulted the quiet town with their arrogant possessiveness. They perched upon the restaurant tables and shouted for their favourite drinks. It hurt me somehow, to see the simple fisher-lads standing apart and watching all this with eyes half-hungry, half-resentful.

There would probably have been more restaurants opening and more 'semi-nude modernity' but for the international Depression, which meant that American and British tourists were fewer and the small towns and villages of southern France held on to their traditional way of life for longer than might otherwise have been the case.

The women spent a week or so in the apartment in the rue Fontanelle. Here Elisabeth had fitted out simple living quarters, where from her studio in the attic she could look over the ever-changing colours of the Gulf of St Tropez to the mountains beyond. Directly below lay the old harbour with nets spread out to dry and well-used fishing boats bobbing in the bay. This was a corner the young had not yet invaded. The order for the chapel furniture was placed with a local antique dealer and a Spanish dining table with twisted iron legs, plus dining chairs of dark Spanish wood, were bought for the proposed hall-cum-dining room in Peggy's new home.

In 1935 Elisabeth began to plan a lengthy camping excursion in the High Alps, but for once Peggy put her foot down. She had been invited to the Jubilee service for King George V and Queen Mary, with a special dispensation to drive in the royal procession, and she was also longing to see her family again. 'Oh, why do you go to England, Pegs?' said Elisabeth at Easter, 'You know you hate the English climate. You'll probably catch cold and get ill and I shan't be there to take care of you. And I was counting the days until we should start off together, our cars loaded up to the roof. Oh, Pegs.' Peggy was regretful but firm and booked her ticket for England. But Elisabeth was not to be left alone, for that summer Polly cancelled her own plans to visit her family in England and went with her to the mountains. It must have been just like old times.

At long last the restoration of the cottage, with its almost metre-thick walls, was finished. Elisabeth's careful design and Peggy's very personal touch in interior decoration combined to create an inviting home. The pick of the furniture and ornaments from the Domaine, the display of Waterford and Bristol glass, the shelves of precious books and Peggy's talent for delightful effects with lighting made it all feel particularly English. And she had a telephone – number 7 Opio. The only truly distressing decision was what to do with John's military prints, for which there was no room. These she presented, together with a portrait of John, to the Sandhurst Military Academy, where she felt they would always be safe.

Her garden had been planned almost from the moment Peggy had crept on to its moonlit terraces one night, while the Italian family were still in residence. Terraces of jasmine were already there and she decided to sacrifice one of these for a mixture of roses and the intoxicatingly perfumed white tuberoses. Around large boulders level with the house she would have purple Provençal irises, her cascades of aubretia, and white cerastium. Parma violets, cyclamen, primroses and tiny narcissi were already in the earth under the olive trees and she would add masses of long-stemmed Russian Czar violets to form a purple carpet on one of the lower terraces. Sweet peas, pale multi-coloured stocks, pinks and tobacco plants would be planted in beds along the walls and, above all, masses of Madonna lilies would line the path down to the terraces. Now all this was well under way. Beyond the garden lay the grape vines from which the wine she never drank was made, for she maintained alcohol made her neck ache and preferred ginger beer and quantities of coffee – always with a cigarette.

The tiny chapel under the cottage was created with devotion for, although she light-heartedly pronounced herself to be 'a sinner', Peggy was deeply religious. Here she placed a Louis XIII altar in painted wood and benches, all found in St Tropez. A stone font was created out of an old trough discovered in a neighbouring cave. Elisabeth's gifts were two great iron candlesticks for the altar and, to hang by the font, the bronze figure of Christ she had found in the mud of a battlefield during one of her missions on the Western Front. In the tiny 'cloister' at the entrance was a figure of a Madonna and Child, 'Our Lady of Malaga', placed there by Peggy for herself, as an admirer of the Virgin Mary, and out of respect to the people of Opio. Even before they were finished, the house and garden were blessed by the Bishop of Gibraltar, who climbed ladders and clambered over broken walls on a bleak, rainy autumn day in order to bring peace to her new, and final, home.

As for the chapel, it was dedicated to her husband John, her parents and, for Elisabeth, to Stewart Robinson. On the boundary wall, to the left of the double wooden gate that led into the courtyard, the local stonemason, Frances Navella, carved a shield upon which, in a replica of John's script, were engraved the words 'Domaine de Fort Escu' after the Norman name of the family. This news was received with mixed feelings by the Fortescues.

In October of 1935 Italy invaded Ethiopia, then Abyssinia, in a display of muscle-flexing and with the aim of gaining control over the raw materials essential for its own economy. But it was not too difficult to push such distant rumblings to the back of one's mind in a golden Provençal autumn.

On a winter's evening, with olive logs aflame in the fireplace of the newly created little salon, Elisabeth and her dog Babs climbed up from the Castello to have supper with Peggy. And Elisabeth was able to say, 'How cosy this is. Aren't you glad to be installed at last in this divine little safe place? Now no one need be lonely any more.'

Elisabeth's passion for the High Alps grew steadily during those quiet years in Provence, while Europe held its breath. She suggested they should rent a mountain hut near the Meije glacier and Peggy readily agreed, loving the mountains – once she had arrived there safely – almost as much as Elisabeth did. They eventually found a simple *bergerie*, or shepherd's house, on a vast grassy plateau under the lee of the majestic glacier, whose massive beauty was omnipresent. Of course all this would mean that Elisabeth would bring Peggy close to a heart attack by disappearing alone into the mountains for hours to fish in streams or search for wild flowers, invariably involving some kind of adventure.

From then on the Castello seems to have been left to run itself for long periods, for the mountains became Elisabeth's chosen place, combining all she loved best – escape, remoteness, fresh air and perfect rusticity. As soon as summer began she immediately felt the urge to spend the months of heat – and frequently even longer ('what fun if we were snowbound') – high up in the cool air at the *bergerie*. They would then load the cars and set off through the wooded hills where the cork oaks grew, on over plateaux of sparse vegetation, scattered with rocks that pierced the thin soil, and climb ever higher, up seemingly endless hairpin bends through towering gorges, past fertile terraces of almond trees and wild cherries until eventually reaching the grandeur of the mountains themselves. Their route would take them through the towns of Castallane, Digne, Sisteron, Briancon (with which they would become so familiar), Le Lauteret and to the Meije glacier. They went to enjoy 'the valleys starred with narcissi and paradise lilies', the rushing stream that ran from the mountains across their plateau, and the pure air that flowed from the glacier – which Peggy always eyed with uneasy respect. Once at their 'divine *bergerie*', Elisabeth would immediately light the lamp, build a fire and unpack 'to get the place cosily arranged first'. This is where she was now most at peace.

Although Peggy often longed to stay in Opio among her flowers and to tend her garden, she invariably kept Elisabeth company, but she sometimes used the excuse of her jasmine harvest to return early. She delighted in seeing the sacks of tiny, scented white flowers safely on their way to the perfume factories of Grasse. Here they may well have joined the little pink *Roses de Mai* in creating Jean Patou's perfume 'Joy', launched in 1930 by the American hostess Elsa Maxwell as the most expensive in the world.

In spite of Elisabeth's possessiveness and need to be in control of most of the events in their lives, there is no doubt that their friendship was of overwhelming importance to Peggy. She admired Elisabeth without qualification and was thankful that life with her was never dull, so there was little time for sadness.

Chapter 14 ❧
SAN PEYRE

Realising that Caroline would now never return to share any part of her life, Elisabeth was able to write to her affectionately, in 1937, on the death of Caroline's grandmother, Violet, Duchess of Rutland, and to send 'all my sympathy and love'.

True to Elisabeth's counsel, Caroline was finding the courage to be herself. Always trying to avoid the boredom of convention, she began to think of an acting career and was only too pleased to be asked to take part in an amateur film to be shot at Cecil Beaton's home, Ashcombe in Wiltshire. This was a rendition of the play *The Sailor's Return* by David Garnett, with Caroline made up as the black heroine Tulip, Cecil as a sailor and John Betjeman as a clergyman. Edith Olivier, devoted admirer of Rex Whistler, friend to everyone and cousin of the actor Laurence Olivier, noted in her diary:

> There is a terrific row with the Angleseys about Caroline being in this because Cecil couldn't resist having it in all the papers, so now she is in high disgrace. It is odd that she should do these *outré* things and get her reputation, for she has that lovely dreaming, aloof character, always seeming apart from whatever is going on, and without enthusiasm or ardour.

Elisabeth would have heard of all this from Polly and was perhaps slightly comforted that her advice 'to be yourself' had been taken.

With Caroline completely in control of the relationship with Rex Whistler, her waxing and waning continued, as it always would. His infatuation was now constant; he would never be able to 'lay the ghost of Caroline'. On two occasions he had her slightly more to himself: when they travelled to Italy and Austria in 1936 with her sister Liz and their cousin, David Herbert, and once more in 1938 when they visited Venice, again with Liz. Here they were entertained by Lady Juliet

Duff, who would one day become Caroline's mother-in-law. Present during both journeys was Raimond von Hofmannsthal, in 1936 as host at his family's Schloss Kammer with his wife Alice Astor, and in 1938 as Liz's lover.

Raimond, a charming, urbane cosmopolitan, was the son of Hugo von Hofmannsthal, an acclaimed Jewish-Austrian poet and the librettist of *Rosenkavalier* and other operas by Richard Strauss. Not long afterwards, Raimond would divorce Alice and marry Liz on a June day in Paris, before the outbreak of war. On her wedding day Liz carried, instead of a bouquet, an edition of Hans Christian Andersen's *Fairy Tales*, illustrated and exquisitely bound by Rex. Cecil Beaton reported that the feeling of her family was of 'the poor, beautiful girl being wasted'. But she had always known she would choose someone different.

As for Caroline and Rex, a snapshot taken on the Austrian trip does not show a couple flushed with love. They sit at a cafe table, looking away from the camera and into the distance, stunningly attractive and less than happy.

Towards the end of the 1930s a fancy-dress party was held at Ashcombe. Now highly successful, Cecil Beaton could entertain in the style he had always longed for. Among the guests were many old friends, including Rex and Caroline. Rex's brother, Laurence Whistler, described the couple's evening: 'For Caroline he [Rex] had designed a Renoir costume: pink-and-white striped dress, bustle, little sailor hat and tiny parasol. She looked ravishing – and hardly spoke to him or danced with him.' But she was not really unkind; it would have been better if she had been, for then Rex would not have swum in a sea of uncertainty. Instead she remained 'like the moon, cold and out of reach'. In later years, suffering no less, he would write, 'I think of you being angry and love you. I think of you being sulky and selfish and I love you much more. And I think of you being loving and sweet and I would die for you.'

During these years and in spite, or because of, this battle with seesawing emotions, Rex did good work. As well as the mural at Plas Newydd, he achieved great acclaim with the set and costume designs for a play on the life of Queen Victoria, *Victoria Regina*, performed first in the United States and later in England. If only life had given him the opportunity, he might, as well as establishing himself as a portrait painter, have reversed the order of preference then accepted for set design: first Oliver Messel then, if he was not available, Rex Whistler. Caroline was delighted about his latest success and was sweet with him. But she had met Audry Carten again, first encountered with Tallulah Bankhead in London in 1934, and Audry was beginning to be a more significant person in her life than Rex could ever be.

In October 1935, Caroline's father, the person to whom Polly felt closest, had made a decision that brought great joy to the three women in Opio. Charles, 6th Marquess of Anglesey (beloved 'Charley'), had grown immensely fond of Opio during his visits there, and now decided to buy the remaining unrestored property on the south side of the hill as a holiday home. This comprised two stone-built houses, facing south and with a view of the wide, sparsely populated valley below and the road that twisted its way through woodland to arrive eventually at the village of Valbonne. The mountains to the west were not as evident as they were from the other houses so the vista was pleasant rather than dramatic. Charley also purchased the grassland across the lane and facing the main entrance, thus protecting the lane's shady tranquillity, which it enjoys to this day. The dilapidated old buildings, set on two levels, belonged to a local farmer and were, as was usual, crammed with peasant families and their children. But the owner wished to sell and, as with Peggy's house, they were all persuaded to move elsewhere. In spite of her genuine philanthropy, Elisabeth was adept at turning local people out of their homes in order to add a chosen friend to her hillside. So the houses, with 4,500 square metres of land, were duly purchased. Now they were four – and almost everyone was happy.

The prospect of having a much-loved, lively family spending several months each year as neighbours brought with it bustle and excitement. Elisabeth, with yet another project to throw herself into, became closely involved with the restoration, although Polly kept firm control of the interior decoration. It was decided to create a staircase between the houses, with wide steps that would wind their way between the upper and lower buildings to the main gate. With old lanterns hung on the walls to light the staircase at night, it was a great success. A covered bridge over the staircase joined the two buildings. A tower and an extra wing were added and a garage built into the hillside on the precipitous turn of the road below. Seven bedrooms and five bathrooms were planned for the main house. Charley was particularly keen on bathrooms, and many were created under his stewardship of Plas

Newydd, true to his pronouncement that 'Every bathroom should have a bedroom!' A swimming pool was dug on a sunlit terrace overlooking the valley, eventually stretching the water supply on the hill to its limit, and two tall and ancient olive oil *jarres* were bought to flank the back entrance to the house, supplying the vital Provençal touch.

Polly, energised, began to organise the furnishings. This she did through the dignified establishment of Charles Pugnaire of Grasse, *Ancienne Maison, Breveté de Sa Majesté La Reine d'Angleterre* (this Queen was Victoria who, for a time, had a fondness for visiting Grasse). From Pugnaire, a white sofa, a *grande canapé confortable avec grands coussins plumes*, was ordered, along with matching armchairs. Lined yellow curtains were to be hung at the salon window (lined curtains being, almost to the present day, an exception rather than the rule in Provence). An antique wrought-iron chandelier, Louis XIV looking-glasses, Louis XIV and XV chairs, tables, desks and oriental rugs were ordered from dealers in the surrounding towns to furnish a rustic yet elegant salon. To create a feeling of lightness, the walls were painted yellow and the ground floor was covered with white tiles, although Charley confided to Peggy that he feared this might impart an air of the public lavatories at Piccadilly Circus. A round-table discussion on the hill decided the new house should be called 'San Peyre' (St Peter) after their part of Opio. 'Nice, simple and dignified,' pronounced Peggy.

But Lady Anglesey never warmed to the Provençal house and she visited seldom. Even some of Charley's children were cool about it, Caroline feeling perhaps that a visit might be awkward and therefore best avoided. Indeed it was Charley, of all the family, who loved his honey-coloured house the most.

Although the garden was planted up quickly with the usual burgeoning flowers and climbers, the drama that was unfolding in Europe ensured the restoration and decoration took far longer than anticipated, and Charley was never to have the pleasure of living in his fully completed home. But from his frequent visits during the 1930s he is still remembered and liked by the older villagers – to some of whom he became 'Le Marquis d'Angleterre'. And later, in 1939 and 1940, a multitude of paying guests, passing through rapidly, greatly appreciated its comforts.

After almost twenty years in Opio, Elisabeth had gathered around her those she could love and who loved or respected her in return. At this time, if you wished to catch a glimpse of the houses of the four friends, you would follow the rue de la Fontaine as it rose from the entrance to the Castello, climbing steeply, swinging sharply in zigzag fashion until it levelled out. Here began the stone boundary wall of Charley Anglesey's San Peyre, with the shaded grassland opposite, sloping down to a belt of pines. About half way along the wall was a deep porch lined, in friendly fashion, with stone benches. The porch sheltered a wooden door, beside which a small recessed arch housed a brass bell. This was the entrance to the garden of San Peyre from which a flight of steps led down to the house below, for here everything was on different levels.

The wall flanking the lane continued for about 30 metres until a slope led to the entrance of Polly's Bastide. Inside, set back in the wide front garden was her cottage with, behind it, its vine-covered terrace and, below, Elisabeth's little chapel-garage and the entrance gates to the courtyard of the Castello. Back up on the rue de la Fontaine, fig and olive trees jostled against the garden wall of the Bastide and in summer and rain the pines filled the air with the scent of resin. A little further along the lane stood the two great water cisterns that served the houses, sitting in their piece of scrubland and the subject of much frustration over the years. Several metres after the cisterns was Peggy's garage, with its staff apartment, and here the lane levelled out briefly before dipping sharply so that, at one point, it seemed possible to step on to the roof of Fort Escu itself. Beyond the house was her spectacular panorama – the best of all the views. Past the high, double wooden gates of the house, the road gradually flattened out, turning first left and then right, curving away through the grassy terraces until, rising once more, it joined the the main road from Grasse to the coast.

It was not easy, standing on the rue de la Fontaine, to see the four houses, lying as they did in their gardens below the level of the road, with the Castello particularly tucked away. The lives of those within were sheltered discreetly from casual gaze.

In 1937 *Sunset House* was published, Peggy's story of the discovery and restoration of Fort Escu and of her life during those years. This is her happiest book, in which it seems she has found a degree of peace and, with Elisabeth, new challenges. Her publisher, Blackwood's, was keen it should be illustrated by Ernest Shepard in the same copious manner as *Perfume from Provence* and asked Peggy to persuade him to agree.

But 'Kip' Shepard had become increasingly famous, resulting in a vast amount of work, and he was reluctant to become involved in another long project of this nature. Perhaps he also felt he had had a surfeit of folksy Provençal scenes. Peggy tried her very best: 'DO, DO, DO try and do it, Kip!'; 'Send me, if possible, a line of encouragement and say YES!' But he was implacable – this was not to be another *Perfume*.

In the end an agreement was reached: Shepard would draw the frontispiece and the cover, and Peggy herself was to send suggestions for these drawings – 'Oh Kip! What a ghastly thing you ask! That I should send an artist like you ideas.' But she goes on to outline for the frontispiece: 'The *déménagement* of the Italian peasants – the scene in the courtyard would be you at your best – the Italian family, papa, mama and countless offspring, the family cat, dog, hens, ducks – the kicking mule, sacks of potatoes ... the pigs.' The cover, too, she designed by letter, sending pieces of Provençal petticoat material and an idea for the drawing of a star with her house in the centre, asking particularly for a pigeon flying above the roof. All this a busy Ernest Shepard drew, just as she described. The only thing she didn't get was the pigeon.

It was now difficult to continue ignoring the outside world and not to become concerned about the uneasiness of European politics. The Russian Revolution of 1917 had been a rude shock to the aristocracy and bourgeoisie alike, not only in France but across Europe. The enduring fear that the old order could be brought down around them contributed to the rise of many right-wing and fascist organisations who felt they were acting in defence of civilisation against communism. In 1936 Léon Blum, a Jewish intellectual, headed France's troubled socialist government in partnership with the communists, striking fear into those who felt this was but a step on the road to a communist state. The country at the end of the decade was a bitter, fearful, disunited nation. There was only one common wish: that they should on no account be drawn into another bloody war.

Even in Opio the ripples extended as far as the entrance to the stony path leading to the Castello. Here, for a spell, a youth wearing a red sweater straddled the low wall and exhorted the local servants not to work for the enemies of the people. He was ignored and his must have been a boring activity in this quiet rural community. But orchestrated discontent was not far below the surface.

As for Elisabeth, Peggy and Polly, it is not clear how much sympathy they felt for the workers of France generally. They do not seem to have spent time in deep discussion of social problems and they regarded the Communist Party with the fear and dislike common to their class. The *après-guerre* of the First World War, which had been both heavy with tragic memories and, at times, frenetically optimistic, gave way to the *avant-guerre* of the 1930s – increasingly morose and ill at ease. Through all this the women continued with their own, rather narrow, lives and activities – until history allowed this no longer.

PART 2

ALL CHANGE

Chapter 15 ❧

MEN IN UNIFORM

After a series of worryingly lean years, the Cote d'Azur in 1939 experienced one of its most successful seasons. In defiance of the anxiety and tension that gripped Europe, suddenly festival after festival was organised along the coast from Juan-les-Pins to Menton. In February, Cannes held its *Fête du Mimosa*, which included the Dagenham Girl Pipers swinging down the Croisette. That Easter was pronounced the best ever, with hotels full and traffic filling the streets. Endless battles of flowers took place. At *La Joute Fleuri* (The Floral Joust) in Nice, army tanks were decorated as 'The Temple of Love', 'The Enchanted Egg' and 'The Butterfly'. There was a *Combat Navale Fleuri* among boats in the bay of Villefranche, and the rowing teams of Oxford and Cambridge beat Toulouse and Nice on the waterway at Cannes. Throughout the summer, theatres, concerts, horse shows and water sports provided entertainment for a wide range of visitors, and on 13 August a spectacular firework display was held in the bay of Cannes.

In the spring of 1939, the entrepreneur Philippe Erlanger had persuaded the French government that the time had come for France to host its own national film festival and that the chosen town should be Cannes. The proposed opening date was 1 September and the venue was to be the pretty wedding-cake casino on the Croisette near the old port. In spite of the increasing threat of war, Cannes tossed its head and continued with the preparations. With summer, so came the stars. Gary Cooper, Tyrone Power and Edward G. Robinson strolled the Croisette. In Antibes the film producer Alexander Korda married the Hollywood actress Merle Oberon, who had starred with Laurence Olivier in *Wuthering Heights*. But soon Merle would fall in love with a young English pilot, whom Peggy befriended in a cottage in Sussex.

The Riviera was holding its own. Henri de Rothschild was at the Villa Meurisse in Monaco, the Aga Khan on the Cap d'Antibes and Winston Churchill at the Château de l'Horizon at Golfe-Juan, cosseted

by the once-stunning American actress Maxine Elliott. The Duke of
Windsor and his jewel-bedecked Wallis installed themselves at the
Château de la Croë on the Cap d'Antibes – a large villa rather than
a château, sumptuously decorated, as befitted a king. On 22 August
the Duke, not yet bored to tears by life on the coast, presided over the
Bal des Petits Lits Blancs, one of the most important charity balls of the
French social season, held that year at the Palm Beach Club at the far
end of the Croisette. The occasion proved to be a last concerted flash
of wealth and sophistication. Fabulous fancy-dress costumes and daz-
zling jewels adorned the rich and famous. The decorations were created
by artists such as Jean Cocteau and Raoul Dufy. Gaiety and laughter
filled the great reception rooms, although the guests were somewhat
subdued during the course of the evening by an uneasy omen – one of
the worst summer storms Cannes had ever known. On the following
day the non-aggression pact between Germany and Soviet Russia was
announced, which boded ill and resulted in a mass exodus of scintil-
lating visitors. Within the week the neon signs announcing the birth of
what would one day become the most famous film festival in the world
were turned off and would not be re-lit for a number of years.

After completing *Sunset House*, Peggy began working on her
autobiography *There's Rosemary, There's Rue*. This was published in
November (to be reprinted three times in 1940). She had worked on
the book in Opio, at the Coastguard cottages and at the *bergerie* in the
High Alps, during the last years of peace. It described her childhood in
Suffolk, the years as a touring actress at the beginning of the century
and her life with John Fortescue. Full of compassion, humour and zest
for life, it would bring in more of the royalties on which she depended
so much. Meanwhile the months of uncertainty rolled on, and in April
of 1940, Polly wrote to Charley Anglesey:

> Darling Potatoe,
> It's a dream of a day – there are some lovely roses on the new
> little bushes in your garden – it all looks very pretty. I fear you
> won't let [the house] yet, as it's so unsettled here. I don't know
> what they are expecting – but Cannes is not to be evacuated in
> the event of war – the whole of Nice is coming there and all the
> hotels are to be taken over to hold the *Niçoise*. There is supposed
> to be a German army in Italy to stiffen up the ice creamers. Your

loving,
Dahlia Imperialis.

Thus did the rumours fly throughout the year. Nice was not evacuated to Cannes but in 1940 many on the French coast, from Menton up to Roquebrune-Cap-Martin, were sent to Nice, Cannes and the surrounding areas. By this stage thousands of refugees, both rich and poor, had already fled towards the south as the threat from a malevolent Nazi Germany increased.

The alarming situation in Europe did not prevent Elisabeth, with Peggy in tow, heading for the mountains yet again for what was to be 'one last lovely summer'. Polly stayed behind at her Bastide, busily supervising the many finishing touches to Charley's house and the planting up of his garden while searching, even then, for holiday tenants needed to defray expenses. During one of the first alerts, Peggy had received orders from the British Consul in Cannes to evacuate British nationals in the immediate area of Opio in case of war but, as Polly told Charley, 'There are only the nurses [from the St Christophe clinic] and me!' Over the next months Polly wrote to Plas Newydd frequently, often daily, as the situation in France deteriorated. Emerging from a rather slothful existence, she was on the verge of rising gamely to the challenges that lay ahead.

France had already been mobilised and stood down twice, first in September 1938 and again in March 1939, in response to Adolf Hitler's designs on Poland and the Sudetenland in Czechoslovakia. Now Germany had already recovered the Rhineland and seized Austria and Czechoslovakia. Mussolini, having made tentative stabs at mediation between Britain, France and Germany, now signed a pact with Germany that established fascist Italy firmly on the side of the Nazi government. Nice, once governed by Italy, had been French only since 1860 and recovering it was high on Mussolini's wish list. This threw the inhabitants of Provence into a state of fear and confusion. The situation caused particular anxiety among the many Italians. Few were in sympathy with the fascists and some had been in France for several generations, having sought a better life from the crushing poverty of rural Italy. On 1 September 1939, as Elisabeth and Peggy returned to Opio from their high pastures, the German Army invaded Poland and the two women descended into a world that would never be the same again.

A definite order for General Mobilisation was issued in France on 2 September and on the next day Britain and France declared war on Germany. Requisition of property, animals, cars, aeroplanes and ships was put sweepingly into place. Six million men between the ages of twenty and forty-five, including every reservist, were called up immediately. For the second time in twenty-five years, all across France they left their farms, offices, colleges and small businesses and became military personnel within twenty-four hours. Monsieur Michel, the Mayor of Opio and owner of the Opio olive mill, surrendered his post to his assistant and became a lieutenant in the mountain troops, the *Chasseurs Alpins*, whose sturdy soldiers in their dark blue uniforms and floppy berets covered the mountain roads with their rapid walk.

The 'Waiting Army' took to the roads of France. Through the Alpes Maritimes vast numbers of men began moving towards the part of the Maginot Line that lay near the frontier with Italy. Truck-loads filled the roads going east to strengthen the garrisons and frontier posts. Civilian movement of any kind was restricted and papers had to be shown constantly. Over the next few months, Opio, with its three hundred inhabitants, was swamped by almost two thousand soldiers who, the locals grumbled, 'took all the bread'. The hill itself became the *Etat-Major* in the *Quartier Général* of the SFAM (the Fortified Section of the Alpes Maritimes) and thus under military law. Because of its splendid perspective, the roof of Peggy's Fort Escu became the emplacement for a machine gun, pointing over the terraces of flowering jasmine towards the road to Grasse in the distance.

In spite of the disruption, the women were delighted to help the war effort, and had already volunteered their houses during the false alarms of the previous year. Charley's San Peyre was immediately requisitioned by a general – pronounced by the women to be 'quite charming'. This was the respected General René Magnien, the officer commanding the SFAM. The plan was that Elisabeth would have six soldiers at the Castello, Peggy four at Fort Escu and Polly four at the Bastide. All officers were to take their meals at San Peyre. When Polly asked her soldiers if she should think of leaving for England the reply was 'Why ever should you? This is England. We are all one country now!'

But with large groups of uniformed men needing accommodation, the numbers expanded rapidly. The Castello was taken over by a general of artillery and every spare corner was needed, including the exotic Arabian Room. Polly's laundry became the office of a colonel of infantry; woodsheds and garages provided shelter for the *poilus* – the private soldiers. The overcrowding was such that occasionally Elisabeth and Peggy had to leave their own beds and sleep in the wooden hut at the end of the swimming pool terrace. In *Trampled Lilies*, her record of those years, Peggy describes those days:

> We scoured the country for planks to cover earth and cement floors; for straw to cover the planks. I tore my evening dresses out of their protecting linen bags which I stuffed with straw to form mattresses; the gardener ransacked the potting shed for empty sacks and olive sheets; we lent mats and rugs and carpets. We dragged forth bath-mats and *peignoirs* to cover the men, anything and everything that might give some warmth.

In September Polly wrote to Charley:

> I daresay you won't get this. I've had no letters for a week – or papers – but the TSF [radio] gives a little scanty news. The soldiers come clattering up to listen. These houses are packed now, nine or ten in mine and God knows how many in yours – I should think forty or fifty including the garage. Elisabeth has been taken on by the army to get provisions in her car, which is nice as she can go to Cannes, we are going today to have luncheon. She is very busy and has fixed up a tiny dispensary where she sits from 11 to 12 and 5 to 6. Yesterday she had a man with fourteen carbuncles! There are endless sore feet. The first general has gone and a new one has come – who is also charming – and comes every evening and sits from 5 to 6. I think his name is something like Spit. The morale here is wonderful and they all say we must fight on until Hitlerism is completely wiped off the face of the earth. I do nothing and Peggy talks and drives everyone quite mad!

The replacement was General Marie-Charles Spitz, who commanded the 66th Division of the French Army and was quickly held in great affection by the women on the hill. Indeed they felt deeply for all the officers and men – their *famille militaire* as Peggy called them.

The *drôle de guerre*, or 'Phoney War', also known by some in England as the 'Bore War', held France in a state of suspension over winter and into the spring. Endlessly the radio and newspapers repeated: *Rien a signalé sur le front.* The situation was bad for the morale of the officers and men of the French military and responsible for a considerable loss of momentum, during which various political groups seized the opportunity for mischief-making. But in the Alpes Maritimes this uneasy vacuum was not felt so much, as the perceived threat coming from the Italian border kept the army there busy with manoeuvres and poised for action.

The French government had sent out an official *Appel a la Générosité* designed to encourage civilians to engage in voluntary activities in order to help the French war effort. Polly wrote:

> Elisabeth and I went to Cannes to nose about – just to see if there was any work. We went to the station where the Yanks have started a canteen. There was a row of perfectly frightful old women [the aid workers] sitting on a bench munching biscuits. There had only been one train full of soldiers all day, and when it arrived they weren't there! We thought we wouldn't care about that job and came home deciding we'd do nothing!

Of course there was no question of doing nothing. As well as her first-aid post, Elisabeth had already done her bit for the *Défense Passive*. This was another project set up by the government which requested local mayors to encourage the population to involve themselves in practical actions, such as digging shelters and creating vegetable plots. She had ordered yards of Turkish towelling and organised sewing parties to make 'gas-masks' for the village children 'like square sponge-bags with an oblong seeing-space cut out wherein we sewed strips of talc'.

In mid-September the Soviet Red Army invaded Poland and the Polish Army surrendered. Within six weeks Stalin and Hitler annexed and divided Poland into east and west regions respectively. The Palm Beach Club on the Croisette sobered up to become a hospital-in-waiting for the French Army. On 3 October, a month to the day after war had been declared, President Franklin Roosevelt (a cousin of Theodore Roosevelt and married to Theodore's niece, Eleanor – who was also Franklin's distant cousin) declared the United States neutral, to avoid becoming involved in another European war. There was a strong feeling of *déjà vu*.

The weather in September had been perfect, but towards the end of the month it began to pour with rain. The soldiers, who had formerly spent the warm, scented evenings sitting on stone walls on the terraces, writing letters and reading or playing cards, suddenly had few places to shelter. Now, at the end of every long day, often racked with anxiety for their abandoned families and with the future horribly uncertain, the men had little to look forward to but an evening crammed together in an overcrowded and chilly garage or barn lit by candles. Opio had no café or bar and, in any case, the army staff discouraged visits to such places, aware that communist provocateurs and fifth columnists were frequently there, only too ready to approach discontented soldiers.

Their officers quickly realised there was someone to whom they could turn for help. Seeing how professionally Elisabeth had swung into action and the ease with which she dealt with the soldiers, they asked her to organise a place where the men could gather and that they could call their own. In the village, virtually stripped by requisitions, one striped non-waterproofed tent was found, set up and became a rather flimsy canteen for up to six hundred soldiers every evening. Card tables, games, a gramophone and writing materials were found. Needles, thread, darning wool and buttons were provided so the soldiers could attempt to mend irritating holes and missing buttons. With the help of the troops, Elisabeth, Peggy and Polly, along with Amy Paget of Château Garibondy plus anyone else they could rope in, served gallons of hot coffee and chocolate from 6 to 9 p.m. Relays of men trudged in off the dark, muddy lanes, stayed for a while, and left warmer and happier, having had a chance to relax and be cosseted by a group of women – even though these were motherly rather than alluring.

As Polly reported, Elisabeth had quickly set up her treatment centre in her studio. Trained as she was from her nursing years, with her expertise and her 'soft, slow voice' she worked once again to soothe the distress of her beloved soldiers. Wearing her soiled Red Cross brassard from the First World War, which she had always refused to wash, Peggy remembered: 'She tended raw feet, sore throats, cut and septic fingers and other minor miseries.' On one late autumn night:

A little fire crackled cosily in a corner, its flames flickering over Mademoiselle's pictures on the walls; the green-painted medicine-chest; Mademoiselle, herself, sitting on a three-legged stool, her small dark head bent over a spirit-lamp as she sterilised something or other

... A big man, with a queer heart and threatened bronchitis, lying peacefully in a real bed with real sheets; turning at intervals dogs' eyes, which filled up slowly with tears, in the direction of his adored Mademoiselle from whom in so few days he must be parted.

For the order had come for the division to move on, destination unknown, and the three women were laden with entreaties to write to the wives and parents of the men with messages of reassurance of good health and spirits – even if it was often not the case.

There were numerous lunches and dinners of *adieu*. A 'Gala Dinner' was given by the officers who had been lodged at San Peyre. The menu for the occasion, created by the regimental artist, still survives. A stork, the insignia of the regiment, heads the page, flanked by the Union Jack and the *drapeau tricolore*. On the left-hand side are charming sketches of San Peyre, Fort Escu, the Bastide and the entrance to the Castello. Food was then still plentiful – the guests ate *sardines grillées* and hard-boiled eggs as a first course, followed by roast chicken, green beans and salad. Roquefort, Belpaese and goats' cheeses came next and, for dessert, 'moka' ice cream with grapes, pears and figs. A good, sensible meal, taken with white wine, a Rosé de Belet [from the area around Nice] and a *rouge de pays* – perhaps the Castello wine.

So the first contingent left and others followed – wave after wave, hundreds upon hundreds of men, who stayed for a while and then gathered together and marched onwards and upwards.

On 1 October 1939 Polly wrote:

I dispense writing paper in a tent, the rain pours in! It's quite impossible to get any money, it's very odd and I can't think why. Neither can the manager, who has shrunk smaller than ever and asked me to take him some carrots. They won't take cheques on an English bank. It's awfully gloomy and depressing, if it feels like this after only a month, what will it be like after a year or more? ... God, how I hate it all. Oh, I musn't be like this – I can't have any guts – and it's the utter boredom of it, mixed with horror at its having happened. Otherwise it's lovely here, and one need not know there is a war on as far as comfort goes, all the same as usual except that I can't go out of the Alpes Maritimes without a permit, or into a military zone – but I don't want to do that.

Le 3 Octobre 1939

Menu

Œufs en tonneaux
Sardines grillées
Poulet   rôti
Haricots verts
Salade
Fromages de Roquefort
de Belpease
de Chèvre

Moka
Raisins . Poires . Figues

Vin blanc
Rosé de Belet
Rouge de Pays
Café

GALA DINNER MENU

Indeed she was already in a military zone, surrounded by swarms of soldiers, most destined for the border towns and the High Alps. Elisabeth now decided to follow them.

By the end of October the first snows had fallen in the mountains and she had been told many of the men in the units stationed there were lonely, cold and ill-equipped for their postings. The combination of the sudden mass mobilisation across France and the inability of the army to equip properly the vast numbers involved, ensured that when winter began in the mountains, their comforts would be few. Apart from those right on the front lines, who had to be well supplied, the 'Waiting Army' was short of everything, including warm clothes. So, with Peggy, Elisabeth settled down to their familiar list-making, but the items were different now. She was determined to provide the troops with as many necessities as she could lay her hands on and at the same time create *foyers* (rest centres) for the soldiers across the Alps. After all, this is what she had been trained for. She decided to 'make each foyer a three-in-one affair'. This would consist of a canteen-cum-games room; a stock of every kind of warm clothing, including underclothes, and a medical store. She also planned to beg or buy stocks of wool and employ the wives of local soldiers to knit the warm garments the men needed so badly.

Always rather obsessive, Elisabeth became totally dedicated to her new project. Rest or relaxation of any kind was now out of the question. All that mattered, once again in her life, were the soldiers of the French Army. With both of them drawing on their respective savings, which they would do with increasing abandon, Elisabeth and Peggy soon had enough bought and donated clothes and useful equipment to 'fill three cars to the roof' and, with Jean, a faithful local chauffeur, set off on their first challenge. They took the familiar road into the mountains through Castellane, Digne, Sisteron and on to the town of Briançon. Here they realised just how much they were needed for, as Peggy wrote, where they had come from 'the jasmine was still in flower and the people of the south still clad in summer attire. So were the first *poilus* we saw, crouched by their anti-aircraft gun in the snow wearing blue cotton trousers and shirts, with noses and hands to match.'

At Briançon they painfully, but with determination, created their first mountain *foyer* and climbed ever higher into the Alps.

Chapter 16 ✿

LADIES WHO DO

The small purple fruit were being shaken from the grey branches of the olive trees on the terraces of Opio. But Elisabeth, in the winter of 1939, had no interest in the charm of the olive harvest. Now committed to setting up and equipping her *foyers* she was already, at this early stage, rapidly depleting her strength and finances.

In November the Red Army invaded Finland, forcing it to sign a peace treaty the following March, and in the same month Paul Reynaud replaced Edouard Daladier as Prime Minister of France. The Communist Party was outlawed and its leaders either imprisoned or in flight. In December, Mussolini's government had made a declaration of non-aggression towards France, but this did little to reassure those living near the border. After one of the heaviest snowfalls the south of France had known, making Elisabeth's work even more hazardous, the vacuum-like early months of 1940 seemed endless. They rolled on in a suspension of uncertainty. But much was going on in Europe and it was all unpleasant.

In April the German army invaded Denmark and Norway and day by day France grew more confused and unsettled. Somerset Maugham in *Strictly Personal*, his account of those years, said of the French in 1939 that, 'When the time came for these armies to fight their battles, with those brilliant and energetic officers to lead them, they could be trusted to acquit themselves valiantly.' But after the Battle of France in 1940 he felt rather differently:

The General Staff was incompetent; the officers were vain, ill-instructed in modern warfare and insufficiently determined; the men were dissatisfied and half-hearted. The people at large were kept ignorant of everything that they should have been informed of; they were profoundly suspicious of the government, and were never convinced that the war was a matter that urgently concerned them; the propertied classes were more afraid of bolshevism than of German domination; their first thought was how to keep their money safely in their pockets; the government was inept, corrupt and, in part, disloyal.

But there were others, such as Maurice Buckmaster, head of the French section of the Special Operations Executive in Britain, which would handle undercover agents going to and from France, who declared: 'Those who engaged the enemy in battle fought with the spirit and courage for which they had been so admired in the last war.' Elisabeth, for one, had no doubts, no qualms. Again in her lifetime France must fight the good fight against the aggressor, with the splendid French Army rising to the challenge as it had in the First World War. And, when the time came, her Army of the Alps did not let her down.

Meanwhile, Elisabeth and Peggy continued their work for the soldiers. Peggy described one of their successes towards the end of that year:

'It is Christmas Eve in one of the many *foyers* we have by this time installed in the High Alps. Picture a huge derelict barn. The soldiers have covered gaping voids in its walls with brown paper and sacks to keep out the snow. Upon a great stove, glowing red-hot in its centre, steams a mighty *marmite* filled with hot spiced wine. A glistening pine tree stands in a corner, and at its foot, half-hidden under the dark branches, the soldiers have arranged a little crèche peopled with brown-cloaked shepherds and gaudy kings. All along the sides of the barn, straw, thickly strewn, forms a sleeping-place for many soldiers and the muffled breathing, stamping and snorting of cows and stabled mules near-by, gives one the illusion of a huge crèche enfolding a tiny one. The scene is lit by shepherds' lanterns and packed with soldiers from wall to wall, some playing cards, some playing lotto, draughts, dominoes or chess; others licking pencil-points as they laboriously indite letters to their families; a studious few reading books; a more frivolous majority joking over the illustrated magazines; a reverent group crouching over the creche ... and a musician, seated upon the corner of a table, playing the accordion.

It was to create scenes such as these that Elisabeth now lived. She became driven by her work, all humour gone, her large, dark eyes haunted by fatigue and obsession. Suddenly, feeling that Peggy did not have the stamina for the task and had become simply irritating, she dropped her abruptly and took others in her place. Peggy, hurt but always forgiving, felt that Elisabeth 'needed me no longer; she was not herself any more. Everyone's personality, and all the gentle lovely things of life were submerged or swept away by the red flood of war.' Instead, Peggy was 'lashed up our mountain [to Fort Escu] by the whip of Elisabeth's tongue to pen propaganda for our friends in America; commanded to accept every social invitation I received and to interest everybody I met in our work for the French Army'. Polly kept Charley up to date: 'Elisabeth and Peggy have come down and E. goes up again in a week – she won't have Peggy any more as she says she is quite useless.'

In a letter to Caroline Paget in later years, Peggy tried to find an explanation for this sudden change of character. She told of an incident when Elisabeth became ill with exhaustion in early 1940 and was persuaded to go to Sunny Bank Hospital for a rest. Peggy had gone down to see her:

> Suddenly – *à propos de rien* – she looked at me in quite a hostile way and said: 'I suppose you think your face matters. It doesn't matter at all. What does matter is that thousands of French soldiers are going to their death not properly equipped'. I merely said that I quite agreed with every word she said and quietly left her. But for ELISABETH to say that. It was just a dreadful moment of bitterness she had and really meant nothing ... for she was sick unto death even then.

Elisabeth was not well. Influenza, which she caught while establishing the first *foyer* at Briançon, was followed by repeated colds and severe sinus trouble. Her will had always been stronger than her body and now this will pushed her forwards and forbade her to give up. Again and again she returned to the Alps, as heedless of those narrow, treacherous and snow-covered mountain roads as if she were going to Cannes on a shopping trip. She continued to create her *foyers* and to equip remote first-aid posts as she went. Now accompanied by younger and fitter companions than Peggy, as winter wore on she often took her skis, the more easily to reach far-flung military stations. The work was relentless and relentlessly she pursued it.

Soon a serious lack of funds obliged her to do what she most disliked: While she would have far preferred to be working in the field with her soldiers, she had to do what others were already busy doing – form a charitable organisation, recruit patrons and a committee and take an office in Cannes in order to raise money for the project. During the 'phoney war' the expatriates of the Riviera had been rising to the occasion. Charitable organisations sprang up, mainly in rooms donated by hotels. The charities were generally complementary to each other and almost always run by strong-minded women. Virtually every expatriate who was anyone on the Riviera was involved in an aid programme or on a committee, sometimes on several at the same time. Organisations were founded to provide aid for families left bereft by the mobilisation, or to provide comforts for the troops, such as *Le Vin Chaud du Soldat* and *La Soupe Populaire* and *Les Optimistes de la Riviera*. An Anglo-American Ambulance Service was formed, as well as an ambitious Anglo-American Home for French Children of the War (sadly soon closed for lack of funds).

Amy Paget, already helping out in the *foyer* at Opio, was on the committee (now running properly) of the *cantine militaire* for soldiers arriving at Cannes station on troop trains. In spite of her advanced age she was fired with compassion and determined to help the men as much as possible. Polly reported to Charley: 'Amy came yesterday. She's furious because she says no one will "use" her and she doesn't see why because she is eighty-two she should have nothing to do. She goes out with a large Provençal bag full of cigarettes for soldiers, but her chauffeur won't ever stop for her to give them – so she is whirled home again with her bag as full as when she started!' Polly herself, rather lonely in the new order, helped here and there and kept an eye on the now ever slower progress on Charley's house. With her dog, Sophy, as her main companion, she spent her evenings playing patience, writing letters and, after her whisky and soda, making a big fire and sleeping in her salon well wrapped in blankets, as she 'liked to see the firelight flickering'.

Elisabeth officially founded her *Foyers des Soldats de France* in Room 153 at the Carlton Hotel in Cannes. She determined to run the programme as economically as possible: money was to be used to comfort the troops, not for setting up a well-equipped office. Letters were typed on plain paper with no smart letter-heading, and sometimes rather erratically. Although one of the smallest committees of the aid charities Elisabeth's was, nevertheless, the charity with the most physically demanding work. But she managed two coups. As Patron she enlisted Henriette, Duchesse de Vendôme, Princess of Belgium. An *habituée* of Cannes in her Château St Michel, Henriette was a true philanthropist who, along with her husband, was described as having '*une qualité de coeur exceptionnelle*'. In January 1931 she had, with the Duke of Connaught, cut the ribbon to inaugurate the improved Promenade des Anglais at Nice. When her husband, Emmanuel d'Orleans, Duc de Vendôme, died a month later, his hearse, followed by members of the royal families and aristocracy of Europe, was pulled by six horses along the streets of Cannes, the crown of France resting on the coffin.

As Honorary President, Elisabeth recruited Madame la Marechal Joffre, the widow of the Commander of the French Army at the beginning of the First World War. Joseph Joffre was fêted as the leader of the victorious French troops at the First Battle of the Marne but subsequently blamed for certain failures on the Western Front and replaced at the end of 1916. Created a Marshal of France, he played a diplomatic-cum-military role in bringing the United States over to the Allied cause in 1917, his efforts being received with various degrees of appreciation by the French government of the time. This connection was possibly why Madame Joffre was happy to put her name to this charity, created to bring comforts to French soldiers and run by an ex-American. Also on the committee was the respected Princess Gennaro de Bourbon des Deux Siciles, born Beatrice Bordessa of a bourgeois Italian family from Chester in the north of England and a founder member of the St Christophe clinic at Châteauneuf. Along with her husband she never, even under threat, renounced her anti-fascist principles and chosen home of France. So Elisabeth's committee was of quality not quantity.

Fund-raising and distribution of aid and money were the aims of these committees and, for as long as they were allowed to exist, they did much good. Tea dances, galas, dinners and sporting events were energetically organised in order to raise funds for their respective causes. Women turned out to these in their slim, wide-shouldered evening gowns, often decorated with appliqué flowers on the neckline, or sparkling with diamante embroidery. Orchestras such as Ray Ventura's played for dancing, and the bars of the grand hotels buzzed with life every evening. There was still hope – of a kind.

'The galas were an agony to us all', wrote Peggy in *Trampled Lilies*, 'for, if we were to interest moneyed people in our schemes, we must put in an appearance:

> *Elisabeth*: I'm not going. I'd rather die than go. I'm not a social person. I hate functions. You must all go and I shall go to bed. Nothing you can say will induce me to go. I haven't any clothes. I'd far rather give three thousand francs to the *foyers* than spend it on a Lanvin dress that I shall never wear again.
> *Chorus of Neighbours*: But you'll HAVE to go. After all, the *Foyers des Soldats de France* is your baby and you'll be expected to go.

In the end she was persuaded, if Polly went too, which she did, most reluctantly squeezed into an old black lace dress of Peggy's.

But sometimes the anxiety and uncertainty all became too much. One evening, after an afternoon working in Cannes, Elisabeth and Polly repaired to the Grand Hotel on the Croisette, from which they each wrote a letter to Charley on hotel writing paper – an action neither of them could later recall: 'Darling,' wrote Polly, 'I am writing this in the bar with the barman's pen. There's been a sort of meeting and I'm so hot and red in the face. Such a sweet letter from you this morning. You may not know it but our friendship means more to me than anything in my life – it always has and always will. There, I've said a mouthful!' And from Elisabeth: 'Dear Charles, You could not believe your eyes seeing Poll and myself sitting in this putrid bar drinking like mad. Sad part is I can't feel any effects, except my face is bright red. How I wish you were here. Is there no escape for us??' Several weeks later, Polly wrote to Charley: 'Did I write to you from the Grand Hotel? Did Elisabeth too? Fancy, I don't remember. All the Cannes ladies are screaming about shirts and socks and scarves and rushing about like mad things – it's really like a bear garden. I think they all enjoy war work.' One does wonder what they had been drinking that evening.

The charitable ladies interchanged aid programmes and attended each other's meetings at the Carlton. Recorded Polly to Charley in April:

There's a committee meeting dear!! Lady Warwick is Chairman. I expect it will be stormy – I know it will be funny and I know exactly what it will be like. E.S. [Elisabeth] will sit and stare and not say or listen to one word. Marjorie [Warwick] will be very official and now and then say she was Mayor of Warwick for eight years. Princess Gennaro de Bourbon, who should be Queen of Naples but isn't, and Mrs [Harold] Baring can't stop talking for one moment. Isabel Pell, an obvious American, beautifully clothed by Chanel and Molyneux, very efficient and self-confident, won't say a word but will probably giggle and [there's also] Muriel Warde [née Wilson, an American-born artist from Chicago] who is as deaf and as lazy as I am – that's all. Interesting isn't it?
Bless you,
Poll.

From an influential American family, Isabel Pell was a flamboyant socialite who refused to keep her preference for women in the closet. Her character is described in *The White Blackbird* by Honor Moore and it was said her family paid her a handsome allowance to ensure she made her home away from the United States. Like Elisabeth at Opio, she had her own 'fiefdom' in the village of Auribeau, above Cannes. With bobbed hair, sporting a distinctive white streak in the fringe, she was athletic and striking. Isabel would be the last love of Elisabeth's life, after celibacy that seems to have been maintained since Caroline had left. She moved into the Castello for a while at the beginning of the war, but the affair was short-lived; as Elisabeth wrote sadly, 'Isabel Pell is dying here.' Fitter by far than Elisabeth and bursting with excitement as the drama unfolded in France, Isabel would soon discard her couture clothes and Tabac Blond perfume by Caron and take to the hills, joining the Resistance and becoming known as *La Dame à la Mèche Blonde* (after her striking multi-coloured fringe). For her escapades she would collect acclaim, a medal and a road named after her in the village of Puget Théniers in the Low Alps. She would also, as Peggy later recorded to Caroline, 'break our beloved's heart, as we knew she would'.

With the early spring of 1940 came a delightful breath of fresh air.

All was quiet again on the hill, for there was a lull in troop movements, when Charley Anglesey and his son and heir, Henry, Earl of Uxbridge, decided, at a time when few people were contemplating a holiday in Europe, to visit Switzerland for a skiing trip. They would then continue to Opio to see Polly and check on progress at San Peyre. They felt no compunction at travelling out of Britain at such a time, for Charley was too old to join a regiment and Henry too young, although later he would see action, becoming a major in the Royal Horse Guards. They thoroughly enjoyed their weeks at Klosters and Saas Fee, 'particularly as there was a welcome shortage of fellow skiers – just a few Germans and an Italian or two.'

Everyone, particularly the now rather solitary Polly, must have been overjoyed to see them once they reached Opio, although for Elisabeth it was perhaps bitter-sweet to be with Henry, Caroline's brother. The weather was good and the men were able to relax, don shorts and enjoy the spring sunshine and their almost-completed Provençal house. While there, Henry used his talents, nurtured by Rex Whistler, to help Elisabeth design two large posters advertising a golf tournament in aid of the *foyers*, to be held in May at the coastal town of Cagnes-sur-Mer, between Cannes and Nice. Henry did the pencil designs and copious lettering and Elisabeth drew and watercoloured two figures at the top. Many years later, Henry, now 7th Marquess of Anglesey, wrote: 'To the left is a khaki uniformed soldier with a golf bag over his shoulder looking apprehensive, and on the right a Chasseur Alpin in blue uniform with alpenstock and snow covered chalet behind. He looks even more alarmed!' As he wrote, the two drawings hung behind him on the panelled wall of his library at Plas Newydd. They had done so for many years.

Charley and Henry only just made it back to Britain in time. As Germany violated the Netherlands in the first weeks of May, they joined the hoards fleeing France in 'an appallingly overcrowded train' to Calais and home.

Polly wrote: 'I can't say how much I miss you and your son. I can't describe it.' And the golf tournament was never held.

Chapter 17 ❧

FLIGHT

The coast was in turmoil, not all of it unwelcome. Those refugees who, looking ahead, considered the Riviera safer than the north, had begun heading south during 1939. Now they were joined by others in increasing numbers. These included many Jewish families, both French and foreign, heeding the warnings towards their people already clearly given by the Nazi regime. Many, although by no means all, of these refugees were well off, and those that were used the hotels, shops and restaurants, so were welcome as far as the local tourist industry and town councils were concerned. But then things happened very fast.

The German invasion of the Low Countries began on 10 May 1940 when Hitler launched 'Operation Yellow'. With overwhelming numbers of Panzer tanks supported by artillery bombardments and the relentless dive-bombing of the Luftwaffe, they swept through the Ardennes, tore a gap in the defences at Sedan and began to push the French Army and its Allies around northern France like pieces on a draughtboard. As the people of Alsace were evacuated into the Dordogne, and Calais was threatened, Peggy knew she had to leave. Feeling suddenly that 'every bit of me was English', that she was no longer of use in Opio, terrified that she might not see her own family again if she stayed but racked with guilt at leaving Elisabeth and abandoning her only home, she worried herself into a state of numbness before the tormented decision was made.

She let Fort Escu for £250 a year to an Englishwoman from Cap Ferrat who wanted to get away from the coast, then threw herself into a frenzy of packing and storing. The rent for the tenancy would go to Elisabeth if times got harder – they did and it was very much needed. Peggy's Fiat, Desirée, was also given to her and would be put on blocks, the expensive tyres hidden elsewhere. Her precious wedding presents, silver, Waterford glass, linen and books were crated up and placed in a back room in the apartment of Gabrielle de Croze in Grasse. Gabrielle was the only close French friend embraced by the group on the hill and had sometimes joined them at the *bergerie* in the High Alps.

As travelling companion and self-appointed protector, 'His Hugeness', as Peggy called him, appeared on the scene. A British ex-military man of great stature with 'a thick thatch of silver hair', he was a 'lord of an island in the West Indies' and had been recuperating in Monte Carlo after an illness. His identity is so elusive that no member of Peggy's family has ever been able to trace him. Together they intended to head for one of the unoccupied Channel ports and 25 May was to be the day of departure.

During those last days at Fort Escu, Elisabeth suddenly put her aid work to one side and spent time with Peggy. She, who refused to leave, was gracious about Peggy's flight: 'But you, Pegs, can probably help much more by doing pen-propaganda in England and talking of our men and our *foyers*. In any case, being English, you are quite right to go.' Peggy and her companion would be accompanied by Peggy's neurotic black cocker spaniel, a birthday present from Elisabeth four years earlier. Called Dominie (it could well have been Dominate), he was a one-woman dog and would bring her pleasure and anguish in equal measure.

The day of departure arrived. In a car owned and driven by their trusted chauffeur, Jean, and with a squirming Dominie pinned in Peggy's arms, they left Fort Escu. Two people saw them off, Irma, Peggy's faithful Italian maid, and Elisabeth: 'A small stone house bathed in sunlight, and two figures, both beloved, standing outside its great gate, silent and like statues of grief ... the slender form of Mademoiselle, whose face had suddenly become all eyes, staring at me. And so, I left them.' The car swept down and away from the hill and the life she had known there and sped down the Grasse road towards the coast.

As Peggy began a long, uncertain journey across France, Polly remained. Why did she stay? She no longer wanted to: 'How lovely it sounds at P.N. [Plas Newydd]. I'd give my soul to be there. Everyone is preparing to shoot high pheasants ... I expect the ice-creamers will become high pheasants here.' The 'ice-creamers' were the Italians, who would become first gamekeepers and then, indeed, pheasants. In spite of the uncertainty, Polly was still in the throes of supervising carpenters and painters at San Peyre and hoped she had found a friend to take Charley's house for the immediate future: 'You ought to get £500 I should think ... she will come only with her butler and cook'. At the beginning of June she wrote: 'I've had every window covered with blue paper as no glimmer is allowed. I never get any English papers so only know what I hear over the air. I don't go to Cannes oftener than I can help, indeed there is no way of getting there, the buses only run now and then.'

With Peggy gone, as well as the last of the soldiers, Polly was often alone, apart from her daytime servants:

> The girls [Elisabeth and her helpers] live at the Carlton, as they have to be on call day and night ... I'm digging more terraces for winter veg – the flowers will have to look out for themselves this summer. I can think of no more local news to tell you. I feel like Jane Austen, never even mentioning what is going on – but I can't – it all matters too much to write about. 'Stormy weather'. Loving Poll

As the Battle of, and for, France raged, Peggy and her large companion were driven northwards along the back roads of France, along with a frantically unnerved Dominie. She was later criticised by some of her fans for having taken her cocker spaniel on the journey and that, in her book *Trampled Lilies,* the story of the mobilisation and her subsequent flight to England, she dwelt too much on her anxiety for his welfare and whether she could obtain a permit for him to cross the Channel. This, while she was surrounded on her journey by a mass of human misery. Peggy explained it by saying how much Dominie meant to her and that she suffered from 'cockeritis', which explanation may or may not have been convincing, depending on the reader.

Heading for the Atlantic port of St Nazaire they passed, fleeing south in the opposite direction, wave after wave of refugees from Belgium and the north trying to escape the ever-increasing horror of the advancing enemy, many leaving behind their crops and cattle to the mercy of the invader. Then news came of the capitulation of the Belgian Army on 28 May 1940, the worst news of the war to date.

Operation Dynamo, the evacuation from the beaches of Dunkirk of over 300,000 British and French troops, including the ill-fated British Expeditionary Force, began on 27 May and was to last for eight days. Many French troops stayed behind to try to hold the perimeter and were consequently killed or captured, causing a feeling among the French that they had been abandoned by the British. Peggy's husband, John, had once written, 'The French soldier follows strictly the military text-book. If he is surrounded by the enemy he will say: "By all the rules of warfare I am defeated," and will lay down his arms. The English soldier, in like position, will fight on desperately and refuse to acknowledge that he is beaten. Through sheer dogged cussedness he may, and often has, turned a technical defeat into a victory.' The circumstances in which the British Army found itself in the north of France in 1940 were perhaps not conducive to this theory, but it would have been interesting to know John's opinion on the Miracle of Dunkirk.

When Peggy and her travelling companion eventually reached St Nazaire it was deserted. A solitary British naval commander informed them that St Malo in Brittany was now their only hope. Wearily they swung across country and headed further north, eventually reaching the port only to find the boat for England had left an hour before. The lull before the next wave of refugees arrived meant, at least, they could now each have a hotel room in which to rest, rather than begging for a bed or sleeping in a railway carriage as so many others would be obliged to do. Peggy now bade Jean, their chauffeur, a tight-throated goodbye, paid him handsomely and saw him off as he began the dangerous 1,000 kilometer journey back across France.

The next days were spent in sending cables to Elisabeth, family and friends, and pulling every string her determined will could muster, in order to get the necessary papers for Dominie. She succeeded, and eventually a telegram from the Ministry of Agriculture in London arrived, giving permission for him to set sail. After a voyage without threats and only a minor hold-up as the Solent was cleared of mines, the boat sailed into Portsmouth. Taking leave of 'His Hugeness', Peggy then went through the purgatory of leaving Dominie in quarantine kennels.

But soon she was, rather dazedly, unpacking her few possessions on an English summer's day in June in a large, comfortable bedroom in her brother's rectory in Hertfordshire, far from the enveloping warmth and grey-green scented hills of Provence.

Chapter 18
Saved or Betrayed?

Although the word of Mussolini had always been mistrusted, the abandonment of his promise not to attack France and the actual declaration of war by Italy on 10 June 1940 shook the Riviera to its foundations. Within a few hours fifty per cent of the population of Monaco fled, adding to the confusion in the countryside. The town of Menton, the area up to Roquebrune-Cap-Martin, the small mountain town of Sospel and the villages following the Italian border into the upper reaches of the Alpes Maritimes were all evacuated. Those fleeing west from the Italians ran into the mass of those fleeing south. This caused, particularly in the Rhone/Aix-en-Provence area, such a tangled mass of humanity that the military authorities, overwhelmed, were obliged at one point to stop all traffic, leaving everyone to sort themselves out as best they could.

In fact the Italians did little in the first few days, except to send their air force on sorties, dropping the odd bomb along the coast, frequently missing their targets. At Marseille they lost planes to anti-aircraft fire, as well as six bombers brought down in the space of a few minutes by a solitary French fighter. That some of the French soldiers carried Italian names and may have had a cousin on the other side of the line could matter no longer. On 15 June the Italians began to shell the French defence lines, forts and towns. Although the French fortifications were strong, there were an inadequate number of troops to defend the length of the border. This fact made their bravery all the more admirable, although they were aided initially by the faulty aim of the Italian artillery, whose shells often fell wide of the mark. But, as the days progressed, heavier shells were used with ferocity to try to break through the undermanned defence line and the situation became increasingly tense.

The battle ran from Menton into the hills and on into the mountains, while overhead Italian planes machine-gunned and bombed the coastline. In this they had a free hand, for there were no longer any airworthy French planes in the area. At one point the Italians landed troops at Menton and reached Roquebrune-Cap-Martin, 7 kilometres to the east of Monte Carlo, but a handful of *Chasseurs Alpins* and French Colonial Troops threw them back to the border. Higher up, a contingent of four hundred French *Eclaireurs-Skieurs*, the dashing mountain guides, held the line in the face of heavy bombardment.

Prime Minister Reynaud had declared: 'Every lamp post of Paris should be defended.' In fact the lamp posts changed from French to German ownership with comparative ease. As the Nazi army advanced southwards through northern France, the French government retreated from Paris to Tours and on to Bordeaux. Paul Reynaud shuffled and re-shuffled his ministers and appointed the ageing Marshal Philippe Pétain, the 'Hero of Verdun' in the 1914-1918 war, as Minister of State. The Commander-in-Chief of the armed forces was changed from General Gustave Gamelin (for failure to defend adequately) to General Maxime Weygand (inclined towards armistice). The government now included a younger general and ex-tank commander, Charles de Gaulle, as Under-Secretary of State for War. De Gaulle's armoured divisions had acquitted themselves with honour but failed in a counter-attack against the Germans.

The Germans entered Paris on 14 June and from then on continued to breach every remaining point of defence from east to west. France immediately appealed to the United States for help, as well as to Britain – planes, above all, were desperately needed to attack German troop movements from the air. Both requests were refused or stalled, and the remaining British troops ordered to return to England. This proved to be excellent propaganda for the Nazi regime, who would make it widely known that 'The English will fight to the last Frenchman'.

Prime Minister Reynaud faltered, then suggested the French troops should surrender and the government move to North Africa. General Weygand disagreed, insisting instead on an armistice – 'A stopping of hostilities by common agreement of the opposing sides'. Reynaud then proposed the 'hypothesis' of an armistice, prompting de Gaulle's resignation and rapidly, in confusion, his own. His government was replaced by one led by Marshal Pétain, with General Weygand as Minister of Defence. Finally, on 17 June 1940, Marshal Pétain, with obvious relief and the certainty he was doing the right thing for France, opened negotiations with Germany: 'It is in all honour and in order to maintain the unity of France ... that I embark to-day on the path of collaboration.' In the south, the French had planned a counter-attack to recapture Menton on the very night the armistice was declared. They were immediately ordered to stop combat. Twelve hours later, in a small blockhouse at St Louis, near Menton, a group of soldiers was still fighting fiercely to prevent enemy troops entering France by that route. It took several French officers of high rank to persuade the six men and their corporal to lay down their arms, evacuate their stronghold and join the New Order.

General Charles-André-Joseph-Marie de Gaulle, of brilliant mind and stubborn bent, had fled to London by boat. He would later set up his Free French office there with his Chef de Cabinet, Lieutenant Hettier de Boislambert, and Aide de Camp, Geoffroy de Courcel. (Lieutenant de Courcel's nephew, along with Madame de Courcel, an expert gardener, now own and care for Peggy's *Perfume from Provence* house at Magagnosc). In his rallying call of 18 June through the BBC, de Gaulle pronounced: 'No matter what happens the flame of French resistance must not die and will not die.' Heard by few in the turmoil gripping his country, it was enough to have him cashiered as a traitor in his absence.

France was now split into two zones, the northern occupied zone and the southern free, or unoccupied, zone – the latter being governed, from 11 July 1940, from the spa town of Vichy. Marshal Pétain became Head of State of Vichy France, and considered his region to be France itself and thus virtually independent, and believed he had saved the whole of his beloved country from yet another encounter with devastation. The demarcation line separating the two zones ran from Orthez in the Pyrenees, north to Poitiers then west to Geneva. The unoccupied zone encompassed the Alps, part of the Massif Central, the Pyranean foothills, the Rhone valley and the Mediterranean coastline, the southern part being an area of much aridity. The occupied zone encompassed the rest, including the recently annexed region of Alsace and Lorraine and the Atlantic coastline.

The British consuls up and down the Riviera were in rather a quandary: as the military situation deteriorated they were unsure what to do with their remaining expatriates as, it seems, was the British government. The blackout had ceased to be firmly enforced and civilian traffic was allowed to take freely to the coastal roads. The British authorities had done nothing to discourage their subjects from visiting or returning to the region in spite of the Italian menace. From May onwards, when the situation in the north became more dangerous, British refugees from Italy, Belgium and northern France had joined others flocking to the south. F.C. Stone, an employee of the British Consulate in Monaco, a neutral principality, recorded in a long memorandum to Anthony Eden at the Foreign Office: 'Constantly augmented by the dwellers of the towns and villages, soon over two million people were crawling at a snail's pace along the roads of France, engulfing on the way military convoys and fugitives from the front. The columns of refugees were bombed and machine- gunned by the Luftwaffe and they buried their dead by the roadside.'

Major H. Dodds, His Majesty's Consul General at Nice (described by Somerset Maugham as 'amiable, without a great deal of energy'), called a meeting of the consular staff of the Riviera towns on 16 June. A British naval officer, sent from Marseille, advised that the evacuation of all British subjects was imperative, but was not sure how this was to be achieved, as few suitable ships remained in the Mediterranean. The Prince of Monaco offered to take British subjects under his protection, but this idea was rejected. The British Embassy, which had moved with the French government to Bordeaux, confirmed when contacted by telephone that 'All British subjects should be strongly urged to leave whilst it was still possible to do so.' How to do so was the problem. And every day more and more became stranded as they escaped from the occupied to the unoccupied zone. During the meeting of the consular staff it became clear that Major Dodds had been instructed by the British Embassy to leave his post and escort the Duke and Duchess of Windsor to a Royal Navy destroyer and on to safety in Spain.

Later, back in Britain, Dodds would declare that the only way the south of France could regain purpose and honour would be for the Germans to occupy it completely, presumably then the majority (if not all) of the population would know who their real enemy was – and that it was not other Frenchmen. He had to wait a while before his theory could be put to the test.

But hopes rose, for on 17 July two British cargo ships, the Saltersgate and the Ashcrest, were suddenly made available. The advice to leave, now became an order to evacuate. If this chance was not taken, the

Sir John Fortescue.
Portrait by William Strang

Peggy on an English beach
in the 1930s

E.H. Shepard with his daughter
Mary at the Perfume from
Provence *house, Magagnosc*

Elisabeth painting Caroline's
portrait in her studio at the
Castello

Peggy in the courtyard of Fort Escu in 1936

Polly Cotton with her dog Babs

Elisabeth in the doorway of the Bastide

Frontispiece to Sunset House by E.H. Shepard
The déménagement of the tenants.

The salon at Fort Escu, 1936

The back garden at Fort Escu, 1936

British government would accept no responsibility for the fate of those who remained. Everyone was to be at the Cannes Customs House early on the following day. What everyone did not know was that the ships were two colliers – iron-decked, grimy coal boats from Liverpool, able to take only 1,000 refugees in total, and not equipped for those. The evening before the embarkation, the Carlton Hotel on the Croisette was brilliantly lit and crowded. Somerset Maugham, staying the night there before joining the exodus next day, found: 'They were in evening clothes, some of them a trifle the worse for liquor, and there was about them an air of hectic, hysterical gaiety, which was sinister.'

In contrast, the scene at the Customs House on the morning of 18 July was despondent. Those who could be contacted, and who had chosen to leave by the ships, were gathered together in the early morning heat. Each person was allowed one suitcase and told to take a blanket and some food. Although some were rich society people who had hung on until the last minute, the majority were older and less well-heeled: retired army officers and colonial civil servants, governesses and employees of great villas and various businesses. Among them were a few just-recovered patients from the Anglo-American Sunny Bank Hospital in Cannes, who had decided to chance the voyage. The other British hospital, the Queen Victoria at Nice, had brought their remaining patients to Cannes, mostly on stretchers, for the hospital had closed its doors that morning, being on the Italian side of the Var River. It was quickly realised it would be impossible for anyone who was ill to embark on such ships, so they were taken up the hill to Sunny Bank, which the matron, Margaret Williams, was determined to keep open and which was about to begin five long, lean and anxious years.

Cars were sold for a song or abandoned on the quayside, and Consul Stone of Monaco recorded: 'A large crowd of French people had come to see this melancholy sight and many were openly affected by the departure of these British whom they had always regarded not only as their patrons but also, in many instances, as their friends.' On the two ships, of which the largest had quarters for a crew of only thirty-eight men, 1,300 were eventually crammed on board, the iron decks burning from a day at rest in the Mediterranean sun. As Somerset Maugham, sailing on the Saltersgate, wrote 'One lady, when she came on board, told an officer that of course she wanted to go first class and another called the steward (there was only one) and asked him to show her

where the games deck was. "It's all over the ship, madam," he replied.'
Also on the Saltersgate were Hedley and Morris, the matrons of the St
Christophe clinic. They had left the children in the hands of Nicole
Vincens from Grasse, a benefactor of the clinic, who cared for it, in
increasing penury, for the duration of the war. And Elisabeth would
be there, for a while, to help.

Rumours circulated about the swift departure of the staff of the
various British consular offices. Major Dodds, ordered to escort the
Windsors, had left quickly, returning only in August as an attached
advisor to the American Consul General at Marseilles. According to
Consul Stone, Dodds now 'regretted his rapid departure'. The Consul
General at Monaco left his office to the care of Stone, without taking leave of the Prince of Monaco or the Monagasque government,
which action was not looked upon favourably. The Consul at Cannes
announced that he would stay – and was gone by the following day. As
Stone reported, there were those who felt the consular officers and their
staff should have considered their duty required them 'to share the fate
of the people under their protection', and that in this they had been less
than valiant. The staff of the Cannes office were particularly criticised.

Polly, along with the other British expatriates, had received the order
to leave now or be left behind. So it was that one morning her maid,
Madame Rita Arnando, unlocked the door of the Bastide and went
into the kitchen to prepare breakfast. On the table she found a note:
'J'ai du partir. Peut-pas expliqué. Miss Cotton.' Polly had gone. It seems
she took one look at the coal boats and decided to try another means
of escape, ending up on an unseaworthy yacht with an untrained crew.
In a Mediterranean patrolled by enemy submarines, her little boat followed the colliers for guidance, first to Marseille, where they picked
up a convoy, and then towards Algeria, hitting a bad storm en route.
During the voyage the passengers on the coal boats were frequently
sure their tiny companion had been lost in the waves, only to see her
reappear bravely each time. Eventually all three boats approached the
town of Oran, which, to their amazement, was blazing with light.
Blackout was no longer necessary, for the French colonialists had that
day accepted the armistice and the Vichy regime.

After perhaps the most arduous journey the passengers would ever
know, the boats arrived safely back in Britain, the yacht trailing about
a week behind towards the end of the journey. On 20 July, Charley

Anglesey's sister Bee, Countess of Pembroke, wrote to him: 'Darling, Polly arrived very tired and has had a peaceful week here – sleeping a great deal. Twenty-seven days in that tiny boat in appalling seas – sharing a bed with a strange woman who stank!' Lady Pembroke was writing from the 'pandemonium' of Wilton House, now an operations centre for Southern Command, where, in the Double Cube Room under the gaze of the Van Dyke portraits, Caroline had danced at her coming-out ball six years before. It was in this room that plans would be laid for the eventual invasion of France.

Not everyone had gone. Some had not heard the order to leave, others had nowhere to go to in England. Amy Paget, at Garibondy, was not minded to leave her family home to a bunch of – she knew not who. In spite of her great age, she set about a different sort of aid, growing hidden vegetables and encouraging her hens to lay in order to supply the occupants of Sunny Bank Hospital and the many others who would have to be fed. Local lore tells of a contingent of German soldiers entering the gate of Garibondy in 1943 to look over the house and being met by Amy draped in a Union Jack flag. It seems they left both her and Garibondy alone. She was, of course, both old and well-connected.

So at least Elisabeth still had one old friend, not too far away.

Chapter 19 🌰
MANY WATERS

Peggy heard of the fall of France sitting by the bed of a wounded French soldier in a Hertfordshire hospital. The ward had been set aside for those Frenchmen who had been injured at the evacuation of Dunkirk – and the radio was on.

She was dressed in her *foyer* uniform, which she and Elisabeth had put together for their aid programme, consisting of a black *Chasseurs Alpin* beret pulled down to one side, a belted navy blue jacket and matching flared skirt. This was the outfit she would wear on all her official duties until the end of the war, sometimes enlivened by flat black golfing shoes wound around the ankle by long ties in ballerina fashion. Peggy had returned, now fifty-two years old, to a defiant Britain of barrage balloons, armed roadblocks and the prospect of rationing – a country in a state of war. So she must have been a little proud of her unofficial uniform, for there were men and women in uniform everywhere and she could feel one of them.

That day in June 1940, deeply shocked and bewildered herself by the news of Marshal Pétain's announcement of the armistice with Germany, she suddenly found herself surrounded by distraught Frenchmen crying with shame, climbing from their hospital beds, even tearing the decorations from their tunics. One image, related in *Trampled Lilies*, stayed with her above all others, as she watched the reaction of a young soldier who had been badly wounded:

> This helpless figure could make no movement of anger or despair, but from the one remaining eye rolled great slow tears. When I thought of him in the watches of the night, symbol of my beloved France, maimed, conquered, dishonoured and heart-broken, my tears flowed too, and, in the morning, I almost felt surprise that they had not stained my pillow red.

Peggy knew then how difficult it would be to make the British understand the trauma across the Channel, but knew too that this is what she must now try to do. Desperately worried about Elisabeth, hating to think that Italian soldiers would now occupy their hard-won *foyers* in the Alps, wondering if her own home would be abandoned or requisitioned, she felt she must, at all costs, organise her thoughts and her life. She was still living with her brother and his family, so the first step would be to find a place of her own where she could live independently and bring Dominie when he came out of quarantine. Perhaps (joyous thought) she would be joined there by Elisabeth, who was now being urged by her friends to retake her American citizenship, make her way to Lisbon and either head for England or climb on the PanAm Clipper to America – the seaplane to freedom. If Elisabeth came to England they could work together for the French once more.

She went into action. Recent welcome royalties from *Perfume from Provence*, *Sunset House* and *There's Rosemary, There's Rue*, propelled her into equipping the home she did not yet have. It was now early August, the sales were on, and it was a good time to buy before the looming Purchase Tax came into being. She bought her furniture mainly at Harrods and, deciding that her future home would be in deep wooded countryside, chose everything to blend with woodland colours: 'A carpet of a tender shade of almond green, little divan-beds covered in green; blankets and sheets, also green; and a chintz for curtains and covers to match the carpet, with a design of buff and russet leaves; the oak, ash, beech, lime and elm of England and the vine and loquat of Provence.' She chose simple, unvarnished oak furniture, her saucepans and kitchen utensils were in shades of green and the cutlery had wooden handles. For Dominie's longed-for return from quarantine there was a basket of plaited rushes complete with green blanket and cushion. He was now all Peggy had of her years in Provence and she missed him sorely.

Trusting, as she always did, that her fate would be guided by benevolent spirits, several weeks later an advertisement in *The Times* presented itself: 'Weekend cottage, unfurnished, without electricity, wonderfully situated, hidden by woods, surrounded by streams. Low rent suitable tenant.' It sounded perfect and, although it was not, it became part of her life. The cottage was in the heart of Sussex, in the parish of Ardingly, and Peggy describes taking a Green Line bus from the local station and driving through, 'one of the most charming villages I have seen' (Lindfield), where she spotted an inn called 'The Bent Arms' – 'all ready to enfold me'. The county was not totally unfamiliar, for her parents had semi-retired from Suffolk to a courtyard cottage in Petworth, further to the west. Here her father had become rector of the ancient churches of Barlavington, Coates and Burton – his 'three little cathedrals of the Downs'. Both parents were now at rest in the churchyard at Burton Park on the road to Chichester.

Everything about the house she chose was a challenge. In a dramatic setting in a deep valley cut through the Wealden sandstone, it stood, a tile-hung, gabled gamekeeper's cottage, surrounded by an expanse of rough grass and shrubs. Beside it were three small lakes, interspersed by little tumbling waterfalls. On one side woods of pine and broad-leaved trees rose up to the fields of the rolling Sussex countryside, and on the other a steep slope, thick with shrubs, climbed to the lawns of Stonehurst, the big house far above. Rhododendron and azalea bushes were everywhere, dotted about the flat land around the cottage and lakes, spreading up the slopes and brushing against the huge sandstone outcrops that ran through the estate. On her walks Peggy would pass 'Big on Little' in the neighbouring Rockhurst Estate. These rocks, the upper as large as a small house and poised on top of one much smaller, caused William Cobett in his early nineteenth-century book *Rural Rides* to exclaim: 'How, then, came this Big upon Little? What lifted up the big? It balances itself naturally enough; but what tossed it up?'

The only motor access was down a steep and narrow track off the Ardingly road, with a one-in-three gradient that a small, sturdy car could just about handle in low gear, provided the ground was dry. She had bought a grey, 7-horsepower Baby Austin, with the assurance it could 'climb a rock face'. Because her cars had to have names, it was christened the 'Grey Pigeon'. This pigeon would spend most of its resting time in the wooden garage at the top of the gradient and rarely made it down to the lakes. The cottage itself had been 'abandoned to the jackdaws' and there was no telephone. All in all, it could not have been more inconvenient and, needless to say, Peggy was determined to love it. So the contract was signed and Many Waters became hers, 'for five years or the duration of the war, whichever is the longer'. They had it just about right. She chose the name Many Waters from a passage in the Bible, Revelation 14: 2: 'And I heard a voice from heaven as the voice of many waters.'

The Stonehurst Estate, of which Many Waters and its valley were a part, was owned by the Strauss family. Stonehurst itself was a large house in the typical late Victorian style. The former occupant had been M.R. Patterson, the owner of the Glasgow firm that made Camp Coffee. The main house stood by the old Roman road that ran northwards through woods and farmland and eventually into Surrey, and was perched far above the deep wooded valley, which abounded in the wildlife Peggy loved. Opposite Stonehurst lay the manor house of Wakehurst Place. Once the home of a branch of the Culpeper family, related to the herbalist Nicholas Culpeper, Wakehurst was now owned by Sir Henry Price, who had made his fortune producing off-the-peg suits and become known as the 'Fifty Shilling Tailor'. The grounds of Wakehurst had been planted throughout the years with trees and shrubs from all over the world and would eventually become 'Kew Gardens in the Country', giving pleasure to countless members of the public who would stroll through its glades and valleys. As with almost all large houses in wartime Britain, both Stonehurst and Wakehurst were requisitioned: Stonehurst as a home for very young evacuee children escaping the Blitz, some with their mothers and mostly from the East End of London, and Wakehurst as a base for mainly Canadian Army regiments.

Peggy's landlady was Mrs Strauss, her 'White Lady' in *Beauty for Ashes*, for she always dressed in flowing white garments. The widow of a wealthy banker, she was a gifted musician, a *grande dame* and rather eccentric. She lived with her middle son, Robert, but in these years of war, both were installed in a couple of the estate lodges, having made way for the evacuated babies and toddlers.

Until Victorian times mid-Sussex had the reputation of being a rather backward region, not over-favoured with great houses or strong aristocratic connections, as were the shires or even neighbouring Kent. The area's only period of prosperity was during the Elizabethan iron industry, when the woods and forests had rung all day with the sound of water-driven hammers producing ordnance for the regiments and ships that protected Britain. From these years came the timber-framed iron-masters' houses that are sprinkled around the area. But it was essentially a rural community and the tradition of local landlords and tenanted farms had preserved the ancient hedgerows and sunken lanes, over which in summer great trees met in high arches, giving the impression of green church naves.

When Peggy arrived, Sussex was still, for many villagers, a fairly primitive place. There was no question of a bathroom in the simple cottages – often only a cold tap in the house and earth closet in the garden. Roads were generally narrow and dusty and people rarely travelled far from their homes. Although many thousands of evacuees had been sent from London to Sussex at the beginning of the war, this was part of the front-line defence area primed for invasion. The beaches were mined and defended with barbed wire and anti-aircraft guns. 'Pill-boxes', concrete emplacements for machine guns, were built overlooking roads and rivers, while agile Spitfires stood ready for their young pilots to hurl them into the air from the runways of small airfields. The planes of the Third Reich droned overhead on their way to bomb London and the docks. It was suspected that Sussex was a base for fifth columnists, so the newly formed Civil Defence Force or Home Guard was constantly on the alert for these clever spies. But, as Peggy announced to her brother: 'If I must be in a war I would rather be of it!'

While she stayed with a sympathetic neighbour, the cottage was quickly mended, made watertight and decorated, with a small bathroom added next to the main bedroom. When the day came for the furniture and household goods to be delivered, this was achieved – dramatically – by lorry, cart and slithering horse, over fields and down steep woodland paths to the bottom of the valley. The delivery men were egged on by Peggy's mixture of nervous energy, extrovert humour and the promise of a plentiful supply of beer once the job was finished. By evening all was safely installed in her new home by the lakes.

But what was missing were books, and especially John's books. A letter sped to Macmillan, John's publisher:

> I am in a gamekeeper's cottage and do miss my books MOST TERRIBLY. Here I have an ABC, and the AA road book, a cookery book and a Bible and I am STARVING for books to read. If you could let me have them at an author's price I should be very grateful for naturally I am even less rich than before. If I could have his [John's] smaller books I should feel less desolate.

Four of John's books were sent as presentation copies, *The Story of a Red Deer*, *The Three Pearls*, *The Drummer's Coat* and *My Native Devon*.

Now Peggy could begin to try her best to feel at home.

Although isolated in her valley cottage, Peggy was not completely alone. Her sister, Marjory, had married into the Arbuthnot family living near the neighbouring village of Turner's Hill, and this led to introductions, for although she declined many social invitations, she was also gregarious by nature and needed to have people in her life. Majory's daughter Fay, who had joined the Army Territorial Service (ATS) was posted to Lindfield, a short bus ride away. Also, a fan of her books, Renée Goldspink, whom she had known slightly in Provence, wrote to ask if she might live near her and share any work she embarked on. Renée, small, sensible and bespectacled, with the air of a brisk schoolmistress, was anything but glamorous, but she loved parties, cocktails, hunting and an active social life. Well-to-do in her own right, she had married a curate but, finding the life of a clergyman's wife not to her taste, had divorced him, returning when he fell ill with cancer and nursing him until he died, for she had a good heart. A luxurious kennel on the Stonehurst Estate, which had once housed Great Danes, was converted into a makeshift home and here Renée was installed, becoming the 'Lady of the Kennels' in Peggy's books and never identified further. Useful (above all, she could cook), she would become Peggy's most faithful and stalwart friend, if not her most treasured one.

Meanwhile, Blenheim bombers attacked the airfields and ports of France and Belgium, and Spitfires, fighting to the death high above Sussex, drew, across the blue skies of an English summer, their beautiful tracery of victory over invasion. And from RAF Tangmere, further south and under the lee of the Sussex downs, the dumpy yet agile Lysanders were beginning their moonlight flights into torchlit flarepaths in the French countryside to drop and pick up British and French agents. The Resistance, out of Britain, was under way.

With Dominie released from quarantine in December, and most appreciative of the valley and woodlands around Many Waters, Peggy began to relax into her new home and plan how she could best help France. But fate would always take account of the words she had uttered so often as a child: 'Let things happen to me, nice or nasty – and go on happening.'

As for Elisabeth, still in her 'old dim house' in the hills of Provence, she was, like everyone else in the free zone, now far from free.

Sussex Map

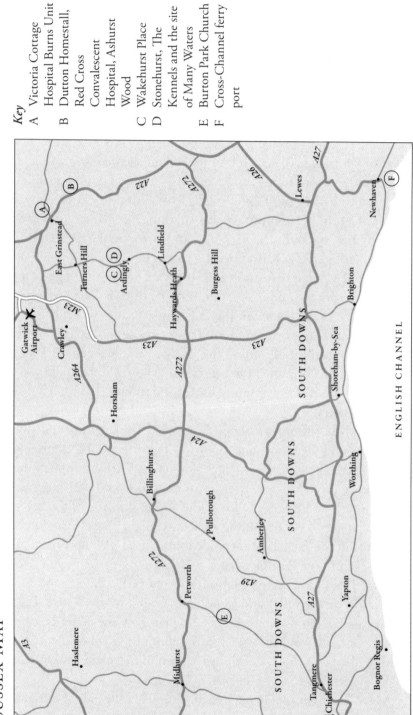

Key

A Victoria Cottage Hospital Burns Unit
B Dutton Homestall, Red Cross Convalescent Hospital, Ashurst Wood
C Wakehurst Place
D Stonehurst, The Kennels and the site of Many Waters
E Burton Park Church
F Cross-Channel ferry port

Chapter 20

RICHARD HILLARY

It was while she was making her home at Many Waters that Peggy met and befriended someone she would never forget – although, sadly, he would forget her. In September 1940, Flight Lieutenant Richard Hillary, whose name would become linked with the history of the Royal Air Force in the Second World War, found himself trapped in his flaming Spitfire and spiralling down towards the English Channel.

One of the handsomest young pilots in the RAF, Richard had flown with his squadron out of Hornchurch, near London on the Thames Estuary. Wearing neither gloves nor goggles – preferring to feel unencumbered – he was, with his companions, defending Britain and seeking to add to his enemy 'kills'. On that particular day he quickly had the chance to hit and damage a Messerschmitt 109. Giving chase, rather than curving away, he fell foul of another enemy aircraft, which opened fire with both cannon and machine guns, causing his Spitfire to burst into flames. He just managed to slide his cockpit canopy open before losing consciousness. The burning aircraft then rolled over on its back, tipping him out into the void over the English Channel. Regaining consciousness just in time to pull the ripcord of his parachute, he slowly followed his burning machine as, seconds later, it dived into that precious strip of water and disappeared from view.

Richard was rescued by the crew of a Margate lifeboat, which had been watching the dogfight from the shore and spotted the descending parachute, but had trouble locating the injured pilot. When they did so, Richard's stunning good looks were no more. Terribly burned on the face, hands and legs, blinded by swollen flesh around his eyes, he was lucky to be alive. But coming back to something approaching real life would be a marathon in itself. When he was shot down he had just seven days combat experience behind him, during which he had accounted for at least five enemy aircraft. He was not resentful. Professing himself to be unpatriotic and believing that the reason for fighting in a war was a means to, 'swiftly develop all one's faculties to a degree it would normally take half a lifetime to achieve', he never ceased to believe that 'in a fighter plane, we have found a way to return to war as it ought to be, war which is individual combat between two people, in which one either kills or is killed'.

In addition to still being alive, Richard had another stroke of luck: the pioneer of reconstructive surgery, the New Zealander Archibald McIndoe, had established a burns unit at the Victoria Cottage Hospital at East Grinstead in Sussex. McIndoe's intricate and experimental operations on the desperately badly burned – his 'guinea-pigs' – would later earn him a knighthood and a place in medical history. After being transferred from Margate, Richard had begun treatment for his injuries at the Royal Masonic Hospital at Ravenscourt Park in London, which used the excruciatingly painful wax-sealing method to treat burns. It was from here that McIndoe collected him and took him south to Sussex, where he had developed his own methods of care.

Educated at Shrewsbury and at Trinity College, Oxford, Richard was born in Sydney to Australian parents. He was an only child. Plump and round-faced as a schoolboy, as he grew older he became increasingly attractive, with his straight nose, well-shaped mouth and 'blazing blue eyes'. Athletic, a gifted oarsman who stroked the champion Trinity College boat two years in succession, he was a linguist and read widely. He also had a complex, existential side to his character, which caused him a good deal of defiant soul-searching.

It was Richard's hands that had suffered most in the accident. They were so badly damaged as to become claw-like and would never really recover. His legs would eventually heal, but it was the injuries to his face that were initially the most distressing. The eyebrows and lashes had been burnt off. The flesh of the lower forehead, the bridge of the nose and the top lip were also all badly burned. To McIndoe came the task of working on a man whose looks and confidence had been striking, enabling him to attract virtually any woman who pleased him – and he was rarely without one by his side. Now he would have to come to terms not only with his changed looks, but also with what to do with the rest of his life. McIndoe's reply to Richard's question as to when he might fly again was 'The next war for you', made in decided tones.

In Sussex, in the early months of 1941, the long and painful skin grafting began. Here Richard fought off depression, recurring infection and intense pain, and established himself as the arrogant *enfant terrible* of the ward – admired by some, disliked by others. In spite of the raw and patchworked look of his face and the claw-like hands, he did not lose his allure. In David Ross's biography of Richard Hillary, there is an account of a fellow patient at East Grinstead remembering: 'He always seemed to have several beautiful girls on the go at the same time.' There were a number of times when we saw a pretty girl rush from the ward, handkerchief clutched to her mouth, crying her eyes out because Richard had jilted her. We were very envious of him.' His fine physique, edgy but intense charm and the remains of his good looks ensured that, for the remaining years of his life, lovely women would continue to float around him like dipping swans.

In between operations, he was sent to recuperate in a luxurious convalescent home for officers, Dutton Homestall, in nearby Ashurst Wood. The house was the home of 'Johnny' Dewar (of the whisky company of that name), his wife, Kathleen, and daughter, Barbara. The family, like so many others, had condensed themselves into the lodge and given the main house over to the Red Cross. It was no time before Barbara Dewar and Richard had formed the sort of relationship that prompted Barbara to give him a photograph of herself in a ballgown inscribed: 'To my darling Richard, with all my love, Barbara'. The flirtation was short-lived and ended amicably, although the episode caused Barbara's mother intense irritation. It was felt by some that Kathleen Dewar was herself attracted to Richard, and that this unreciprocated feeling turned into unfriendly aggression. In later months a fearsome quarrel erupted between them, in front of other patients, in which Kathleen accused Richard of taking advantage of his injuries and hiding behind them in order not to have to return to flying. In her fury she called him a coward – an accusation never to be forgotten.

Peggy had been introduced to the owners of some of the large houses in the neighbourhood. So it was at Dutton Homestall, one day in February 1941, she was invited to lunch so that Richard, 'who wants to write and doesn't know how to begin', could meet and talk with her. In fact, Richard had never read any of Peggy's books, but Kathleen felt that discussion with a 'real' writer might encourage him to follow through his idea of putting his experiences down on paper. A good dry day meant Peggy could drive her car right down to the door of the cottage and collect a quivering Dominie, frantic with excitement at being included in the outing – so frantic he nearly killed them both by leaping, when a passing motorcycle backfired, first onto the steering wheel and then down between her feet, causing her little car to swerve and almost collide with an army lorry. By the time they reached Dutton Homestall, Peggy's poor heart, which always had so many reasons to pound faster than it should, had slowed down somewhat and she was shown into a large room where 'silhouetted against a sunlit window, stood the tall, lithe figure of a young man'. At that stage Richard's grafts were still very white and incomplete and one arm was supported on 'a kind of tennis-racket contrivance with loops on the rounded frame to straighten crooked fingers'. She remembered: 'He wheeled towards me, and stood with his gallant head thrown back and the bright sunlight shining full upon that marred face, the burning blue eyes, streaming from strain staring defiantly into mine. "Look well at me", they seemed to say. "But damn you, don't you DARE to pity me." I was being tested. Thank God I passed that test.'

It was Peggy who brought up the subject of writing, suggesting Richard might like to visit her for tea at Many Waters, where they could talk quietly. A date was fixed, on which she gave her maid Kitty the afternoon off, for Kitty was engaged to a boy in the RAF and Peggy was concerned the meeting might be upsetting for both her and Richard. At 4 p.m. exactly the tall figure, wrapped in his Air Force blue overcoat, knocked on the door. Peggy, clad in slacks and never sure he would actually come, sprang to open it. In his diary, Richard described that day:

> I walked on; and round the next bend I found my reward. Like proud courtiers, streams of cascading water poured down from the wooded hills, to subside in respectful homage in the quiet pools around the cottage. It was enchanting. I rang the bell, in some fear that the good lady had forgotten; but the door opened, and she welcomed me like an old friend.
>
> First I was shown the cottage, which should be priceless for the view from the bedroom alone, and then we made our own tea, toasting buns at the fire. After this she talked; of the lovely house which she and her husband had built together in Provence; of his death and how she tried to live there alone, but could not; and how she rebuilt Sunset House, of her leaving

France after Calais fell and taking this cottage, 'to be alone to lick her wounds'.

As she talked of Provence her face grew animated and it was not long before I found myself upstairs in the midst of a pile of photographs; views of the house, of their *bergerie* up in the Alps, to which they escaped when the Midi became too hot; of their carpets of narcissi; of magic-scented tobacco plants bursting in fertile abundance everywhere; and finally of the sky in the Alps, lowering and heavy before a storm, and fleeced with white streaks of trailing glory in the ensuing peace.

Who were 'they' who escaped to the Alps? Peggy had visited them only with Elisabeth and Polly, never with John. Did she speak of Elisabeth, left in Provence? If at all, certainly very little, for Richard did not mention her in his account of that afternoon at Many Waters.

He responded immediately to the calm of her pretty studio-bedroom on the first floor, with its welcoming log fire, bowl of spring flowers, pictures and books, all enveloped in the greenery of the grass and woods outside. It is here that he first spoke of the Circles of Peace: 'For years I have been looking for the Circles of Peace. This is the centre of the Circles of Peace.'

So began a pleasant friendship and Peggy, always compassionate – and also susceptible to compelling men – took Richard, for a short time, under her wing. By now he had read *Perfume from Provence* and been inspired by it, judging from his diary entry, which has something of Peggy's style about it. Although he did not write his best-selling book *The Last Enemy* at Many Waters, Richard certainly used the cottage to make preliminary notes and a rough draft of the Introduction. Peggy had said he might use the house at any time so, 'it was with joy in the weeks which followed that sometimes, as The Blackness [Dominie] and I returned from his riot in the woods, I did see smoke rising from my chimney from a fire lit by Richard Hillary.' Until one day he rang the telephone in one of the gardener's lodges and left a message for Peggy to contact him as soon as possible. After toiling up the precipice and ringing back, she was greeted with a joyous 'I've got a job! I've got a JOB,' and asking if he might come to tea that afternoon to tell her all. Thrilled with his news, she descended her hillside and waited – and waited. In the darkness of early evening one of the gardener's children brought down another message, which said Richard had been called away for a meeting with Lord Beaverbrook, then running the Ministry of Information. She never saw him again.

Richard was sent to the United States by the British government with the intention of giving lectures throughout the country on the state of the war in Europe. It was his own idea, basically approved of by Archibald McIndoe, that he should contribute to the efforts being made to encourage America to join the Allies. However, McIndoe was concerned that the work on Richard's face was unfinished and he would have liked to have completed it before it was displayed before his medical colleagues in the United States.

Initially all went well, until the moment the British Ambassador met Richard in Washington and felt immediately that the reaction of American mothers might be one of horror that their sons could become so disfigured in combat, thus producing the opposite effect to that desired. Consequently, the decision was made to restrict him to reading his speeches over the airwaves and writing articles and pamphlets on the British cause. This was a great blow. Not only had his plans been dashed, but the verdict that he was too damaged for general view could only have been humiliating. What he had tried to rise above in England had been brought home to him only too brutally in the United States. But, staying in New York with the rich and kindly Edward and Mary Warburg, Richard was provided with the sort of comfort, friendship and admiration that helped to ease his disappointment. Mary was possessive of him and made sure he accompanied them to parties and the theatre and was included in the social life of the city. And here at last he could begin to write properly, as Peggy had urged him to. Writing was difficult. His damaged and crooked fingers could hardly hold a pen or pencil and he found a Dictaphone difficult to deal with, but Edward Warburg encouraged him, providing a room in which to work and introducing him to the publishing world.

The finished book, called in the United States *Falling Through Space*, was published there in February 1942. The speed with which the book was written during Richard's busy stay in America, which included another operation on his face (disapproved of by McIndoe), prompted suspicion that he had professional help. Even if this was the case, no one but Richard could have produced the basic material, and his character, described in detail by so many people, comes through on every page.

In spite of his injuries having been brought so much to the fore by the controversy over his appearance, lovely women clustered around Richard in the salons of New York and Washington as they had in London and Sussex. One in particular met and quickly won him – the actress Merle Oberon, who had married Alexander Korda in Cannes in the summer of 1939. Their affair was entirely satisfactory to them both, and came at exactly the right time for Richard. To possess such an internationally acclaimed beauty must have been balm to his injured pride and, although when he left for England in the autumn and the affair came to an end, their affection for each other endured. Merle did something else for Richard: she gave him the address of her good friend Mary Booker. An admired beauty and part of the London social scene, Mary was divorced, mother to two girls, and forty-four to Richard's twenty-two years. Her calmness and maturity attracted him immediately, resulting in an affair of passion combined with a sort of convoluted intellectual torture.

But Richard missed the camaraderie of the pilots' mess and the concept of 'kill or be killed'. Although almost all his close friends had indeed been killed in action, he longed to be part of all that once more. In April 1942 he went back to East Grinstead to have more operations, which included work to try to straighten out two of his fingers, with the goal of being passed for operational flying once more. McIndoe hated to see his pilots, who had been through so much, go back on active duty: 'You've done your stuff, and now the other silly sods can get on with it.' This did nothing to deter Richard. During the course of the year, further operations, examinations by medical boards, refusals and yet more operations followed one another monotonously.

The planned British publication of *Falling Through Space* was a high spot. But this was not a title Richard liked – and nor did someone else. Denise Maxwell-Woosnam had become a close and valued friend. She had been engaged to be married to Peter Pease, a fellow fighter pilot of Richard's whose plane had also been shot down by a Messerschmitt during the Battle of Britain, but he had not survived. Richard had greatly admired Peter's character and also described him as 'the best-looking man I have ever seen'. He had been impressed by his quiet confidence, his integrity and firm belief in the sacrifices needed to save his country, so different from Richard's own reasoning. In his vulnerable state, Richard was greatly affected by Peter's death. Denise, devastated, had visited Richard in hospital and there began a friendship of importance to them both, for they began to meet often, as Denise would say, 'Pulling each other back from the brink of despair'. With Richard back in London, the couple spent several evenings trying out alternative titles for the book, none of which seemed right, until one night, left alone, Denise picked up a Bible that had belonged to Peter. The pages fell open at 1 Corinthians 15:27. 'The last enemy that shall be destroyed is death.' On an impulse she rang Richard and heard him shout triumphantly 'That's it!' They both felt Peter had sent them, from somewhere, a message.

Published in June 1942, *The Last Enemy* was dedicated to Denise. In those days of paper shortage 15,000 copies were printed initially. They were sold out within a few weeks and, after that, it was impossible to keep up with the demand. Interviews and publicity filled the summer months and increased the hope of Richard's friends that he would now discard the idea of flying and take up writing as a career. But, ever obstinate, he had not given up. Working at an RAF desk job, he continued to attend medical boards to try to get himself passed as fit to fly. Relentlessly persuading and insisting, in November 1942, by sheer force of character and against the explicit wish of McIndoe, he got himself accepted for night-flying training on bombers. Mary Booker, although not wanting him to take to the air, felt she did not have the right to try to forbid it – and was perhaps hoping it would put an end to his increasing moodiness. Significantly, Richard had admitted he was more afraid of what people would say if he did not return to flying than what would happen if he did. It seems as if Kathleen Dewar's taunting words still rang in his ears.

Peggy had often thought of Richard since he had visited Many Waters, and the news of the success of *The Last Enemy* filled her with joy and pride: 'I awaited his letter telling me of his achievement – or perhaps he would just send me a copy of THE book which we had so often discussed. I waited in vain, but though human enough to be disappointed, nevertheless I knew that in spite of the disparity of age, nothing could change the friendship between us.'

Having at last got his way, Richard was posted to the bleak RAF Charterhall airbase in Scotland and, on a freezing night in early January, accompanied by his radio observer Kenneth Fison, the father of two children, he set off in his twin-engine Bristol Blenheim for the second flight exercise of the night. Below him, in an office near the airfield, a letter from Archibald McIndoe, expressing his opinion that Richard was not ready to resume flying and should return to Sussex, had only just been opened by the squadron's doctor. It had lain in a drawer for two weeks while he was on leave.

The night-flying exercise involved Richard and Kenneth Fison tracking a fellow pilot on radar – an operation in which the two pilots took turns. While waiting for the other aircraft to become airborne, Richard began to fly in great circles around a beacon. The summing-up by those present at the time was that, part of the way through the circuit, the control surfaces began to ice up and Richard, struggling with his crooked hands, lost control of the plane. In a matter of seconds, the aircraft ploughed into the ground and exploded, killing both him and his radio operator. Richard was twenty-three.

Peggy, now far from Sussex, heard of his death while she was 'watching the hawks wheeling and swooping suddenly from the sky' above a high tor in North Devon. Filled with emotion, she quoted, on his behalf, the seventeenth-century poet Henry Vaughan's lines: 'I saw eternity the other night like a great ring of pure and endless light.'

Chapter 21 ❧
MEFIANCE

How did the months following the capitulation affect Elisabeth and the inhabitants of the unoccupied zone? With the creation of the Vichy State, communications with the outside world, which had been blocked during the Battle of France, were now gradually re-established, and Peggy and Polly were able to exchange news with Elisabeth once again. She was grateful for these letters and cables, sent reply pre-paid, for they made those unreal times 'seem less long'.

The majority of the lively, elegant expatriates who had lit up the Riviera had fled. Apart from local people and refugees, there remained only a sprinkling of mainly elderly expatriates and the actors and singers such as Danielle Darrieux, Maurice Chevalier and Charles Trenet who would be allowed to come and go, as their services were required. The Aga Khan and the ex-Khedive of Egypt were still there in 1941, but soon left. Families of royal descent, such as two branches of the Bourbons, stayed, as did some exiled Russian princes and various widowed duchesses and countesses. Prince Jean-Louis de Faucigny-Lucinge, noted in his memoirs: 'Some of these elderly ladies, almost without exception beautiful in their time, now took to bicycles and could be seen pedalling slowly through the streets of the town, veils floating in the breeze and frugal provisions in boxes on the back.'

Painters such as Henri Matisse and the artist-photographer Jacques-Henri Lartigue watched their step and lived quietly in Nice and Monte Carlo respectively. Pierre Bonnard worked in his villa at Le Cannet above Cannes. These artists visited a lithograph gallery in Cannes, run by a young man called Aimé Maeght, who, many years later, in memory of his young son, founded the Fondation Maeght near the hill town of St Paul de Vence, now one of the most famous galleries in France. Marc Chagall, a Jew, found himself trapped near Marseille and was spirited away to New York with the aid of the American-funded Emergency Rescue Committee. And the writer and artist

Jean Cocteau, who always liked to dine at the top table and was now uncertain which way to sway, maintained that he was asleep and the passage of history was simply his personal nightmare.

As far as the indigenous population of the Alpes Maritimes was concerned, apart from those who felt a profound sense of relief that they would now be governed by Marshal Pétain rather than the communists, the mass of people went about their daily business under a cloak of stunned apathy. The Italians had been allowed, by the terms of the Italian-German agreement, to occupy fully only the land won from the French during their assault of June 1940. This territory included Menton and its immediate surroundings, plus the strip of villages and pastureland that ran up through the Alps along the border. The Italian Command was installed in Nice and their military scattered throughout the south from the Italian frontier to the Rhone but, outside their own designated strip, they were not permitted to consider themselves occupiers. On the railway that ran along the coast, the trains went back and forth constantly, loaded up with French arms, tanks and munitions to be taken away to Italy as spoils of war. But the total invasion of Provence by its Italian neighbours had not taken place and the region's inhabitants and their numerous refugee visitors, both rich and poor, now had to face the prospect of life in Vichy France.

Marshal Philippe Pétain's Vice-Premier was Pierre Laval, an ex-Prime Minister of France whose rough peasant appearance belied his business acumen. He was considered by many to be self-seeking and caring nothing for any political system. Extremely rich through acquisition of newspapers and radio stations, he was chosen by *Time Magazine* as 'Man of the Year' in 1931. He had used his control of the media to promote propaganda supporting Pétain and Vichy, until his proposal of a military alliance with Nazi Germany had caused Pétain to sack him at the end of 1940. Reinstated in 1942 in response to German pressure, Laval would become the 'Evil Shadow over Vichy' doing the Nazi bidding with renewed vigour, although he would claim his appeasements and trade-offs were made solely with the aim of protecting France, its colonies and the French themselves.

In an area deemed 'unoccupied', as long as it behaved itself, the ageing and strongly Catholic Petain expounded his National Socialist ideals and 'guidance' for social behaviour under the New Order. *Travail, Famille, Patrie* were paramount. Exercise, games and youth camps were strongly encouraged in order to promote clean and healthy living. Married women were discouraged from working in state offices unless their husbands were unable to provide for them. Others, in education and administration, were urged to give up their jobs to men unless they were totally self-supporting. Mothers were expected to stay in the home, look after their family and be discreet and biddable. They were to be honoured as the bearers of the children who would carry forward the future of the *Patrie*. Schoolchildren were taught, and expected to sing, the patriotic song, *Maréchal, Nous Voila*, praising the Marshal. Swimming costumes and shorts were banned away from pools and beaches, along with trousers for women. And, in the puritanical spirit of Vichy, the Préfet of the Alpes Maritimes would order the internment of around two thousand prostitutes and homosexuals in a camp near Sisteron in the High Alps. Other rules followed swiftly, either from the Nazi High Command or Marshal Pétain's own Vichy government. There was to be no crossing, without permits, between the occupied and unoccupied zones; it was absolutely forbidden to aid escaped Allied military personnel in any way, under pain of imprisonment or worse. In the south, the police had orders to round up all escapees and send them to Fort St Jean at Marseilles. As a result, escape lines sprang up rapidly, run by those who knew the possible consequences of their actions.

Fêtes of all kinds were encouraged, providing they furthered the ethics of the New Order, although, following Pétain's conviction that general moral laxity had contributed to the fall of the country, public dancing was banned. Those who flouted these orders were deemed to be 'enemies of France'. The guardians of the morality of Vichy France ensured that entertainment in the south was closely monitored, while in Paris under the Germans, nightclubs and restaurants were soon again in full swing for those who could afford them – unless, of course, one was Jewish and therefore less than welcome.

At this time there was no direct contact between the population of Vichy France and the German armed forces. Only Germans in plain clothes or on the Armistice Commission, checking that the terms were being adhered to, circulated in the region. They initially went to great lengths to win over the local people with courtesy and discipline, and seem to have had little inclination to linger on the Riviera after their periodical inspections, preferring Marseilles and Aix-en-Provence. But those in plain clothes were often also the Gestapo, and their role was to watch for any sign of resistance among the population and to keep an eye on the behaviour of their own agents as they went about their business. They were everywhere, and adept at recruiting locals, often disaffected young men whom they paid to spy on their neighbours and friends and report any sign of dissidence. For the person on the street there was soon a fine line between compromise in order to live and eat and collaboration – and that formerly rather pleasant word took on a whole new meaning.

In those summer months of 1940, as the sun beat down on the terraces and sparse shrubland of the hill country and, far below, the Mediterranean shimmered through its palette of blues from dawn to dusk, an atmosphere of bewildered suspicion hung over everything as heavily as did the heat. In a world that was, in the following years, to become increasingly topsy-turvy, *'méfiance'* – a potent word meaning not only 'mistrust' but also 'beware' – became the order of the day. In Cannes, members of the French *Service d'Ordre Légionnaire,* the forerunner of the dreaded *Milice* (a French paramilitary organisation, which held itself above the law), destroyed the statue of King Edward VII, a gesture about which the Cannois felt uneasy, knowing how much he had loved their town and how he and his fun-loving entourage had helped to swell their coffers.

The south of France, in spite of its much-vaunted bounty of grapes, olives and citrus fruits, was not a productive agricultural area and the population quickly began to suffer from lack of food. January of 1940, even before the defeat, had already brought restrictions – the marching army had priority. Restaurants at that time were allowed to serve each client only one meat dish of no more than 100 grams, and that in exchange for coupons. Then came the order that no meat at all should be served on Mondays and Tuesdays and that butchers' shops should close on those days. Friday was then included, encompassing the traditional religious abstinence. Coffee, rice and soap began to become scarce and, as early as February, ration cards were introduced. In March the patisseries, once filled with their delectable little works of art, were told to close three days a week and the sale of alcohol was forbidden on Monday, Tuesday and Wednesday. When Vichy rule began in July 1940, a new decree restricted the serving of sugar in hotels and restaurants and *le petit café, non sucré* became the order of the day. The black market, which was to become a necessity, swung quickly into action.

In the autumn of 1940 the Nazi army, less than courteous, entered the free zone and dug up and annexed the potato crop in the Durance Valley of the Luberon. Olive oil, wine and citrus crops throughout the south were compulsorily purchased for shipment to Italy and Germany. The work of the French Red Cross became increasingly ineffective following the declaration of the armistice, and supplies collected in Britain could not be sent for fear they would fall into enemy hands. The American Red Cross was allowed to operate, providing aid particularly for children, until America joined the Allies at the end of 1941.

As for Elisabeth, although her freedom was curtailed, her position at this time was not dangerous. She was not Jewish, had been born in the United States – still a neutral country – and had been French for a decade. Her *Foyers des Soldats* programme having been brought to an abrupt halt at the armistice, she began helping with the resettlement of the many thousands of refugees from Menton, the north and re-annexed Alsace and Lorraine who were flooding the south. Weak and now suffering from anaemia, she nevertheless threw herself into this new project, visiting, negotiating and organising. Villagers remember seeing her dashing along the country roads in her Peugeot, often with a carload of children to distribute to their new homes. In those dark days when children became separated from their parents, those increasingly at risk were, naturally, Jewish. Elisabeth began to hide some of these vulnerable waifs. Twenty-five years later a Mr Kolinski, now living in the United States, drove into the courtyard of the Castello and asked to see the room in which he was given sanctuary during the war. A Polish Jew who had lost his parents in a concentration camp, he visited again the attic room in which he had been hidden. He had known there were others hiding nearby, heard but not seen. The resettlement of refugees was done in conjunction with the Relief Committee of the Quakers, based in Marseille. It was one of their main programmes in the south at that time, along with the care of French prisoners of war and those in the emerging French concentration camps. Although she was not particularly religious, Elisabeth's Quaker genes had not deserted her.

The Castello opened its doors wide to others as well. It rapidly became full of women refugees, causing Elisabeth's protective cook, Madame Arnando, to remark they 'lived off her, ordering good food and luxuries and using her money'. When the United States entered the war Elisabeth's American funds would have been affected. But the United States government kept lines of communication open with Vichy, facilitating matters for those Americans still in the south of France, and the Swiss banks had set up a loan arrangement to help expatriates who had lost their income. In any case, almost all Elisabeth's capital had gone into the *foyers* and there was little left.

From 1942, throughout France, the quota of non-French Jews ordered to be deported to the east, where they were told they would 'live on the land in a specially created state in Poland', began to be ruthlessly pursued. Soon no Jew, French or otherwise, would feel safe anywhere. Philippe Erlanger, founder and later president of the Cannes Film Festival, spent most of the war years in semi-hiding in Nice and Cannes. He became one of the organisers of a group that raised money from the Jewish community in order to send vulnerable Jews from the coast to what was, hopefully, more security in the hills. Working against great odds, this group was actively supported by Angelo Donati, an Italian Jew based in Nice. A director of La Banca Commerciale d'Italia and with an entrée to the Vatican, he juggled his two lives with courage and aplomb. With the renowned 'Father of the Jews', the Catholic priest Père Marie-Benoît, he and others like him, worked secretly and ceaselessly.

And all over France many were humming a popular tune, *'J'attendrai'* ('I will wait').

Chapter 22
DOGS AND MONKEYS

Having survived the freezing winter of 1940, when the lakes by Many Waters froze into miniature ice rinks and the valley lay at the bottom of a bowl of snow, in June of the following year Peggy succumbed to bronchial pneumonia. In the subsequent heatwave, and burning with fever, her thoughts turned to the many happy weeks spent at the *bergerie* in the freshness of the High Alps under the lee of the Meije glacier. Once recovered she began to write, and over the next two years, with many interruptions, she worked on *Mountain Madness*. Of all her books, it probably describes best the character of Elisabeth and the relationship between the two women. Full of accounts of mountain life, of the daunting grandeur of nature, pastures of flowers and hair-raising adventures, it did well. In wartime Britain, in the throes of a paper shortage, it was reprinted three times between December 1943 and 1944.

After that harsh winter, spring brought great beauty to the valley and slopes around the cottage. The woods filled with primroses and bluebells, followed by the flaring colours of the rhododendrons and azaleas that grow so well on the acid soil of that part of Sussex. But, in the midst of all this loveliness and as spring flowed into summer, Peggy would sink down under the green branches of a great tree with Dominie in her arms and, in her own words, 'howl'. For 'we must lose one more home, and go in search of some other habitation – and it nearly broke my heart to contemplate such an exile.'

Over the previous months, unable to find a role in which she could help the plight of the French, she had become involved in resettling the victims of the Blitz, then raging over the cities of Britain. Bombed-out, homeless families were spread around the countryside and large houses were offered or requisitioned and had to be equipped for those who had often lost everything. The evacuation programme 'Operation Pied Piper' had nearly doubled the population of mid-Sussex at the start of the war, many evacuated children being sent south to a strange kind of safety. House owners, some welcoming, some reluctant, were paid ten shillings and sixpence for the first child and eight shillings and sixpence for each of the others. The children came to a county where anti-tank blocks, two metres high, were placed along the beaches and 6-inch-calibre guns were taken out of storage, ready to repel any enemy ships sighted in the Channel. Some of these guns brought back memories, for they were last used on the battle front of the First World War.

The victory of the Battle of Britain saved the country from invasion in the summer of 1940 but from then on, until May of the following year, hundreds of German planes, often pursued by Spitfires, passed over Kent and Sussex on their way to bomb London, the docks and industrial cities. Although the enemy did not waste bombs on rural counties, the great fear was that some would be jettisoned as retreating aircraft lightened their loads in order to escape the Spitfires. The raids lessened once Russia switched sides and joined the Allies in the late spring of 1941, for the Luftwaffe was kept busy on the eastern front, and that beautiful summer was remembered by a schoolteacher at nearby Ardingly College for 'the tranquillity and peace of perfect summer days'. But there was always the danger of a lone raider, and a bomb had fallen on Ardingly village, killing five people. Even more tragically, in 1943, another (accompanied by machine-gunning) hit the Whitehall Cinema in East Grinstead, near Archibald McIndoe's Victoria Hospital, killing over one hundred and injuring many more.

Suddenly, to her delight, Peggy was sent for by the Free French Headquarters at Carlton Gardens in London and enrolled in a newly formed organisation, under the patronage of General de Gaulle. This was the *Amis des Volontaires Français*, the *AVF* – the English name being the 'Friends of French Volunteers'. She was asked to be a propaganda speaker and fund-raiser for the 'Fighting French' on the platforms of Britain. Honoured, thrilled and terrified at the idea, Peggy accepted immediately. She set out to try to explain to Sussex audiences, sceptical at that time, that 'France is with us, she was just sold and betrayed!' Her lectures went on to say that General de Gaulle had asked her to talk about France because of the spirit of hostility that had arisen in England after the capitulation. She described the turmoil of the general mobilisation, which had decreed that men were obliged, within twenty-four hours, to leave their homes and families to their fate, only to find themselves poorly equipped and clad. She illustrated the pathos with the story of one man who carried a bundle as he shambled along with his new regiment. The bundle turned out to be a baby, for his wife had died a few days before, and he had no one with whom to leave the child, so was allowed to march with it until he could find someone who would take it in. As her confidence grew Peggy's lectures became more fluent. She held herself well, had great presence and was able to capture her audience with her vibrant actress's voice which made the talks a success – although it is doubtful whether all her anecdotes would have pleased General de Gaulle.

Never ceasing to write, *Trampled Lilies*, her book on the mobilisation in France, the creation of the *Foyers des Soldats* and her subsequent flight to safety in England, was published in 1941. Although a vivid and personal historical document of those months in Provence, for several reasons it did not do as well as it deserved, selling only 12,000 copies by the end of the war. The increasing paper shortage contributed to this but, above all, it seems the British people generally were not susceptible to the plight of French soldiers. But Peggy was doing her utmost to remedy this and was settling into her new life and task – until fate intervened once more.

On renting Many Waters she had been assured that the cottage was just outside the 32 kilometre zone from the coast, inside which any house could be requisitioned by the army at any time. Now she was told it was actually 5 centimetres inside the boundary! It was rumoured that almost all the now-settled evacuees in the area would have to be moved once again and perhaps she too would be displaced *en masse* with everyone else. And there was another problem. There had always been an old, proud red setter named Romulus at Stonehurst House. Hitherto friendly and accepting, his disposition changed when his former companion, a setter bitch called Rema, was brought back to the Strausses. Rema had been given away, but her new owner found a large dog too much to handle in wartime, and she had been sent back to her former owners. Romulus became aggressively protective of his returned love and one or two trial encounters between the three dogs proved to be a dismal failure. The setters had the run of the estate and now Dominie could never be allowed out on his own, and must be confined to the cottage for the greater part of the day, for the two dogs would attack as soon as they caught sight of him. Short, tense walks with Peggy, snatched when the setters were having their midday meal, did nothing for the condition of her heart, already strained by years of negotiating intimidating mountain roads and, latterly, toiling after Elisabeth in order to equip yet another *foyer* in a remote village or lonely frontier post. The anxiety of protecting Dominie from violent attack, combined with the prospect of perhaps being forced to become an evacuee again herself, was suddenly all too much, and Peggy, very sadly, decided Many Waters must be abandoned for the foreseeable future. So, still paying rent but bolstered by a fresh transfer of book royalties, she began the search for a new home.

A 'Siddal Special' touring caravan was well equipped and large enough to accommodate Peggy, Dominie and later Renée Goldspink – who never stayed behind for long. The interior was clean, comfortable and satisfactory except that the colourful upholstery had to be exchanged for a soft green, for the caravan must try to be a substitute for Many Waters. She christened it 'The Ark'.

The Ark having been sent ahead, in late autumn of 1941 Peggy and Dominie headed to Devon. Armed with proposals from French Headquarters for the lectures she would give in the West Country, she went first to Manaton on the south-east side of the Dartmoor National Park. Here John Fortescue's favourite niece, Joyce, was living with her husband, Colonel Peter Carew. Very tall and full of brisk common sense, Joyce was running the local Land Army and had given permission for Peggy to park her caravan on their land. To judge from a photograph taken at the time, Joyce seems to have chosen a rather uncomfortably exposed site on the moor for the Ark. And although life was made easier by Renée, who now joined Peggy and 'to my enormous relief, took over the cooking', the wildness of the moor and the cutting winter winds proved too rude for a semi-permanent home. They decided to find a warmer site so, on an early summer morning in 1942, the Ark having been sent ahead again, they left Dartmoor and took to the road once more.

This time they headed north-west, towards Exmoor and Fortescue country. Peggy did not ask to park her unwieldy home among the rook-filled trees and murmuring streams and waterfalls at Castle Hill, John's family home at Filleigh, near Barnstaple. Perhaps the house had been requisitioned and, in any case, her background as an actress and her quick tongue had prevented closeness with the main branch of the

Fortescue family. Instead she arranged with the Stucleys, cousins of the Fortescues, to pitch camp at their home, Hartland Abbey. Further west than Castle Hill, in a gentler climate and a mile from the Atlantic coast, Hartland was ancient and beautiful. Built in the twelfth century, it was set in a sheltered valley among banks of rhododendrons and home to peacocks and rare black sheep. Above the house the walled gardens sheltered peaches, pears and nectarines. There was a deer park and terraces, that had been the monks' vineyards, and through the grounds a small stream ran from the Abbey down to the sea far below, which 'crashed and sucked on to its treacherous, rocky coastline'. John Fortescue had loved Hartland and here, during his bachelor days, had written many chapters of his *History of the British Army*. He and Peggy had visited the house on their honeymoon, when she too had fallen under its spell. The Stucleys, now living in the lodge, had let the house to an evacuated prep school, whose undisciplined pupils had done their best to cause as much damage as they were able. Shortly before Peggy arrived, the school had been evicted and a great clearing-up was in progress – for the Abbey had been let again.

Like the Carews, it seemed as if the Stucley family were not too keen on caravans. The Ark had been taken, with enormous difficulty by the estate workers, up a steep one-track lane and placed on a narrow grass terrace set in woodland. As it was impossible for Peggy's little car to climb from the lane onto the campsite it was parked at the Abbey farm, making it necessary to set out on foot, in all weathers, to get anywhere – shades of Many Waters once again.

Positive as always, Peggy eulogised about her new surroundings:

Once there, its position could not have been more perfect – half-way up a great tor, in a clearing of woods, facing south, with a wonderful view across the valley. Through bird song and the music of little hidden streams and pixie wells boomed the distant roar of Atlantic rollers as they crashed against great rocks. Overhead, hawks soared and swooped.

There was a temperamental water pump, which meant that water would sometimes have to be brought up from the house. But although, as ever, complicated, it was all green and peaceful and a home of a sort.

Her last visit with John to the cushioned comfort of the Abbey itself had been in 1914. Now, twenty-seven years later, she was there again – this time on a hill in the parkland, in a caravan with no running water, a little black dog and Renée, whom she referred to as 'a wartime acquaintance'. 'What a fantastic kaleidoscope is life', she reflected, and if she ever felt grievance or discontent she did not transfer it to her books or the people around her. The Stucley family, in contrast to the Fortescues, appreciated her qualities and would ask her to become godmother to one of their children.

On the day after her arrival Peggy flung herself into a flurry of activity, organising supplies of milk and food and finding someone to scythe, tidy the campsite and provide supplies of fresh water. That done, she descended to the chaos of the Abbey to meet the new tenants – Helen Joynson-Hicks, the daughter of the 1st Viscount Brentford, and Marion Ellison. Helen, six feet tall and corpulent, was, with Marion, who was tiny and equally plump, the owner of the Three Wise Monkeys Club, whose members soon filled the Abbey and its grounds with youth and laughter. The club was not an evacuated night-spot from the West End of London but a rather avant-garde finishing school for daughters of the well-connected and well-to-do. The name came from the motto of the Three Wise Monkeys, 'See No Evil, Hear No Evil, Speak No Evil', and no one was allowed to use the words 'pupil' or 'school'. As well as being taught to run a household efficiently and be a relaxed and charming hostess for the suitable young man she was expected to marry, a Monkey was also trained to be bright, cultured, enthusiastic and innovative. A wise policy, for the post-war years would place far more demands on these young women than their leisured mothers had known. The competent Misses Joynson-Hicks and Ellison drove around the county in a 1912 Morris Cowley convertible, which brought great *élan* to the local village on shopping days.

Peggy was delighted to have this youthful exuberance so near. She often visited the Abbey and became involved with the club's projects and theatrical productions. The girls took to riding or walking up to the caravan to have coffee with her, enjoying her extrovert personality, the sense of humour she took care should never desert her, and the gusts of rich smoker's laughter that punctuated her anecdotes. This mutual respect and close association would, in due course, give rise to a rather extraordinary plan between Peggy and Helen Joynson-Hicks.

As in Sussex, now the schools, clubs, colleges and Women's

Institutes of Devon rang to the sound of Peggy's exalted tones as she proclaimed again the plight of defeated France and the determination of the Free French to liberate their country. Endlessly fund-raising, she took to the roads of the county, driving long distances alone and often in the dark. From inland towns to seaports she lectured constantly. But the inevitable bout of exhaustion brought on yet another attack of her chronic health problem and this time it was more serious. After nearly fainting in the street during a visit to London, she was obliged to consult a doctor immediately, to be told her system was poisoned and she was on the verge of toxaemia. A stay of several weeks in the city for yet another debilitating set of treatments was a low period, for she felt she was almost at the limit of her now delicate health.

To her doctor of that time Peggy dedicated a copy of her auto-biography *There's Rosemary, There's Rue*: 'To Doctor Hugh Gordon, the only doctor who respected my intelligence enough to tell me the truth, believing, I think, that I had courage enough to bear it.' This is when she must have learnt she had an enlarged heart, on which subject she commented, typically, to her niece, Fay Arbuthnot, 'I didn't think anyone's heart could be too big.' But, as she would do again and again, she rallied, and returned to Devon and the caravan, summoning her considerable will-power to keep going. Polly Cotton heard of this episode and gave her version of it: 'Peggy Fortescue is living in London, she's ill, she's got intestinal toxaemia – whatever that may be – it sounds disgusting.'

During that year of 1942 France increasingly needed all the moral and practical support its Allies were prepared to give and, as the year wore on, attitudes in England softened and Peggy's audiences grew more sympathetic to the cause, making fund-raising easier.

Meanwhile the letters from Elisabeth had become ever more worrying.

Chapter 23 ❧

FADING

Elisabeth's former life on the hill must have seemed like a distant dream. Fort Escu, the Bastide and San Peyre were empty. Their owners, the friends she had gathered around her, had fled, as had the two nurses, Hedley and Morris, on their coal boat. The close, relaxed companionship of loved neighbours was a thing of the past. So, in August of 1940, Elisabeth invited her neighbour, Jeanne Holroyd Reece, and her daughter, Diane van Dommelen, to move into Polly's Bastide. Jeanne had by now been deserted by her Albatross-publisher husband John, who had doubtless moved on to another of his five wives. It would be wise, from now on, to try to keep the houses occupied, for so long as they were empty they were liable to be requisitioned once again, this time with unknown consequences.

Elisabeth, deeply saddened that her beloved France had been defeated so rapidly and was clearly about to suffer, was obliged to adapt her life to the Vichy New Order. Now there was only one way to learn what was going on in the world outside, and that was through one of the most precious and dangerous possessions of the wartime years – that other weapon, the radio. She hid her own in the great chimney in the salon and here, despite the incessant jamming of the airwaves by the Germans (lessened after midnight), she and trusted friends learnt what really was happening outside the prison that France had become. She would have heard of the seemingly unstoppable early successes of the German Army, coupled with the increasing tyranny of the Nazi regime in the north towards those on their growing list of 'undesirables'. But the triumph of the Battle of Britain must have brought joy and hope.

It was not long before the Vichy-controlled broadcasts and German-controlled *Radio-Paris* were seen to be no more than self-serving propaganda. Soon the children of those who hated the occupation and the New Order would chant within the safety of their homes '*Radio-Paris ment, Radio-Paris est Allemand*' ('Radio-Paris lies, Radio-Paris is German'). The punishment for listening to a clandestine radio was severe – and would become increasingly so – but this was no deterrent to Elisabeth. The broadcasts from the English-language BBC or, under its auspices, *Les Français Parle aux Français* from the Free French, were fragile links between her quiet hillside and England. During the latter programme, over the space of four years, General Charles de Gaulle would be permitted to make sixty five-minute speeches to the people of France. For him, too, the radio was indispensable.

At the end of each night-time gathering around the radio at the Castello, the group, which included Monsieur Michel, the young Mayor of Opio and his wife, would raise a toast in the house wine. Monsieur Michel had been demobilised after the occupation and returned to his post at the *mairie*, before eventually leaving to join the growing ranks of the Resistance. Proposed by Elisabeth, the toast was always the same, '*A la Victoire*', for she did not doubt for one moment that it would come at some time in the future.

In England in November 1940, Polly Cotton had written to Charley Anglesey: 'Elisabeth Starr is going to the USA, end of this month, so that's alright. I expect some day or other she'll turn up here with the American Red Cross. Anyway I'll be much happier about her when she's out of France.' She went on to urge him to cable Elisabeth, 'agreeing about the gardener but not mentioning money, as they make such a fuss about money in cables'. She added that in a day or so it would be her own birthday – 'I'll be older than God'. She would be sixty-three and her own war effort was just about to begin.

Elisabeth did not turn up in England with the American Red Cross or any other organisation. In spite of rumours between her friends over the next couple of years to the effect that she was about to leave or had a seat reserved on a plane, she never did. With her determination and in spite of her 'vile body', as she now described her increasingly delicate state, she could surely have summoned the strength to leave in the early stages of the war. But she felt committed to France, and perhaps, with her pride, found it impossible to contemplate giving up her own home and becoming a guest in the house of a friend in England or America, to neither of which she felt she belonged. She cherished space and freedom dearly. In addition, she had invested so much in the *Foyers des Soldats* programme, as had Peggy, that her funds were dwindling and the idea of perhaps having to rely on charity would have been very hard. Above all, it must have been unthinkable to abandon her beloved Castello to be invaded by persons known or unknown – and then finding it ruined or impossible to reclaim.

As time went on she became increasingly trapped both by her fragile health and the grip of the New Order. Her days were filled with looking after the other three houses, organising staff and the grape and olive harvests, exchanging letters and cables with England, working with permitted aid agencies and running her own *domaine*, which now included her refugee guests. Money came from Charley at Plas Newydd under 'Trading with the Enemy' regulations, so she was able to pay wages and attend to the maintenance of San Peyre.

What did Elisabeth see, in those early years of the war, that might have given support to her unwavering belief in the eventual victory of the Free French? She would surely have been delighted and relieved when President Franklin Roosevelt signed the Lend-Lease Act in March 1941, which gave him the power to direct every kind of material aid, including food, to the war effort in Europe without the United States actually entering the war; she would have despaired when the Nazis invaded Greece and Yugoslavia the following month; been joyful when the Germans attacked the Soviet Union and the Russians became an ally instead of an enemy, and felt pride and hope when the United States finally entered the war after Pearl Harbor. The country of her birth was again, and at last, coming to the aid of her beloved France. But the United States would indulge in a complicated game with Vichy France, almost to the end of the war, President Roosevelt holding to the belief that this was the France with which one must ultimately negotiate. The involvement of the United States would bring complications for Elisabeth. Even though she had been a French national for twelve years, it was also widely known she was American by birth, and Peggy noted that later her home was spied on by the Gestapo.

The end of 1942 saw the fortunes of war begin to swing imperceptibly, like a great tanker, in favour of the Allies, and the German Army was defeated at El Alamein in November. But these events did not help France. Lack of fuel meant that increasingly there was no heating and no hot water. Gas and power shortages made cooking increasingly difficult. Camping stoves and, in the country wood fires, heated small meals. As there was no petrol for the population, the rare unofficial cars, the *gazogènes*, were propelled by encumbering charcoal-burning stoves perched on the back, and makeshift bicycle rickshaws appeared on the roads of towns and cities.

Queues outside shops often began as early as 4 a.m. when word got around that new supplies had come in – and such supplies did not last long. The grapes and citrus fruits of the south were forcibly purchased in great quantities and shipped to Germany, milk was requisitioned and rice became non-existent. Horses were seized by order – the odd one concealed riskily among cows in their byres – and to slaughter an animal was illegal. The permitted squares of hard soap became the '*Savon National*'. British submarines patrolled the Mediterranean (painted blue for that sea and green for the Atlantic) and blocked supplies from North Africa. Those supplies that did get through were taken by the local authorities or seized by the occupiers. If there had been any surplus foodstuffs left in the agricultural north, there was no transport available to get them to the needy south, even if this had been permitted.

Swedes became a staple food. Bread was scarce, black and badly made from, among other things, the fruit of the carob tree, and sometimes so vile it brought people out in boils, from which Elisabeth now began to suffer. 'Coffee' of grilled barley and acorns was almost undrinkable. Items of food, taken for granted so lightly in the past, disappeared for years to come. Those who were ill or old, and too poor or proud to buy from the now lively black market (the *BOF – Beurre, Oeufs, Fromage*), often died quietly of malnutrition in their homes. Children, their tummies swelling from lack of protein, frequently succumbed to tuberculosis and rickets.

Vegetables, salads, figs and grapes had always been grown for the Castello's use in the past. Elisabeth and her staff had reared chickens, rabbits and the odd pig. A new addition was a cow, which she named, defiantly, 'London Pride'. But the whole area was covered by 'Inspectors' charged with searching for food for the remaining French Army, now confined to barracks, or to be shipped to the occupied zone or Germany. In a bid to avoid requisition, cars were put up on blocks, their tyres buried in the countryside. Vegetable plots had to be hidden among bushes and behind houses and, with market stalls now almost bare, there was simply not enough produce to adequately feed Elisabeth's household of refugees. A trip to Cannes would have procured some kind of supplies through the *BOF* dealers on the terrace of the Carlton Hotel – but this would most probably have been against her principles, even if she could have got there. When her activities with the refugee aid programme came to an end, so also did her petrol allowance, leaving only bicycles, an unreliable bus or an un-requisitioned donkey and cart to descend from and return to the hills. People ceased to travel.

As for Sunny Bank, the small Anglo-American hospital in Cannes settled down to an uneasy existence. This period in its life is described in Elsie Gladman's book *Uncertain To-morrows*. Elsie, a nurse, now worked in a marooned hospital staffed by two other nurses, an English doctor and a few brave local French girls – brave, for the English were regarded as enemies by the authorities. Initially the hospital was supported by the American consul, who did all in his power to help as long as he could – particularly regarding transfers of money and loans. Discharged patients, with nowhere safe to go, became residents in an outbuilding. As time went on the greatest concern was, as always, lack of food. Leaves were cut off potato plants in the hospital garden in order to avoid detection, puddings were made with strange flour, water and saccharin and the hospital had no milk, of any kind, for months. Wood began to replace leather for the soles of shoes, then hand-woven raffia slippers often replaced shoes, as every material need became ever more impossible to obtain. There was frequently neither electricity nor gas and thus no heating or hot water. The only remaining transport would soon be requisitioned.

Towards the end of 1942, as Elisabeth grew weaker, Diane van Dommelen, of whom it would always be difficult to say whether she was rather good or really rather bad, began to help increasingly with the running of the Castello. After all, Elisabeth had helped Diane's stepfather, John Holroyd Reece, with livestock matters ten years before. She had taught him much about poultry-keeping and, in between publishing his stylish paperback books for the European market and sitting on the boards of French banks, Reece had learnt about sitting hens and hatching out guineafowl. Consequently Diane knew how to run a smallholding and, as the months wore on, began to take over the organising of the house and estate, finally moving, with her mother Jeanne, into the Castello itself. The Bastide now became empty – not a satisfactory state of affairs, but one that Elisabeth would remedy.

She was fading away – and suffering as she did so. During 1942 she had sought treatment from a specialist in Cannes for the anaemia, now accompanied by carbuncles, that was weakening her so much. Dr Suzanne Perles, a blood specialist, had come to the south with her family, as had so many other Jews fleeing the terrors increasingly meted out to them in the occupied zone. Not permitted to set up her own practice, she was accepted by a courageous local doctor who allowed her to use his surgery to see patients. Dr Perles treated Elisabeth, and Elisabeth told her of the empty houses at Opio.

One of Elisabeth's last letters to Peggy, which must have been written around October 1942, took her three weeks to complete: 'I have septic carbuncles in all vital places, but I'm trying to keep the flag flying.' The carbuncles were also inside her ears and on each of her fingers, which were now permanently bound up. Then a cable: 'We are all growing much too slim. Very difficult to console Babs [her dog]. Can you anyhow send parcels?' Peggy tried, by every possible channel, through every friend who might be in a position to help – but to no avail. For on 8 November 1942 'Operation Torch', the Allied invasion of North Africa, began. For this Elisabeth must have been more than glad, but in response to this threat, the Germans and the Italians invaded Vichy France. In another bewildering change for the people of the south, communications were cut once more and sending aid parcels became impossible.

It was the Italians who, in a deal with the Germans, were allowed at last to occupy the south militarily. They sent, as the advance guard, their most glamorous soldiers: the tall, handsome *Bersaglia*, the elite mountain troops. Dressed in black, with feathers flying in their helmets, they drove triumphantly through the towns of the Riviera in cars and on motorcycles. It was the Italians who flew their flag over their headquarters at the Hotel Gallia in Cannes and whose uniformed presence was greeted with subdued mockery or, on occasion, discreet familial embrace. And it was the Italians who reined in the increasing persecution of the Jews in their part of Vichy France. This was occupation at last, but not of a terrifying kind – although the Gestapo swelled its own ranks throughout the area.

Elisabeth would have learnt that the Russians were gaining ground and had won the battle of Stalingrad and that Field Marshall Montgomery's Eighth Army had taken Tripoli. So perhaps 'A La Victoire' rang out with more confidence in the salon of the Castello than it had done a year before. But she would not have known of the surrender of the Italian government to the Allies a year later, bringing with it the truly fearful, total invasion of the south by German troops. For she died at the beginning of 1943 after the harshest winter of the war to date. She was fifty-four. At the end her anaemia and chronic skin disease, aggravated by malnutrition, were 'the last enemy'. Her body gave up the struggle on 25 February. She died in her Castello and the death certificate stated 'heart failure', but could have said so much more.

With her youthful beauty and charismatic character Elisabeth had been loved and admired. But the lasting relationship for which she longed had eluded her. Although one cannot know whether she and Stewart Robinson would have gone on to share their lives, he had died tragically, leaving her to face the world in the aftermath. Both Lucy Upton and Dolly Watts had left for the different experience of marriage. Caroline Paget, to whom perhaps the relationship had been no more than an initiation, had come and gone as quickly as one of the fireflies that darted around the Castello terraces. The liaison with the dashing Isabel Pell at the beginning of the war had done little to console.

Although supported by a different kind of friendship with Peggy, Elisabeth had spent her adult life sublimating a deep loneliness. This she attempted to do in a manner that was engrained in her Quaker ancestry – helping others in two world wars, creating the role of benevolent 'Mademoiselle' in her lovely, simple village and escaping to small cabins in wild corners of Provence.

In the back of her copy of *Tristan and Isolde* is a poem, in an unknown hand but with the words 'Opio 1934' underneath in Elisabeth's writing. It is called 'The Road' and is dated the year she had met Caroline:

> For all we sought and missed or left unclaimed,
> For all the dreams we had and lost, for youth
> Ruffling his hair, suppled by Time and tamed,
> For love denied, or seen with too much truth
> For all of us who die before we live
> For all the crippled feet on the long road
> You made for angels – we forgive you, God.

It was not permitted that she be buried, as she had wished, on the terrace which led out from the studio of her courtyard cottage – 'so cosy' as she had thought the idea. Instead she was laid to rest in the little Opio cemetery, looking up to her Castello across the valley. In those wartime years there was only a token headstone, but all the village came to say farewell and, in the spring, the children planted pink carnations on her grave in the form of a 'V' for victory.

Polly had been able to correspond with Elisabeth fairly regularly until the Allied invasion of North Africa, usually about the situation with the houses and the increasing hardships in Provence. But in March 1943, in a letter to Charley exclaiming over his latest granddaughter, she adds, 'Did you see the cable about Elisabeth Starr? I'm afraid it's hopeless, as they would never have cabled unless she was dead.' Polly, who always stated that she never really needed anyone – and so patently did – seems to have added the news of Elisabeth's death almost as an afterthought. Perhaps it was too painful to elaborate on, and perhaps Elisabeth would have understood.

Peggy heard of this second death, as before, high up on her Devon tor at Hartland Abbey. Whereas the news of Richard Hillary's crash in January had brought profound sadness, Elisabeth's death brought wild distress. She had been so powerless to help her. She dealt with it in her own way, rushing out in agony into the woodland behind her caravan, where she suddenly saw, on a sunlit bank of early daffodils, 'the lovely little head of Elisabeth – and she was laughing for joy'.

Chapter 24 🌰
Now is the Time ...

for all good men to come to the aid of their country.
Typing Exercise

A homeless Polly had about nine different addresses during the war years. Although she was now in England, she did not cease to write letters to Charley at Plas Newydd, and through these it is possible to pin her down from time to time. For a woman of sixty-three, whose life over the past thirteen years had consisted mainly of reading, walking around the terraces of her neighbours' properties and writing her steady stream of letters – a routine punctuated by local excursions and leisurely summer visits to Britain – things were to change radically.

On arriving in England, Polly was cared for at Wilton House by Charley's sister, the Countess of Pembroke, and recovered quickly from her tortuous weeks on the small yacht: 'It's so wonderful to be home and not at the bottom of the sea.' Longing to go to Anglesey and Plas Newydd, for she was never happier than when she was there, in July 1940 she wrote, 'I'm hoping that you will be able to let me a cottage where I can keep chickens and grow cabbages. Do you think that is possible?' But for some reason this plan did not materialise and August found her stoically in the midst of the London air raids and visiting Caroline's 'charming rooms over a lovely fruit and flower shop'.

Then suddenly, the following year, she is in Hayes in Middlesex and has become both a lodger and a factory girl. Perhaps a combination of straitened financial circumstances, no permanent home and a desire to 'do her bit' brought an elderly Polly to live the life of an energetic forty year old. To Charley, in November:

Shall I tell you my day? I am called at 6.00 by Mrs Clusky, who is very nice. I then have breakfast in the parlour and when that is over I set out by moonlight for the factory. It's about a mile

and a half. I need not really go so early but I should hate to be
late. When I arrive, I put on galoshes and a long blue coat and
a white hat – I look a fair treat. I'm called an operator! They've
put me on a machine – a very simple one – but it's rather fun.
I've broken it lots of times. We work till 12.00 when we have an
hour for lunch in a huge canteen – the only time we can smoke.
It's half a mile from where I work. We finish at 6.30 and I stagger home. The workers are all perfectly charming, mostly from
Sheffield and the North. They already call me Polly. The work is
five and a half days a week, plus a turn at night shifts.

She goes on to ask if Charley has any butter to spare as the canteen
food is 'filthy', although Mrs Clusky gives her a good dinner when she
gets home and cocoa at bedtime. All rather a contrast to a November
evening in Provence when, after a supper prepared by her maid, she
settled in front of a roaring fire with a glass of whisky and her dog
Sophy curled at her feet. One hears no more about Sophy, almost
certainly taken in by Elisabeth.

In May 1943 Polly is living at Glebe Place, Chelsea, and has another
job, at a factory named Boldings, 'making airplane and submarine
parts. The hours are 8.30 a.m. to 8.00 p.m. and 8.30 p.m. to 7.30 a.m.
night shift, which I start with. I'm very pleased about it – I manipulate a
capstan lathe.' At one point she finds herself sitting beside, 'a lady from
Poona who looks like a bulldog and on the other side Lady Albemarle
– who once had that peculiar case, when all the women of England
took her side and all the men his'. She is only there for a day or two and
then goes down on to a lathe: 'I much prefer sitting with real factory
girls.' Polly continued to move and work throughout these years and
began another factory job as late as July 1944. When she pauses for a
rest she 'feels shamed to have idled for four months'.

During this time, Caroline and Audry Carten had moved into a
flat in Paultons House on the corner of the King's Road and Paultons
Square in Chelsea. Now no matter what followed, Audry (whom she
called Omar) would always be the most 'significant other' in Caroline's
life. They shared the flat with Audry's brother Kenneth who, after the
war, would become the theatrical agent for Noel Coward and Laurence
Olivier.

Towards the end of the 1930s, Caroline had fulfilled her ambition of becoming an actress by joining the Oxford Repertory Company. A review in the *Evening Standard* read: 'In Lady Caroline, who acts under the name of C. Bayly, the Manners beauty is heightened by a sultry languor and sharpened by a sly and elfin charm.' Manners was the family name of Caroline's mother, and the Manners girls were known for their loveliness. The review went on to say that Caroline 'preferred to act in minor roles, mostly in the provinces, in order to get a thorough grounding in the profession'. Her aunt, Lady Diana Cooper, described her at this time: 'Caroline was a dream of physical beauty, long classic legs, brief modern pants, Garibaldi shirt, her beautiful sulky yet smiling face very small in a Zulu shock of hair.' How easy it was for her to submit to the discipline of a life on the stage one can only guess, but she was to do so for several years and then take on another and far more demanding task.

As the months wore on and the threat of war loomed ever nearer, frustration with his work and his love for Caroline plunged Rex Whistler into a sort of desperation, coupled with an increasing feeling of inadequacy. On a visit to his friend Edith Olivier at her little house at Wilton he implied he now, 'wanted to go to the Front and be killed', and, not necessarily with this as a definite aim, he began the process of finding out how to become part of the drift towards war. At this time the art historian Kenneth Clark, director of the National Gallery, was preparing a list of official war artists. Rex, not being 'modern', was not invited to apply. This was a mistake. He would have made a splendid war artist; he was capable of working amazingly quickly and would have honed his particular talents to produce highly sensitive records of great precision. It is the nation's loss that he was not appointed.

Rex's fame and quiet charm had ensured he was now entirely socially acceptable, having been invited to both Sandringham and Balmoral as a house guest. For better or for worse he was fascinated by royalty and the aristocratic *milieu* and seemed to need to be a part of it. Still dogged by the urge to do the right thing, he made several futile attempts to be accepted by a good regiment, using his artistic talent, but to no avail – it was regarded as a rather embarrassing irrelevance. In the end he succeeded in spite of and not because of it, and by the time France finally fell he was a subaltern in the Welsh Guards which, after rain-soaked manoeuvres on Salisbury Plain, he described as 'The Mud Guards'.

Diana Cooper, writing to her son John Julius, described the new Rex after he and Caroline had dined with her one evening in July 1940: 'Rex Whistler and Caroline came to dinner last night, Rex with a tough military moustache. He says there are not so many hairs, but each one is as thick as a hedge, so they make a brave show.' And, in an anecdote about his inexperience:

> He was told suddenly to form his men up and march them to church. Every order he shouted produced greater chaos, soldiers scuttling in opposite directions, forming sixes and sevens instead of fours (or is it three now?) ... Standing in a row to be inspected, he realised he had forgotten his collar. The Colonel inspecting felt this so apoplectically that he was robbed of speech, which did not return to him until he came to the next officer, who got the full blast of blimp rage for having a loose shoelace. Poor Rex, he's not suited to the life.

Rex's paints and talent went with him into the army, and they were used constantly, leaving a typically humorous trail and leading his fellow artist, Alfred Munnings, to remark: 'Rex Whistler is just for fun painting framed pictures in mess halls, and stuffed salmon. He's in the Army almost for fun, not a job.'

Everyone was doing something. Perhaps influenced by stories of Elisabeth's bravery in the First World War, Caroline left the theatre and, choosing one of the toughest jobs, donned a uniform and became a driver for the Light Rescue teams who would dart around London during the Blitz, dealing with the wretched results of the bombs intended to destroy or demoralise its citizens. With shifts of two days on and one day off, she stuck with this dangerous and heart-rending work through the early years of the war, until she could stand it no longer.

Chapter 25 ✖

OPIO TO ALGIERS

After Elisabeth's death, Diane van Dommelen expelled some of the Castello refugees and put the remaining occupants of the house on a strict budget. To her chagrin, Elisabeth's will was kept locked away in her lawyer's office. Madame Arnando, who gave Elisabeth her meagre last meal, told how she was sacked the day following Elisabeth's death, and departed unpaid, leaving, to her lasting grief, her precious Escoffier cookery book in the kitchen. Diane was now the chatelaine, a role she fulfilled with gusto, for she was sure the Castello would now be hers – and made no secret of the fact. But there is also evidence that she continued to hide vulnerable people, even when it became extremely dangerous to do so. Two communist schoolteachers, Monsieur and Madame Dardaillon, taught in the nearby village of Le Rouret and gave lessons to two Jewish children hidden in the Castello. This couple also brought to a fine art the act of entering the local *mairie* at night, under pretext of using the telephone, to stamp false papers, *les faux papiers*, in order to help people escape deportation.

Since November 1942 the south-east of the unoccupied zone had been more or less settled under Italian military rule. This meant that, after the terrifying Vichy round-ups of non-French Jews across the south in July and August of 1942, Jewish refugees (especially of French nationality) now felt more secure. The Italians had little tradition of anti-Semitism and for this reason, and because they resented being dictated to by the Germans, they contrived to block the Nazi–Vichy effort to deport Jews to an unknown fate. For the fact this minefield was negotiated with skill by his ministers, Mussolini must be given credit.

Dr Suzanne Perles, who had treated Elisabeth for anaemia and been told by her about the houses on the hill, now arranged to rent Polly's Bastide. Here the family felt safer, away from the coast. The household comprised Dr Perles, her husband, who was also treasurer to a group of local resistants, and their three children, Alain, Nicole and a younger son, plus several friends. One of these friends was a young man named Claude Marcus, although, by sleight of hand, he had sensibly changed the name on his identity card from 'Marcus' to 'Marais'. His age was entered as seventeen, although he was nineteen, for this enabled him to escape the *Travaux Forcé*, the Forced Labour decree that sent young men to work in the fields and factories of Germany. Claude's parents had sent him up to Opio from their apartment in Le Cannet, on the hill behind Cannes, for in spite of the relative benevolence of the Italians they felt he would be safer away from the town.

The summer progressed through its simmering heat. Bicycle rides were taken, with no hindrance, around the neighbouring countryside and to and from the coast. The cicadas sang and grapes (soon to be picked and almost all requisitioned) ripened on their gnarled stumps. Food became ever scarcer. A great fig tree grew in the front garden of the Bastide, and figs could quickly be eaten before the 'Inspectors' spotted them. Since then figs have always been a favourite fruit of Claude's.

Charley Anglesey's San Peyre was also let. The Bogobzas were from Marseille, an unsafe place from any angle. Monsieur Bogobza was Jewish and his wife Catholic. Of their children, the youngest had suffered from polio and was partially paralysed. Mr Bogobza was remembered for his gentleness and, each time he fetched the bread from the *boulangerie*, for giving sweets to any loitering village children. During these months the two families would visit Diane at the Castello for lunch or dinner, pooling their meagre rations. She was supportive and friendly.

In July of 1943, the month that Claude joined the Perles at Opio, American forces captured Palermo in Sicily. Mussolini was suddenly arrested and Marshal Pietro Badoglio, known for his cruelty during the Italian occupation of Ethiopia and Libya, took over. Badoglio pronounced his intention to carry on with the war, but at the same time began negotiations with the Allies. This dithering policy boded ill for Italy and the Italians. In September, Mussolini was rescued by the Germans and re-established a fascist government at Lake Garda in northern Italy, thereby creating 'two' Italys. On 1 October the Allies entered Naples in the south and on the 13th the Badoglio government declared that Italy was at war with Germany. In the south of France there was a mass rush eastwards towards the border by retreating

Italian troops, jettisoning their arms, munitions and uniforms en route, pursued by the Germans, who had moved swiftly down and through the south. The Vichy regime became virtually impotent and the Nazis took control of the whole of France.

Now the hills of Opio had other visitors – solitary Italian soldiers, either deserters or separated from their units, trying to reach the Italian border. The families in the houses on the rue de la Fontaine gave these hunted men what little food they could spare. And the Gestapo now had open season.

A brutal awakening disturbed the peace in the early morning of 23 December 1943. One of the sons of the Bogobza family, having rushed across the terraces, warned the Perles at the Bastide that the dreaded black Citröens had swept up to San Peyre and the Gestapo were arresting everyone at the house. The rest of the Bogobza family had tried to hide in a deep cupboard carved out of the wall beside the fireplace in the large salon, but were quickly discovered. Flung into a waiting van, they were driven off to their fate. Only the son who had warned the Perles would escape and manage to survive the war. On hearing the news, the group at the Bastide rushed *'comme des fous'* out into the countryside and into hiding. The following morning they telephoned Diane at the Castello, who confirmed all was now quiet. This enabled them to return to the Bastide for the last time to collect their most vital belongings before moving back to Cannes. Opio was no longer the place to be.

The Anglesey family were never informed of the tragic event at San Peyre, and Elisabeth was not there to witness it, for there is no telling what she might have tried to do. Doing nothing had never been an option.

Claude's parents, still living in their apartment in Le Cannet, now decided to move to Pau on the edge of the Pyrenees, which they felt could only be safer. About the same time, Alain and Nicole Perles and Claude Marcus, lying low with the rest of the Perles family in Cannes, made a decision: they must cross the mountains into Spain and somehow get to North Africa and join the Fighting French. Preparations for the journey took all of January 1944. Organisers and guides had to be trustworthy. The expenses were great and the whole expedition would be in the lap of the gods. Eventually a rendezvous, in Lourdes, was arranged with a contact and the three set off separately to meet first in Pau. During Claude's journey a strange incident occurred. Nearing Toulouse a man entered his train compartment and, after a moment, began to whistle a new Irving Berlin song, familiar to Claude and only heard on the BBC: 'This Is The Army, Mr Jones'. Although bewildered, Claude was very careful not to react. Even a casual tune could open the path to the interrogation room and deportation.

Once reunited in Pau with Claude's parents, the three friends then travelled to Lourdes to meet their contact, a craggy-faced Basque, who would arrange for them to be taken over the mountains to Spain. He told them what to take for their journey – this being the bare minimum with, above all, warm clothing, for they were to walk long hours at night and sleep in barns during the day. As part of the transaction they were instructed to leave half a five-franc note with Claude's parents before their departure, the other half to be given to their guide once they were safely in Spain. This would, hopefully, be brought back to France to complete the note and prove all was well. They had no choice but to trust him.

On the day before their departure the three returned to Pau to take leave of Claude's parents and gather their belongings together. Now, tense with anxiety, they decided to spend their last afternoon in a cinema. Claude would never forgive himself for those two lost hours away from his family.

That evening they travelled by bus to Navarrenx, about 50 kilometres west of Pau. The escapees were seven in all: Claude, Alain and Nicole plus four others, three men and a distinguished blonde woman who introduced herself as the Comtesse de Moussac. Their guides were a father and son, and the first stage would be to cross the 30 kilometres of the forbidden zone before reaching the frontier. Anyone discovered there who was not a resident was either arrested or simply shot. The first night consisted of plodding across endless fields, clambering through hedges and barbed-wire barriers, avoiding the villages that housed German units and barking dogs. After a day spent sleeping in a barn they set off once more and were almost immediately stopped by the forward guide, who had spotted a German patrol on the small country road they were taking. Ordered to flatten themselves at the bottom of a ditch, two very long hours were spent stretched out in the cold and damp. At one point Alain leant over and whispered hoarsely in Claude's ear, 'Heaven is where one can cough.'

Charles, 6th Marquess of Anglesey, in court dress

Charles Anglesey at San Peyre in 1940

Caroline Paget and Rex Whistler in Austria

Many Waters, West Sussex, 1941

Peggy and Dominie, Sussex, 1943

Richard Hillary before his accident

Peggy and The Ark on Exmoor (the Grey Pigeon in the background)

*Students of the Monkey Club
picking grapes, 1946*

Diane van Dommelen

Caroline Paget entering the gate of the Castello, 1947

Caroline and friend in the pool garden at the Castello, 1947

The third night they began climbing steeply – and at the same time it began to snow heavily, for this was February in the Pyrenees. Unable to continue, they spent a freezing night in a huntsman's cabin in front of a meagre fire, all seven, friends and strangers, huddled together for warmth. On the following morning things began to improve, for they could now walk in daylight. A long hard climb took them eventually to the top of the pass of Larrau, where they were told they now had 'one foot in Paradise'. Then came the descent into Spain. For twelve increasingly exhausting hours they scrambled down, following a rushing mountain stream, until they came to the farm where the guide's responsibility ended. All in all, their journey had been charmed: no injuries, no shots fired and no border guards hiding in the bushes ready to arrest them. The guide was handed the other half of the five-franc note and they were on their own.

Spain had a strange relationship with the Allies. Supposedly neutral but overshadowed by Franco's strong Nazi sympathies, it nevertheless traded its general laxity towards fugitives against insurance for the future and Allied provisions. But the system was unpredictable and anything was possible.

After resting, the small group continued to trudge through the snow towards the frontier village of Orbaiceta, deciding en route that there was no point in trying to avoid any kind of Spanish control. This was fortunate, as on entering the village they immediately ran into two *carabinieres* in their black swept-back hats. Taken to a police post, their papers were checked in a relatively friendly fashion. Here the Countess observed: 'To think that you considered avoiding them, when they're so handsome.' That night was spent in a guarded villa and from there they went to Pamplona, where they ate in a restaurant, rather surrealistically surrounded by captured American airmen. Then on to the open prison village of Leiza in Navarro where they were told to rest, in order to recover their strength before internment.

Internment began in Urberuaga – a real prison camp, surrounded by watchtowers and barbed wire, where the regime was strict and the food scarce and bad. After a spell here it was on to Molinar de Caranza, between Bilbao and Santander, and it was there that Nicole was separated from the two men and sent to a women's camp. But the Spanish were playing their cards carefully, relaxing rules as the war swung ever more in favour of the Allies, now poised for action across the Mediterranean. Everyone in the camps was waiting for the next convoy that would take the lucky ones to Algeciras, on to Gibraltar – and freedom. So it was a very good moment when Claude and Alain were told they could travel to Madrid to join the next group leaving Spain, and go there alone as long as they promised to behave themselves and not escape.

In the space of twenty-four hours they changed from prisoners to tourists. Embassies and consulates in Madrid were hives of activity. That of the Free French, although less luxurious than the Vichy Consulate, was far more animated. Here Claude and Alain went each week for pocket money, news of the war and, as always and everywhere, the ration of cigarettes. As 'clandestine expatriates' their papers had to be stamped regularly by the Spanish authorities. Nicole, released from her women's camp, had now joined them, so all three were together once more when the long-awaited day came.

Forbidden by the British to embark for North Africa from Gibraltar, on 1 May the group took a train to Algeciras, from where launches ferried them to the Ville d'Oran, an aging ferry anchored off Gibraltar and now crewed by the Free French Navy. Along with about 100 other escapees from France and 800 British soldiers and officers, they were now on an Allied troopship, crossing a Mediterranean where German submarines patrolled and attacked constantly. In spite of these hazards, by the end of the war around 20,000 had escaped from France and made their way through Spain to join the Free French in North Africa.

Docking at the bustling port of Oran, the trio were fascinated by the sight of tiny, roofless cars scuttling around like so many ants – they had seen their first jeeps. Once in Algiers, Claude and Nicole began training as interpreters for the United States military while Alain, to his joy, was accepted as a student pilot for training in the States.

The 12th Tactical Air Command of the US Air Force included four Free French squadrons. And it was as an interpreter that several months later Claude found himself flying in a Dakota, as a member of the invasion force, and not without emotion, across the bay of a still-occupied Cannes.

Landing near St Tropez, soldiers and airmen went rapidly to La Foux near Ramatuelle, where a holding camp had been set up under the pine trees. Apart from one other soldier, Claude was the only

Frenchman. Here he discovered another American marvel – washing-up liquid.

While aircraft strafed the retreating Germans relentlessly as they fled towards the north, ground troops fought their way along the coast, through Fréjus and Agay and onwards towards Cannes. Claude, anxious to get news of those members of his family who had stayed on the Riviera, was now given permission to travel eastwards under his own steam. It was on 25 August, six months after beginning the trek to freedom, that Claude entered Cannes, newly liberated by the Americans.

The victor's return was muted. Having no transport, he borrowed a well-used woman's bicycle and began the long climb towards Le Cannet. Pedalling along the Boulevard d'Italie, he passed another cyclist who he recognised immediately. Dr Perles was on her way down to Cannes and was astonished and thrilled to see Claude and have news of her own children, Alain and Nicole. Suzanne Perles and her youngest son had been hidden in the Convent of the Bon Pasteur in Cannes and her husband had also survived the occupation of the south. There was much news to exchange, but there was one answer she could hardly bear to give Claude: his parents had been taken at Pau in May. He would not see them again.

Claude has always said that, in spite of the events through which he lived there, he has fond memories of the charm and tranquillity of the rue de la Fontaine and its houses. He remembers the beauty of the surrounding countryside and, above all, the great fig tree in the garden of the Bastide. But although he has had a holiday home in another part of Provence for many years, he has never been back to Opio.

Chapter 26 🌰
RETURN TO MANY WATERS

Peggy, still encamped at Hartland in Devon, could at last return to Ardingly. Romulus, the male red setter, had received a blow to his head, probably from a car, for the dogs had roamed at will. Now almost blind, he was never let out unattended, so the wild races through the woods with his mate Rema were no more. Dominie and Peggy were free to walk when and where they wished and Peggy was now assured she would not be evacuated from Many Waters.

As the Allies marched into Rome, an event followed immediately by the landings on the Normandy coast on D-Day in June 1944, Peggy settled once again into the cottage in the valley, with Renée Goldspink installed, as before, in the Kennels above. In a matter of days, Hitler's 'secret weapon', the V-1 bomb, the doodlebug, made its evil appearance over southern England. These pilotless 'planes' with a wing span of over 6 metres and a noise 'like the exhaust of a gigantic motor bicycle', shooting flames from their tails, roared over the villages of Sussex towards their target – London. Pilots from southern airfields scrambled to try to catch and shoot them down over open countryside before they reached the city. Their successors, the rocket-shaped and silent V-2s, held a different terror, for, as there was no noise, there was no way of knowing who would be the next victim. The bombing of their launching sites in northern France by the RAF put an end to these sinister missiles.

Peggy quickly became chairwoman of the Sussex branch of the *Amis des Voluntaires Français* (the AVF) and flung herself into the work 'with the driven ferocity of the over-tired and unhappy'. Again lecturing across the county, she ended her long days by writing appeals for funds for the Free French to anyone she felt might be sympathetic. At this point in the war, General de Gaulle was complaining bitterly that Churchill and Roosevelt were withholding much-needed funding and equipment from his Free French Army. In fact, the tension between the three leaders was on a knife-edge, so much did Roosevelt mistrust de Gaulle, his ambitions and his *Forces Française de l'Intérieur*, and so much did Churchill object to de Gaulle's arrogant intransigence and displays of ire towards the British government. But now the British people and the press were firmly behind the general and his Fighting French, so soon to enter the battlefield of France. And Peggy knew only too well what France would need when it was liberated: everything. Fund-raising must be maintained at all costs.

In August of 1944, the *Sussex Daily News* ran an article on a great Bank Holiday Fair. On the terrace of Stonehurst, high above Many Waters, a luncheon for one hundred guests, organised by Peggy, included the duchesses of Norfolk and Richmond and Gordon, Lord Leconfield of Petworth House, the Acting Ambassador of the French Committee of National Liberation, General Sicé (President of the French Red Cross), a baronne, a countess, and the great and good of the county. The *entente cordiale* flourished in Ardingly as the guests consumed, at lightning speed, lobsters, fresh and smoked salmon, chicken, ham and copious fruit salads, which disappeared down those well-bred throats until the buffet was no more. Robert Strauss, Peggy's landlord, had turned up trumps. She had persuaded him to become treasurer of her branch of the AVF and, after initial hesitation, he had more than done his bit. From London, by various means, he had produced a feast the like of which had not been seen for four years. Meanwhile, far below in the valley around the lakes, others guessed the weight of a cake, placed pennies on squares, played darts, skittles and the wheel of fortune, took pony rides and splashed under the little waterfalls.

Peggy had pulled it off. Her idea she could raise yet more money for the Free French by holding a summer fete in the Stonehurst gardens had been amazingly successful. They were blessed with wonderful summer weather but the temperatures of over 80°F (27°C) along with the necessity of constantly climbing and descending the precipice to and from the big house, had made the organisation anything but easy. As she wrote feelingly:

In the late fifties one's legs prance less easily than in youth; muscles ache as one climbs steeply; one's interior seems to be suspended upon an ever-slackening string; one's heart beats in one's nose, and conversation, if any, is made in gasps. Humiliated and infuriated by the approaching anti-climax of AGE, one pauses at intervals pretending to absorb the beauties of the surrounding scene, but in reality to inflate one's bellows, hoping that the companion will not notice one's distress.

An auction on the house terrace, held on full stomachs and accompanied by plenty of good cider, produced a total beyond expectations. Along with the games, rides and picnic teas served out of Many Waters, the grand total came to the most satisfying sum of over £700. This, together with a personal message from Queen Elizabeth, read out by Peggy, had made the whole 'crazy idea' worthwhile.

But now Peggy had other plans for, somehow, she must think of a way to pay tribute to Elisabeth.

Chapter 27 ❧

LIBERATION

In the south of France the resistance movement had taken time to reach the vigour of its counterpart in the occupied north. But, although slower in getting started despite the influx of, mainly communist, Spanish *Maquis* (the remnants of the defeated Spanish Republican army), towards the end of the war the southern resistance grew rapidly in numbers.

Several events swelled the ranks of the Resistance or, as they were called if they took to the hills, *le Maquis*, after the scrubland in which they hid. When, in June 1941, Russia entered the war on the side of the Allies, many members of the French Communist Party formed groups of what became the *Francs-Tireurs*. At the end of 1943 when the Germans invaded the south, members of the French Armistice Army (those members of the French forces allowed to exist but confined to barracks by the Germans) formed their own military resistance, *Les Groupes d'Armée*. These professional soldiers despised the unstructured *Maquis* as much as they were disliked in return.

In that year the *Service de Travail Obligatoire* (Forced Labour) swung fully into action throughout the whole of France. What had been a campaign promising good conditions and compensation for those willing to work in Germany became, in the light of increasing unwillingness to take up the offer, simply deportation. This threat was now so great that to join the Resistance, although a tough and comfortless life, was infinitely preferable to the risk of being sent to Germany. As a result, new recruits swelled the ranks of the *Maquis* considerably from the end of 1943 and into 1944. The *Maquis* lived, like the outlaws they were, in the forests and scrubland of the hills. Insufficiently clothed, often cold and hungry, they relied on friendly farms and villages for food and occasional shelter, applying pressure if supplies were not forthcoming. Allied agents got money and arms to them when and where they could.

At the beginning of 1944, General de Gaulle brought the majority of the groups together as the *Forces Françaises de l'Intérieur*, the *FFI*, which included the Free French abroad, enabling de Gaulle to speak in the name of France as the liberation approached. It was the *FFI*'s evocative *Croix de Lorraine* armbands that would flash through the streets of Paris in 1944 as they fought for their city.

In the misty dawn of 15 August 1944, a group of United States parachutists of the 1st Airborne Task Force, together with French and British paratroops, landed on a plateau in the Massif des Maures in the Var. The units had been drafted from war-torn southern Italy, Corsica and Algiers. Some of the Americans were members of the OSS, the Office of Strategic Services. Founded initially in 1942, the OSS was the forerunner of the CIA and in Washington its members were known as the 'Cloak and Dagger Boys'. But now they were to co-ordinate the actions of the different resistance groups and provide badly needed equipment and trained men to aid them in sabotage activities in preparation for the imminent Allied landings in the south of France. The programme operated under the auspices of the Special Projects Operational Centre, with the blessing of General de Gaulle.

The parachute landings were followed by over 400 gliders, carrying men and equipment, which endeavoured to land in the area of the Argens Valley near the village of Le Muy. Many of these lightweight machines missed their landing spots, only to crash in pieces among the vines and trees surrounding the plateaux. The troops were detailed to protect the right flank of the American Seventh Army as it landed on the southern coast and made its way up through France. It was essential to control Le Muy, about 24 kilometres inland from the town of Fréjus, for from here a spider's web of roads led in all directions and to block these effectively would be to block the movements of the enemy army. So began Operation Dragoon.

On the same day in August, US Forces, and a small British contingent, landed on the coast east of Toulon. With them was General Jean de Lattre de Tassigny and his Free French troops. This brilliant and respected soldier would lead the French 1st Army as, with two United States battalions under his control, it fought its way through to Alsace and across the Rhine to Berlin. Also on that summer morning landing craft raced on to the beaches of Cavalaire-sur-Mer (now called the Plage de Débarquement), Pampelonne (near St Tropez), St

Raphael, St Maxime, Dramont and Antheor. In between Cavalaire and Pampelonne lay Elisabeth's now abandoned coastguard cottages – the scene of happier days. The Germans were in no position to defend the coast properly, and Toulon and Marseilles were swiftly opened up by General de Lattre and around 60,000 prisoners taken, at the cost of nearly 6,000 Allied casualties.

The Allies swiftly made their presence felt by land, sea and air. Under bombardment from Allied planes and shelling from their ships at sea, dedicated to taking out the batteries and enemy gun emplacements in the hills above the coastal towns, swastikas were pulled down from public buildings and the *drapeau tricolore* raised in their place. Although accepted fatalistically as a necessity by the population, the Allied attacks were frightening. During this time an Allied bomb landed on a crowded Nice railway station killing many, while others lost their lives when a railway bridge near the town was destroyed, along with the train travelling across it. In one month, with the help of resistance groups, the Allied Army swept north and west to Avignon and up the Rhone valley through the centre of France. It was generally acknowledged that the unexpected rapidity of the advance was due to the courageous fighting and sabotage carried out by the Resistance.

Although Cannes was far from heavily defended, a company of the Task Force suffered heavy casualties as it approached the town, being pinned down by enemy troops equipped with heavy guns and dug in on the east bank of the Siagne River. But on 25 August, the day Paris was liberated, so was Cannes. Tears, kisses, flowers and wine flowed.

A prominent member of the Resistance in Cannes, the schoolteacher Ange-Marie Miniconi, was responsible for saving the Croisette. The German Army, headed by its local commander Colonel Schneider, was still in the town on 23 August, when Miniconi learnt the Allies planned to take the town on the 24th. He had also learnt that Schneider had received orders (similar to those given to the occupying commander in Paris) to destroy municipal buildings and installations, including the town hall and the law courts. In addition, parts of the Croisette were to be reduced to rubble in order to provide a defence wall, in case the Allies braved the mines on the beach and attacked from the Bay of Cannes.

Tracking the demoralised German colonel to his private dining room in a café opposite the station, Miniconi offered him a safe conduct out of the town, along with his staff, in exchange for leaving Cannes untouched. In the early hours of the following morning, Schneider took Miniconi and his group to the Hotel Splendide at the eastern end of the rue d'Antibes. Here, in a basement, he unlocked a large black metal box – the master control for detonating the explosive charges – and handed the Frenchman a pair of wire cutters. One by one Miniconi gingerly severed the web of wires until all were disconnected. A plan found in the cellar showed that, in addition to the municipal buildings, every hotel and villa between the Casino by the old port and the Palm Beach Club at the eastern end had been mined through drains under the Croisette. The Carlton Hotel alone had been allotted fifty canisters of explosives. The Croisette would have been completely destroyed.

Colonel Schneider refused Miniconi's offer of safe conduct and by dawn the German troops began their retreat. A week later Schneider was court-martialled in Nice by his superiors, accused of dereliction of duty and executed by firing squad.

As for Sunny Bank Hospital, the difficult years at the beginning of the war had become even more so, when the Nazi troops took over the south completely in the autumn of 1943. The English church in Cannes had been closed and the English library ransacked, some disapproved-of books burnt, and others, if they were of value, sent to Germany. The Sunny Bank Hospital staff were ordered to present themselves regularly at the *mairie* in order to have their fingerprints taken. Plain-clothes agents visited the hospital to search for people in hiding and all patients had to be checked and signed for. At first, British citizens were confined to the town limits and later, as an Allied invasion threatened, ordered to go beyond 100 kilometres of the coast. Others, more suspect, were sent to a concentration camp at Grenoble and these included Sunny Bank's Dr Ginner, leaving the hospital in the care of a French doctor, who took a great risk in being involved with the British. Although increasingly under threat of evacuation to the hinterland, the nurses and patients were always reprieved. A radio hidden in the basement kept the staff abreast of events in the world outside. So it was with both hope and fear that in August of 1944 the nurses spread a great home-made Red Cross flag over the courtyard in front of the hospital as the Allied bombers thundered over Cannes, in order to knock out the gun emplacements on the hills behind them.

Sadly, the hope of freedom was mixed with horror, with the discovery of savage reprisals. On the same day that the German troops withdrew, eight prisoners at the Gestapo Headquarters at the Villa Montfleury, resistants from the local area including one woman, were grouped together and shot. It was the Gestapo's final gesture to the people of Cannes. This was a repetition of the massacre of a group of resistants held at Nice, who had been taken out into the countryside and shot on the day news of the Allied landings reached the Gestapo in that town. Among them was Hélène Vagliano from Cannes. Brought up in England, of Franco-Greek extraction, her bravery in refusing to name her fellow resistants under repeated torture made Hélène a martyr of the Resistance. A street in Cannes bears her name.

The liberation of Nice was trickier than that of Cannes, and the town was not freed until 30 August. There, the first young Americans, not stopping for the proffered wine and carnations, paused only to ask a group of local *Niçois* 'Where are they?', before pushing on in hot pursuit. The Task Force, now joined by the swashbuckling American-Canadian 1st Special Service Force (the Devil's Brigade), fought their way eastwards towards the Italian border. The border was long, the terrain tough and the fighting often bitter. The Force lost many of its men, killed or wounded, in the operation. In the town of Draguignan in the Var there is a beautifully kept cemetery where those who did not survive the liberation of the south of France lie, far from home.

The United States Army set up a Civil Affairs operation in Nice and Grasse, 'to administer the activities of all the people of all the nations who have gathered along the Riviera'. The audacious Isabel Pell, the subject of Elisabeth's last relationship and now respected by many for her work with the Resistance, was closely involved with this. The programme was nevertheless an uneasy one, and both Americans and French were more than happy when control was handed back to the French authorities.

Polly wrote to Charley from yet another digs in London, this time in Old Church Street, Chelsea: 'What about Opio now? Isn't it exciting? I can't wait for the news. I do hope we haven't destroyed St Tropez – but I expect we have!' But, taken quickly by members of the Resistance and paratroopers, the town, apart from damage to the port caused by bombardments, had survived intact.

It was in the north of France that Rex Whistler met his death. He had seen rather less of Caroline once he joined the Welsh Guards, although his feelings for her were painfully constant. About her work on the Light Rescue team he wrote: 'I think of you so continually with dread and anxiety and such admiration too. It is thrilling and magnificent and lovely to know you are being actually heroic, isn't it?' It was a typically loving note, now expecting little in return.

Rex continued to draw and paint while he was with his unit, finishing the designs for a revival of Oscar Wilde's *An Ideal Husband*. His very last murals were drawn on the walls of the Old Ship Club at Bosham on the Sussex coast. Over several convivial nights a fat Bacchus seated on a barrel and a naked girl tied to a stake, flanked by an ogling guardsman and a satyr offering grapes, were created in response to well-lubricated requests from fellow drinkers. On the fourth night, with his fellow Guardsmen, he crossed a choppy English Channel and prepared for combat. It was July 1944 and 'Operation Goodwood' was filling the skies and roads of northern France in the follow-up to D-Day.

On the verge of battle Rex wrote three letters: to his mother, to his elderly soulmate Edith Olivier; and to a close woman friend, Imogen Gage of Firle Place in Sussex. In the top of each he inserted a piece of mistletoe, picked from the tree above his tent. There was no letter to Caroline.

As Platoon Commander, Rex was ordered to support a group of Canadians who were to take the village of Giberville in Calvados but, contrary to expectations, the village had not yet been cleared and a small group of Germans were still fighting hard. Jumping down to try to free his tank, which was stuck in a tangle of wires in a gulley, Rex was hit by a mortar shell. Among summer orchards and fields full of the corn he had so often drawn into his cornucopias, he died instantly. His neck was broken in the blast, leaving him outwardly unblemished. Dressed in shirtsleeves and wellingtons, he was laid out beside a hedge, 'looking as though he were asleep'.

In Connecticut, Cecil Beaton, deeply affected, wrote in his diary: 'Now his potentials were all unfulfilled, and Rex, the person suffused with effortless charm, so romantic and youthful of appearance, with his bold, ram-like profile and pale tired eyes, would never grow old.'

Chapter 28 ❧
BROKEN THREADS

The world was in a state of flux. Victory in Europe Day had come and gone in May of 1945. President Roosevelt did not live to see it, for he had died in April and the new President of the United States was Harry S. Truman. It was impossible then to foresee how fundamentally Germany would change, face up to and strive to redeem the actions of the Third Reich. Great events are not mentioned in Peggy's books and letters. Accounts of the death camps of the Final Solution, the carpet bombing of Dresden and the atom bombs dropped on Japan are not included. She stayed with what she knew best, and that was her life in France and England.

Many people in Ardingly were extremely busy in that summer of 1945, for The Elisabeth Starr Memorial Fund for the Relief of the Children of Provence, was up and running. Peggy designed its symbol of Elisabeth's seven-pointed star and registered it under the War Charities Act. Using up what would be almost her last reserves of energy, she attacked the whole idea with her usual determination. The writing of her latest book, *Beauty for Ashes,* on the war years in England and postwar France, was put aside. Instead she began to send out piles of appeal letters, often working until the early hours of the morning. Once again long lists had to be made – this time without Elisabeth.

In spite of continuing hardship in England, the response to Peggy's appeal was overwhelming. The combination of her fame as an author and an awareness of Elisabeth, the *Mademoiselle* of her books, had moved people to give what they themselves could ill afford to part with. Gifts of clothes, shoes, toys, medical and household goods, cots, blankets and such essentials as needles, thread and buttons, unobtainable in France, flooded in. With the aid of the ladies of the local Women's Institute these were sorted, packed and stacked in spaces offered by sympathetic villagers in Ardingly.

The Fund made the thought of returning to an empty hillside in

Opio more bearable. Peggy had no option but to return, for Fort Escu was her only home and all her possessions of any value were in Provence. Even if she had considered going back only to sell the house, this would have been a virtual impossibility in a prostrated Europe where, for the British, transfer of money was limited to the smallest amount. The French themselves were not in a buying mood. Organising the Fund would help to keep Elisabeth's memory alive, so the project became a vital *raison d'être*. It gave her, 'courage to return and to strive, in loneliness, to take up the snapped golden threads of our so happy life.'

The Mayor of Grasse, a doctor, was one of those who had accepted her offer of material aid, made through French headquarters in London and it seemed natural to work from his town, so near to Opio. But visiting the liberated countries was fraught with difficulties. Apart from the travel permit, for which a serial number had to be allocated, if one had no bank account in the country of destination a total of only £5 was allowed, plus £10 in French currency (around F2,000) for the duration of the stay. At that time a taxi ride in Paris could easily cost F1,000. Once inside France it was forbidden to move around without a special permit. As for food, 7 kilos of this was allowed, as luggage, in order to spare the strain on the rations of a near-starving Europe, now largely dependent on American aid. Although Peggy would be able to use her French bank account for additional transfers, escalating prices in France would be a real problem for some time to come.

Now she had to wait for her permit.

In June 1945 as the Allies divided up Germany and the United Nations Charter was signed in San Francisco, her serial number suddenly came up. Furious packing and organising were crammed into a few hours and Dominie left behind with friends. The frantic rush pitched her breathlessly on to the Newhaven ferry for Dieppe and then the train for Paris – laden with luggage and her 7 kilos of food. In an intact but hungry city, full of the noise of American lorries, jeeps and the clatter of wooden-soled shoes, for there was no leather left in France, she set about the frustrating process of gathering the necessary papers to regularise her situation and register her charity. Once this was achieved, her greatest stroke of luck was the exciting offer of a seat on an RAF bomber flying to Marseille. From there a military car took her swiftly to Opio and home.

So it was, in the heavy heat of a quiet summer afternoon, with the only sound the rasping chant of the cicadas, that she reached out to pull the, now rusty, chain on the bell by the entrance gates of Fort Escu. When Peggy had left in 1940, her pretty maid Irma had been wearing a lemon-coloured house dress, with her head tied around by a scarlet silk handkerchief and her feet in scarlet sandals. Now she was almost unrecognisable. Rake-thin, in ragged clothes, with her toes hanging out of her broken shoes, she collapsed into Peggy's arms. It was impossible now to fail to understand what the years of Vichy government, German occupation and the added misfortune of three years of drought had wrought.

The tenant from Cap Ferrat had long since left and the house was encased in a Sleeping Beauty bower of overgrown foliage and creepers. The pine cone laden branches of untrimmed cypresses fell wide of their trunks, wisteria and climbing roses scrambled over the entrance terrace and up the sides of the house, blocking the shutters open or closed. Briars had leapt the dry-stone walls surrounding the garden and sprawled into the lane outside. Irma, quite alone, had only been able to tend the vegetable patch in order to keep herself alive. The mere fact of her being there probably saved the house from requisition or theft.

Once through her front door behind the now very shady terrace, a weary Peggy was stunned to find that all was immaculate. In spite of the lack of cleaning materials, Irma had washed and polished everything that could be made to gleam and shine. For five years she had tended the house in the hope Peggy would return. Peggy did not yet dare tell her that, very soon, she would have to leave again for England,

The effects of war became evident again in the little kitchen. Although still full of the mod cons of the day, that Elisabeth had so carefully organised, nothing worked. With no electricity or fuel, Irma had installed the laundry boiler upon which it was possible to cook very simply over a small fire of olive twigs. Supper that night was 'a minute cup of vegetable soup and some haricot beans sauteed in a few drops of precious olive oil'.

At dusk that evening, she went out into her overgrown garden on the silent hillside and prayed for at least the comfort of a firefly. And after a moment they came flickering over the terraces from the direction of the Castello below and she felt that perhaps Elisabeth had tried to send her a greeting. Tomorrow she must descend those terraces and visit the house – a visit that daunted her for more than one reason.

In *Beauty for Ashes* Peggy writes a short paragraph recognising (a nameless) Diane van Dommelen as 'the courageous woman whom she [Elisabeth] had sheltered during the war and who, thank God, was there to nurse her with a matchless devotion when she fell ill'. She makes the point that Diane had been there as a guest, compliments her 'devotion' and never mentions her again. But her private letters show she mistrusted and feared her. Diane was an unknown quantity and this added to Peggy's dread of walking into a Castello that Elisabeth had left, never to return. Even Elisabeth's little dog Babs had died three days before, so that anticipated link had now gone. As she approached the entrance the following day, she strove to protect herself psychologically, imagining that, although unseen, Elisabeth had come to meet her and was welcoming her back to the house, their dogs running at their heels, as in the happy days before the war. But it was Diane who greeted her, heavy with an air of possession and defiance, coupled with the inference that Peggy would now be welcome only by explicit invitation. It was a painful and humiliating experience.

However, in the village itself everyone was overjoyed to see her again, for she was the first English person to return to the area and therefore a sign that things might eventually return to normal. Here she learnt, from those whom Diane had invited to the Castello over the past two years, that the ring Stewart Robinson had given to Elisabeth had been worn constantly by Diane after Elisabeth's death, but removed as soon as news came of Peggy's return to the village. Elisabeth had worn the ring all her life and had always made it known she wished it to remain on her finger when she was buried. What Diane did with it was never discovered. It was not all that would be found to be missing.

The Mayor of Grasse was allowed a small supply of petrol, so trips of assessment were made throughout the area, the Canton du Bar. The answer to what was needed was, as always, everything. Peggy had returned to what was a destitute land, ravaged by occupation and drought, and in a worse state than the countryside of northern France.

The little St Christophe clinic was grievously short of funds and had suffered from lack of maintenance. Though its devoted matrons, Hedley and Morris, would return to take it back from the small French staff who had run it valiantly during the war years, the clinic did not survive as it had been founded. A French organisation for orphaned children, the *Rayon de Soleil*, took it over for a spell and the buildings were then restored and became the attractive home of a retired British Ambassador. The matrons moved to a small house at Magagnosc, near Grasse (where Peggy and John had owned Domaine Fortescue) and lived there until 1963, when they returned to England to spend their twilight years in a residential hotel near Haslemere in Surrey.

Three weeks later, to Irma's chagrin – for she feared that, once back in England, her mistress would decide to stay there and not come back to a frugal and unheated winter in Opio – Peggy prepared for her return to Sussex. There she must pack up the contents of Many Waters and arrange for the shipment of the 108 cases of donations for the Fund. Another RAF plane full of lively, sun-tanned South African pilots, was produced for the return journey, which took her from Marseille to Croydon. Once back in Sussex she probably did not dare to ask herself whether, if given the choice, she would now prefer to spend the rest of her days in England. But, although feeling keenly the effect of 'the snapped golden threads' on her Provençal hillside, she knew she must return there.

Peggy's now over-strained heart would probably not have allowed her to do all that was necessary to vacate her cottage without the help of Renée Goldspink. In spite of her protestations, Renée was forbidden by Peggy to accompany her back to France at this stage, but she worked valiantly, packing, carrying, preparing meals and generally being a tower of strength. Even so, in endlessly pouring rain, Peggy had to climb the steep slope above Many Waters time and time again to deposit at Renée's 'Kennels' the packages and bags that would travel with her as hand luggage. She did not record her thoughts on saying farewell to her small cottage, deep in its verdant valley.

One important item would not accompany her. In a twist of fate so unfair to someone feeling so alone, Dominie, her black spaniel, suddenly and distressingly died. A delay in treatment had led to jaundice, too far gone to be cured. Peggy tried desperately to save him, sitting for three days by his basket, persuading him to take tiny sips of liquid. When he lost the fight she tried hard to understand, calling on her faith to support her: 'Perhaps He means His crusaders to stand alone and be of single mind and heart.'

Chapter 29 ✖️

SOME VERY HUNGRY MONKEYS

Peggy now began her excruciating return journey to Opio, laden with hand luggage that included, among much else, two small electric stoves, two electric boiling rings and a typewriter – all of which she called her 'bluggage'. There was no RAF plane at her disposal this time, now it was the cross-channel ferry – followed by a nightmare journey across France in a standing-room only train. And in the midst of it, no matter how difficult life became, she always had to attempt to carry out the tedious morning treatment on her face.

It was October 1945. The French Third Republic was being voted into history, making way for the crisis-ridden Fourth Republic which would see twenty different governments come and go over the next ten years. Into this uncertain new life, for better or for worse, she returned for good.

In a France suffering badly from the effects of war and occupation and in the grip of political turmoil, nothing functioned as it should. The Communist Party, once banned, was now flexing its muscles with a vengeance, these having been highly developed in the Resistance. Russia was sliding its fingers into Eastern Europe and beginning to be seen for the threat it would become, and talk of a resumption of the war was everywhere. Prices were unrealistically high, the food shortage grave, and the only way to keep a reasonable table was to pay the enormous cost of black market food – impossible for the vast majority of people and certainly for Peggy and the villagers of Opio.

The still scarce and almost uneatable bread was now made with a mixture of maize and ground olive kernels – terrible for Peggy's skin condition. Consuelo Vanderbilt Balsan, ex-Duchess of Marlborough, always thoughtful, regularly sent little parcels of white flour from America 'which saved my life'. Shops were virtually empty and 'fear made those who grew crops hoard them for their own families or sell them at exorbitant prices'. There was virtually no meat and, in spite of the miles of Mediterranean Sea, hardly any fish, this being snapped up as soon as it was caught. Ration tickets bought pasta, a little sugar and some vegetable fat. People still queued endlessly for vegetables and other staples and the coming winter was viewed with apprehension. Only the food parcels from abroad, with their tinned fruit, meat and fish, could be depended upon. The dire lack of transport continued, for there was still little petrol for the few cars or lorries, and the Nazi army had destroyed most of the locomotives. Insufferably crowded buses and trains were for the brave or the desperate.

But now Peggy was back and must re-make her life as best she could. She was overjoyed to find all her precious ornaments still crated up and safe in the Grasse apartment of her old friend, Gabrielle de Croze. Grasse had been a Gestapo headquarters towards the end of the war and the knock on the door was as feared there as elsewhere, but all Peggy's possessions had been well hidden and were intact, including John's books, that meant so much to her. Bringing everything back to Fort Escu and, with Irma, making the house a home once more, was a high spot at a difficult and uncertain time. Once settled in she would write to her family, 'I am alone now on my hillside'.

Soon afterwards the Grey Pigeon (the Baby Austin) arrived, having been driven from Many Waters as far as Paris by the Quakers and from there by the French Red Cross to Opio. Its familiarity made Peggy feel a little less cut off. And no sooner was everything unpacked and put back in place than the 108 cases from Sussex, for the Elisabeth Starr Memorial Fund, arrived at the front gate. Too soon began the heavy task of sorting and making up packages. Everything had to be hauled up the slope into her garage above the house and securely locked, as the contents were worth millions of francs on the black market. She was terrified of theft for, 'extremely odd refugees of all nations' regularly broke through the gap in her fence and took a short cut down through the terraces to the Castello path below and on to the village. These pitifully destitute and displaced people were everywhere.

Following the packaging came the distribution, which involved months of driving, often on narrow, uneven mountain roads and some-times in the dark as winter approached. Often alone, she heaved heavy bags up steep tenement stairs in high narrow houses and searched tire-lessly for remote cottages in the countryside, where she had been told help was needed. The inescapable local committee meetings brought with them the need for careful diplomacy with a proud people who desperately needed foreign aid but sometimes resented that need.

Working for the Memorial Fund put paid to her remaining stamina. From the end of 1945 to the end of 1946 Peggy toiled without cease, and from then on would never really be well again. But, for a while, there was moral support. The Quakers were once more operating out of their base in Marseille and could now be joined by their American and British colleagues. Peggy often gave them a bed for the night as they made their aid assessments throughout the area, and their help and companionship must have been welcome. During the war, and under immense difficulty, the French Quakers had continued to supply food to schools, prisons and concentration camps. At the end of 1943, when the German Army occupied the south, the Marseille centre could function no longer but, with the Liberation, swung back into action. The American Quakers were now able to purchase, through Portugal and Switzerland, great quantities of dried milk, cereals, dried fruit and tinned food for distribution to the needy, and especially the children. The British Quakers, with their ambulances, accompanied the liberating army of General Philippe Leclerc from Paris to the battlefields of Germany. Other groups tended to the new prison camps, those of the German prisoners of war, for the Quaker 'sees a brother in every man, without distinction of race, religion or nation'.

In spite of hardship, things were stirring down on the coast. In Cannes, in July 1946, the Palm Beach Club, restored and without its accompanying blockhouses, had staged its first entertainment since the Liberation. On 19 September a Battle of Flowers on the Croisette, followed by a magnificent firework display, heralded the delayed opening of the first Cannes Film Festival held in the late-*belle époque* Municipal Casino. Here the great hall was equipped as a cinema and the artist Jean-Gabriel Domergue created sumptuous decorations for the festival receptions. To the British who were slowly returning, it was of great significance that the bust of Edward VII was reinstated in Cannes by the *Cannois* themselves – a small gesture towards the *entente cordiale* he had so vigorously endorsed.

In that year Peggy did a rather extraordinary thing. Although she would, a year later, still be describing France as 'a very sick country, unstable and fraught with corruption', she set about using all her powers of persuasion to urge Helen Joynson-Hicks and Marion Ellison to take Charley Anglesey's house, San Peyre, for a year and bring over a group of girls from the Monkey Club. The lease was to run from June 1946 and would cost £250 for twelve months, paid in England. How they managed the basic foreign allowance is a mystery – perhaps they were awarded a special dispensation or had a transfer arrangement with Peggy.

It seems a reckless thing for them all to have done and rather surprising that the two women succumbed to Peggy's persuasion. But it is easy to see how overjoyed she would have been to have a flock of young, lively British girls in one of the empty houses. Strangely no one seemed daunted, still less the families who encouraged their daughters to participate – the plan probably being promoted as character-building and mind-stretching. In spite of this, the two directors themselves remained firmly in England, sending staff to run the project. In September fourteen well-reared girls descended on Opio and moved into Charley's house. It was all in great contrast to the Gestapo's arrival there in the winter of 1943, when the Jewish family was taken away, never to be seen again. Details of that event were not told to the new arrivals.

The house was sparsely furnished, for, due to the war, by no means all the items on the list prepared by Polly before the war had been delivered, and there had also been a couple of burglaries. But it was adequate, and somehow extra beds, along with tables and other necessities to equip a schoolroom, were found. The girls were to improve their French, do general studies and hone their skills as hostesses. Brisk little Gabrielle de Croze was brought down from Grasse to be their French tutor, a task she performed diligently. And they would also be given another interesting project – picking grapes!

Barbara Bossom, then Barbara North, at almost eighteen the youngest of the group, kept a diary of her stay there, which brings to life those months at the end of 1946. As they arrived in Opio the *vendange* was just beginning and, once settled in, the girls were told they too would be involved. Dressed in crisp pale dresses and greatly enlivening the local scene, they were taken to the vine terraces where they worked – and worked hard. Supervised by both their matron and the local foreman, they picked grapes at Peggy's and surrounding vineyards, providing very welcome free labour.

As well as their studies, the girls prepared meals with what was available, acting as hostesses at lunches and dinners that included the Mayor and his wife and, of course, Peggy – who they thought was charming, elegant and very friendly, even if she did make them pick her grapes.

Free time was spent walking in the countryside, visiting Grasse and Nice or travelling down to the coast on tightly packed and highly scented buses, adorned with market provisions and the odd sought-after live chicken. Occasionally there were invitations to Cannes from those friends of the girls' families who had gradually begun to reappear on the Riviera, and here they would get an excellent (probably black market) meal. They sunbathed on the beach at Cannes or Cagnes-sur-Mer where, Barbara noted with interest, there were occasional topless female bathers, a fashion statement new to the girls. On the few occasions when there was hot water (a fact always noted in Barbara's diary) there was a dash to wash hair. On some days there was no water at all.

The English girls' reward for the hard work of picking grapes – the *vendange* celebration – was both unforgettable and greatly appreciated. In contrast to the sombre mood of the time this was an oasis of fun and gaiety. Barbara remembered:

> The dance at the end of the *vendange* was wonderful and took place in a sort of village hall. There was a splendid oompah, oompah band, 'squeeze boxes', wind instruments of every sort and much heat generated by sweaty farm workers, happy and enjoying dancing with the dozen or so of us English girls who they had been working with in the vineyards. Their arms pumping violently, round and round we went, stamping feet and with much hilarity. Unfortunately, there must have been a busy-body reporter present because news of this glorious evening reached the eyes (or maybe ears) of Miss Joynson Hicks and Miss Ellison who threatened to come out and read the riot act. Very stupid of them, as the *entente cordiale* generated by all this was enormous. Luckily for us, both Misses J-H and E were deemed to be of such huge size that a *wagon-lit* could not accommodate them, so they never came.

Autumn progressed, and in spite of the brave efforts on the Riviera, the basic problems of France, and especially the south, were felt as keenly as ever. The girls woke to breakfast of the usual dry bread, spread with unpleasant jam (no butter) accompanied by acorn coffee without sugar. Their diet was locally grown vegetables and, occasionally, some lamb. Barbara fondly remembers her own food supplement gathered from nearby trees – figs dried in the sun, split open and filled with a walnut. But they were always hungry, and the Club became sorely in need of basic rations – their plight was such that they saw no alternative but to ask for help, although they all felt very embarrassed at making the request, knowing as they did how little food there was for the French themselves.

Barbara, as the youngest and slimmest, was sent on what she felt to be a 'desperate mission'. Terrified that her French would fall far short of the task and of the reception she might receive, she was sent to the Mayor of Opio to beg for food. With trepidation she set off on foot, down the hill of the Quartier San Peyre, across the valley and up the western hill to the main village and the *Mairie*. The prospect of asking for food was daunting, but she was to meet Monsieur Michel, Peggy's 'charming young Mayor', the respected ex-resistant who had now resumed his post. Although Barbara cannot remember his response, she was surely received with sympathy and courtesy – after all, he was known to be kind and she was young and pretty.

In spite of these difficulties Barbara, like Claude Marcus, loved the peace and beauty of the village and the friendliness of the local people. Both particularly remembered the figs. But the other girls were almost all older than Barbara and she began to feel homesick and longed to return to England. Her pleas must have been heartfelt, for her mother agreed she could leave Opio at the end of term. In the last week of November, after a night during which she was too excited to sleep, followed by a rough channel crossing, the train drew into Victoria and she was home once again.

How many adults have blamed their parents for what they now see as a weak decision made during their childhood? Barbara summed it all up: 'It was a brave idea and I only wish I had stuck it out to the end. I can't think why my mother let me leave after only one term.'

Chapter 30 🦋
CAROLINE RETURNS

Caroline Paget wept when she learnt that, after all, she really had inherited the Castello. But it seemed her name *was* there, in the will, and the short visit to Opio of almost ten years before had resulted in her becoming the legal owner. The bequest brought back the once distant sadness of Elisabeth's devotion and the whole situation was fraught with difficulties. She could not afford to maintain a large, very old house that had been untouched for years, in a land where nothing was obtainable. Opio was a long way away and money transfers were still extremely complicated.

Her first reaction was to abandon any idea of taking on the property and simply put it in the hands of local agents, in order to find a buyer as soon as possible. But those British who wished to settle in France had to apply to the Bank of England to become an 'emigrant' and were then allowed to transfer only £1,250 a year for a period of four years. If they wished to purchase property, it had to be paid for out of this sum, leaving little to live on. The French were not disposed to buy large properties and, in addition, there was a determined sitting tenant in the shape of Diane van Dommelen. But perhaps a sense of obligation to Elisabeth's wish, a lingering memory of her shy devotion and above all, Peggy's absolute determination that Caroline should become mistress of the Castello, prevailed. From Fort Escu the letters flew.

Caroline was toying with the idea of returning to the stage, when in November of 1946 her mother, Marjorie Anglesey, died. It was a bad blow. As her uncle, Duff Cooper, recorded, it was 'Caroline who loved her best and who has least else'. A couple of days later an unwitting Peggy sent Caroline a long and complicated letter relating to the Castello. Unaware of her grief, the letter was full of problems about strips of land, *cadastres* (property plans) and difficulties with the water tanks. She asked that Caroline should try to re-establish the bird sanctuary and forbid *la chasse* on Castello land as Elisabeth had done, 'becoming frantic if she heard shots on her property and instantly fleeing [sic] forth to hunt away the trespassers'. This alone illustrates Elisabeth's courage, for to descend on an armed and irate Provençal hunter is not for the faint-hearted.

Peggy and Caroline had never met, for Caroline had not returned to Opio since 1934. Peggy now pleaded with her to come out soon – perhaps with Polly in the spring: 'I can't tell you how terribly sad and lonely Elisabeth's lovely Castello looks now. I never go NEAR it if I can help it. Come and love it and make it live again.' The two were soon friends and Peggy's letters began to address Caroline as 'My Little Darling' and 'Darling Heart' and within months Caroline was confiding in her, as she had with Elisabeth.

The immediate problem was Diane. That Peggy feared her is clear, but why she feared her quite so much is more of a mystery. It was true that Diane had changed from the rather aimless daughter of a twice-abandoned mother to the forceful chatelaine of one of the largest private houses in Opio. She was a woman of complex personality. That she was courageous and principled enough to hide Jewish children and be a supportive friend to the Jewish families who rented the Bastide and San Peyre was well known. Also, she had remained in the village and was popular with some of the local people, and perhaps this was another reason Peggy trod cautiously, though resentfully.

One must hope and assume that Diane had indeed nursed Elisabeth with care and devotion and this was probably so, for the staff, who were deeply fond of their *Mademoiselle*, were still working in the house when she died, and would presumably have ensured Elisabeth was well looked after. But Diane made no secret of the fact that she genuinely thought Elisabeth had changed her will to leave her the Castello and was devastated when she found it was to go to Caroline. In a state of denial and defiance, she stayed put.

Soon after her return to Opio, Peggy was told by Elisabeth's lawyer that a pencil line had been run through Caroline's name in the will. He was also Peggy's lawyer, so she was allowed to examine the document – which presumably Diane was not. Peggy put the crossing-out down to the period of sad bitterness Elisabeth had gone through when France was threatened and she was exhausted by her work for the *foyers* and weakened by illness. She wrote to Caroline:

The fact that she did it in pencil – which could be erased when the bitterness passed, is to me very significant. Then [came] ill-health, for she was sick unto death even then, and vagueness and lassitude and the belief that she could change things at any minute ... and the pencil line was not rubbed out. IT IS NOW! She [Elisabeth] always dreamed of you in the future, loving and caring for her Castello as she did and now you're here to save it from disintegration and desolation.

Perhaps their pragmatic lawyer, respected by the expatriate community had, after a discussion with Peggy, agreed the line should be rubbed out. The pencil line is rather a mystery and, if Diane's name had been put there too, no one would ever say.

At the Liberation the Castello had become open house. Diane, described as quick, vivacious, pleasant and in control, was admired by those who flocked to her parties. She was cultured and an amateur singer and had drawn other singers and amateur actors around her. Appreciative audiences listened to productions of *Rigoletto* and *Antigone* – the latter being a Greek myth reworked during the Occupation by the playwright Jean Anouilh into a thinly veiled attack on the Vichy government. In addition she was memorably expert at whistling between her teeth, an asset much admired by her visitors!

On the first Christmas after her return, Peggy had been invited there, and it must have been a cruel experience to be received by Diane as hostess in that much-loved place. In a passage marked PRIVATE she wrote:

Caroline, I can do nothing against that fierce possessiveness and since I came back I've never been taken inside E's room or studio (save for one awful orgy in that sacred place on Xmas Day 1945 when I was invited to a party in the sacrosanct studio and found a mob of drunken peasants, chauffeurs and refugees and Diane embracing everyone and mad with excitement – Oh).

She refers to the house as being over-populated with 'disreputable freaks'. To add insult to injury, Diane asked Peggy to renew the lease on the Alpine *bergerie* with her: 'In case those people [the Pagets] come out and take possession, I want a place where I can put the things that

Elisabeth really, really gave to me'. The request was politely declined.

Peggy now began to learn more of Diane's various wartime activities. To Caroline: 'I was not invited into the old familiar haunts – I knew too much of what WAS once there, having a photographic memory. But I will whisper outside the wall to the Castello that you are soon coming as a loving protector.' She was told by villagers, to whom they had been offered, that Diane had dug up and sold the tyres from Peggy's Fiat, 'Desirée', and had obtained enormous sums for them. She did, however, manage to summon enough courage to recover the bodywork and sell it, the proceeds going towards a Peugeot *camionette* to take her vegetables to market, a practice from which her gardener Edouard profited greatly.

There had been two burglaries at San Peyre, once during the war and again in 1946 before the Monkey Club took the lease. All the china, glass, linen, most of the rugs and the curtains had disappeared – along with a Butagaz bottle, as precious as anything else. According to Peggy, the police had proof that Diane had herself taken goods from the house over the years and sold them, but could do nothing unless Charley Anglesey brought proceedings. This he was most unwilling to do, as it would complicate matters even more for Caroline and be generally unpleasant for the Paget family, who now owned two houses on the hill in Opio. Furthermore, it would not have been very good for the ever fragile *entente cordiale*.

The realisation that everyone had been in such desperate straits for money and food and could live only by barter and exchange, coupled with her fear of the younger woman, meant that Peggy would never accuse Diane, although she was certain she had been at once caretaker and thief. The others back in England were more relaxed, being grateful to Diane for simply being there and guarding the houses during the war, trying to keep them occupied, and thus protecting the buildings from 'undesirables'. But Peggy was more than relieved her own Fort Escu had been in the loyal hands of Irma and not subject to the ministrations of Miss van Dommelen.

Charley did not return to his pretty house on the side of the hill, for he died in February 1947 after the worst winter in Britain for fifty years. It was a terrible second blow for the children, who lost both parents in less than three months. Henry, the only son, inherited the title and became 7th Marquess of Anglesey. Just as Caroline had to deal with the Castello from afar, now Henry had to do the same with San Peyre, neither of them having hitherto been involved with either. The combination of Caroline's distressing war work in the fire service, coupled with the double shock of losing both her parents so close together, affected her badly and she confided in Peggy, who responded with compassion: 'Never tell me you are a weak character, darling. After all you endured during the war and two ghastly heart-breaking shocks in succession. I think you have survived all this quite marvellously and your courage and self-control stagger me. Clear up all business and START AGAIN.'

In June of 1947 Polly and Caroline came to Opio together – Polly to check up on the condition of the Bastide and Caroline to get to grips with the problem at the Castello and its stubborn occupant. For once the two older women were in agreement. As Peggy wrote to Caroline:

> Bravo, darling. Poll came up with your letter to her [Diane] and we read it together with the deepest admiration and relief! I know how hard it must have been and how exhausting! Half an hour of Diane and her dramatic and insincere vehemence kills me dead – and you had nine hours of her. *Mon Dieu*. But you managed the affair in a masterly way, letting her give notice to quit – and giving her permission to take what she liked of Elisabeth's was the cleverest thing of all. You felt something was due to her and most important of all now you will say 'such and such a thing was there, I know it was but I gave D. full and free permission to take away what she liked. Your treatment of the whole situation shows a masterly patience and strength. Poll let her have the rent of her house, you have made a magnificently generous gesture, and all we get is hate.

As many of Elisabeth's possessions as could be loaded onto a mule cart were taken away by Diane. She had various jobs over the next thirty-five years or so, running restaurants, including the Auberge de Camarades at Tourette-sur-Loup, higher into the mountains, and finally managing an antique shop on the main road at neighbouring Le Rouret. Here she settled into a dark little terraced house opposite the Place and near the bar-café, living on slender means but finding solace in wine and cigarettes. She haunted the Castello for many years, as long as Caroline was not in residence, and the tenants would learn of the old days and that, by rights, it should all really have been hers. She lived to an old age, her last years beset with ill health, one of the expatriate waifs of the south of France. She is buried in a pauper's grave at the edge of Le Rouret cemetery and traces of her name can just be made out on a tiny wooden cross.

Peggy went back to England in that summer of 1947. She had undergone an operation to remove gallstones in July: 'They have built a wall with them'. She decided to convalesce near her family and, renting out Fort Escu, went to stay with her sister Marjory at The Malthouse at Yapton in Sussex. She then had another minor operation at a hospital in Chichester. The wound refused to heal and the procedure was later roundly criticised by her doctor in France. After the operation she moved to Rose Cottage at Limmer Hill near Wokingham, where she settled in for August, looked after by an old woman, 'who cooks and does lamps'. In that sweltering summer, in a certain amount of pain and anxious as to how to keep her penicillin cool, she began to recuperate slowly. She was filled with joy on learning that Caroline and Polly would be returning to Opio for several weeks in September, at the same time as herself.

Back at Fort Escu, after a short spell during which the hill felt just a little as it had done in the past, Peggy was alone once more. At least she still had her Fund for the children to fill her days and her justification for staying. She realised she was becoming too old even to contemplate the upheaval of moving back to England permanently, and the physical side of her aid programme was now taken over by others younger and fitter.

With Diane's departure, the atmosphere around the Castello lightened considerably, and in October Peggy went into the attic there to retrieve the boxes that held what remained of Elisabeth's possessions. Many things were damaged by damp but among them was a small pile of memories: a *Foyer des Soldats de France* beret; a tattered Resistance flag with a home-made 'V' in yellow sewn on; a set of First World War medals and her proudly soiled Red Cross brassard, worn in both wars. All these were now taken to the Fort Escu chapel to be hung on the walls or placed on the broad stone slab by the window.

Clothes went to *L'Assistance de Grasse* to be given to the poor, except for the blue *foyer*'s uniform coat and skirt, which were given to a young girl in the village who had no warm clothes for the approaching winter. Six pairs of long, slim shoes, too narrow for anyone else to wear, were sadly sold only for the leather. Piles of letters received and drafts of letters sent, were burnt in Peggy's garden. Elisabeth's jewels, including her mother's diamond pendant and Corinne Robinson's ring and brooch, were never found.

Nor did Peggy find Gouveneur Paulding's tortured diary of his amorous adventures in the 1920s, which would be spotted by another in later years. But she did discover an ancient metal lantern. On a long stem and with a conical roof topped by a cross, it had been fitted for electricity and used in Elisabeth's black and white bedroom. Now it would sit by her again, for over the next year Peggy and Caroline designed a permanent headstone for Elisabeth's grave. As soon as Francis Navella, their much-loved mason, had enough petrol to spare, the rough stone, placed there during the war, was taken from the grave and carved. The inscription reads:

Elisabeth Starr de Castel de San Peyre. Decédée 23 Fèvrier 1943 à Opio

Above the inscription is her symbol, the seven-pointed star, and in the star is a V for victory. The round base at the bottom of the old lantern was cut off and the stem sunk into the rock at the top right hand side. Age and rust have left only a remnant of the stem.

The grave was complete and would remain so, for with part of the proceeds of the various rentals, Diane had bought the plot in perpetuity – perhaps under direction from Elisabeth, perhaps in a gesture of good will. But, for whatever reason, in the village town hall the name on the plan is listed not as Elisabeth Starr but as Elisabeth van Domm.

Chapter 31 ❧
INTERESTING TENANTS

Le Géneral de Gaulle remercie Lady Fortescue du l'aide généreuse qu'elle n'a cessé de prodiguer aux Voluntaires des Forces Françaises Libres. La France libérée n'oublie pas ses amis des temps difficilies. 15 Janvier 1946.

So ran the citation on an attractive illuminated certificate. January 1946 had been a significant month for General De Gaulle, for it was then, in exasperation with all around him, that he stepped down as head of state and retired from politics, declaring, *'J'attendrai'*.

By the end of the 1940s things were running rather more smoothly in France (apart from its politics). Although in 1947 prices were still sky-high after devaluation of the franc, (a kilo of dried haricot beans costing F350 instead of F4 and a three-minute telephone call F72 instead of F6), the situation slowly improved. The three-year Marshall Plan, the massive and timely American aid programme for Europe, kicked off in June 1948 and quickly began to make a difference.

Caroline was now receiving some money for her olive crop – with a more than generous share to her overseer. Peggy hired a local couple to run the Castello and this they did well, in an arrangement more or less profitable to all. Their moving in was sealed when they were spotted driving a large pink pig up the lane to the house – *'On s'installe'*.

At Fort Escu the garden was cared for and blooming. In spring, the Czar violets still carpeted the lower terraces and bowls of these long-stemmed little flowers were placed throughout the house. A guest at that time felt it was 'a beautiful spot if ever there was one, where Jean the [new] gardener dug the vineyards below and the kitten romped around in the chapel'.

More British, and some Americans, retired or no longer in uniform and longing to return to the south of France, were reappearing on the coast and occasionally in the hills. Irma, who had guarded Fort Escu so faithfully during the war, married rather suddenly and left to live in the village with her Italian husband. Now Thérèse, a gangling and competent *Normande*, a *bonne à tout faire*, took over the housekeeping, caring for Peggy with eager devotion. Peggy was persuaded to take on a puppy, another black spaniel – a bitch this time. As disobedient and devilish as Dominie, she could never replace him and Peggy made sure that others would feed and exercise her, wishing never to become so attached to an animal again.

Just before Christmas of 1948 her book *Beauty for Ashes* was published. The story of her war years in England and her subsequent return to France, it shot into the best-seller lists. In austerity Britain 10,000 copies sold in the first four days and W.H. Smith at King's Cross and Euston called it 'The Book of the Hour'. 'I feel it's my swan song', Peggy said, 'and only wish it was.'

Renée Goldspink, the most faithful presence in Peggy's life, had by now followed her to the south and realised her own dream of buying a Provençal home. Robert Strauss, the landlord of Many Waters in Sussex, had advised Renée well on her investments, leaving her even more comfortably off than before the war. Her villa, Le Castelet, stood on a hill near the village of Peymeinade. A substantial house with a grand staircase that descended into a large reception room, it was ideal for the parties she loved to give. It is remembered by her guests mainly for the vertiginous drive up to the front door. Renée would remain Peggy's most devoted, if rather lightly regarded, friend.

As for Peggy, she now found herself, with mixed feelings, more and more involved with the running of the other three houses on the hill. She supervised preparations for the increasing number of holiday tenants, organised the gathering of the olives and grapes by the villagers, and the division of the proceeds between owners and labourers. The tiles on the roof of San Peyre had begun to leak, soaking the upper floor, and the great beam in the wall over the entrance gate to the Castello had started to splinter dangerously under the weight of centuries. She seemed to be constantly on call. Was this a business arrangement? Possibly. Was she taken advantage of? Probably. But she was wise enough to refuse accepting power of attorney for the houses: 'NO, not for that family [the Pagets plus Polly] for they all change their minds every two minutes'. Caroline was unfailingly courteous in her dealings with the older woman, agreeing amicably with her various plans and suggestions. There is no doubt that Peggy was a valuable asset in Opio.

People began to have daydreams about buying the Bastide or San Peyre. Sums were tentatively suggested and mulled over – but for the moment indecision reigned. Lady Diana Cooper (who even toyed very briefly with the idea of buying the Castello herself), worked hard at finding tenants. They came and they were interesting.

As early as June 1946, (when Diane was asked to move from the Castello to the studio across the courtyard) the artist Augustus John had been a guest. He painted the 'secret garden' and called it *The Swimming Pool at the Castello, Opio*. In the painting, the moon lilies around the pool are no longer there, but Chateauneuf is glimpsed through trees that have sprung up from the terraces below. The picture shows the little wooden cabin (long gone) where Elisabeth and Peggy camped out for a while when the French soldiers filled their houses in the General Mobilisation of 1939–40.

In July 1949, the young writer Ludovic Kennedy and his fiancée, the dancer Moira Shearer, took the Castello for two weeks. With her Rossetti-like red hair, sensitive face and tall slenderness, Moira Shearer had entranced Britain with her dancing in the film *The Red Shoes*. In his autobiography, *On My Way to the Club*, Sir Ludovic wrote of the Castello as 'an old building on the side of a hill a little way down a lane, and a tiny garden with fig and orange trees and a swimming pool which took all of three strokes from end to end'. One slight disappointment was the lack of fruit on the orange trees in the garden. Sir Laurence Olivier and Vivien Leigh, the previous tenants, had eaten most of them. The Oliviers had asked for the gates of the courtyard to be closed and saw no one during their stay there. They both rested and Olivier painted – although his paintings have not surfaced as did August John's view of the swimming pool. Vivien Leigh had been diagnosed with TB several years earlier, which slowed down her acting career, and their marriage had become less than happy. Perhaps a spell at the Castello calmed, for a while, their troubled relationship. Visitors also arrived from America, including two oil queens, who were quickly named Madame Shell and Madame Mobiloil by the villagers.

When the prospect of selling the Castello hovered for a while, Peggy fired off letters to Elisabeth's contacts in America. Dorothy Kelleher, a friend of Corinne Robinson's daughter, Corinne Alsop, replied in 1948:

I've thought so much of you in that divine place. I can hear those bells, smell the flowers and feel that air. I can understand only too well how you must feel about the possible sale of the Castello and I only wish I could buy it. The horrible truth is that no-one has any free money. America is going full out to arm herself and Europe – and everything is going that way. Even if I were free – or Corinne or any Alsop [Corinne had married and became mother to the journalists Joe and Stewart Alsop] – to go and find peace and live in that divine place, we still couldn't do it on account of taxes. And the very people who have the money to buy it would be afraid of possible war. The Castello is so beautiful and so far – and so much more beautiful because it is so far.

Such was the thinking at the end of the 1940s.

Chapter 32 🌰

ONE WEDDING ...
AND ANOTHER

In October of 1948 Henry, the young new Marquess of Anglesey, married Shirley Vaughan Morgan. Through her father, Shirley was even more closely linked to France than was Henry. With a naval background, Charles Morgan was a novelist, playwright and essayist, his books being better appreciated in France than in England. Devoted to France (he was made an Officer of the *Legion d'Honneur* in the 1930s), he took up his pen to produce pro-French propaganda in Britain during the Second World War and to speak directly, through their newspapers, to the Fighting French. After the Liberation he was asked to read his poem *Ode to France* on the stage of the newly re-opened *Comédie Française* before General de Gaulle, and in 1948 he was elected an *Associé Etranger* of the *Académie des Sciences Morales et Politique* of the *Institut de France*. It was a rare honour for someone from Britain, previously only accorded to Rudyard Kipling.

The new Marquess and Marchioness of Anglesey would lead lives very different to those of their parents. Henry, as well as fulfilling his official duties, became a military historian. Among his works are eight volumes of *A History of the British Cavalry* and the biography of his famous ancestor, *One Leg, the Life and Letters of the 1st Marquess of Anglesey*. While bringing up five children, Shirley became National Chairman of the Women's Institute from 1966 to1969. Sitting on the boards of organisations dealing with broadcasting, museums, drama and dance, she would become a Lieutenant of the Royal Victorian Order and a Dame of the British Empire.

A year later, Caroline followed her brother Henry into matrimony. Sir Michael Duff, the 3rd Baronet and owner of the Vaynol Estate at Carnarvon, was determined Caroline should marry him. He was seven years older than her and they had known each other all their lives, having both been part of the rather *outré* set that revolved around Caroline's cousin, David Herbert. Michael was the boy next door, whose estate, enclosed by a seven-mile stone wall and five lodges, lay a short journey by motor boat across the Menai Strait from Plas Newydd. The only son of Sir Robin Duff and Lady Juliet Lowther, when he was seven he had lost his father in the 1914 retreat from Mons. His mother, the daughter of the 4th Earl of Lonsdale and the Marchioness of Ripon, was frequently absent from his life. Energetically gregarious, a patron of opera and ballet, she was a close friend of Sergei Diaghilev and an admirer of Rudolf Nureyev. Lady Juliet Duff lunched, dined and travelled with her wide circle of friends and acquaintances and is mentioned in virtually every diary and memoir of the period.

Vaynol was an ancient estate with a neglected medieval-cum-Tudor manor house in its grounds, and a new hall built in 1793. The surrounding land had been actively exploited in the eighteenth century by its then owners the Assheton-Smith family, for the lucrative slate extraction that was then in full swing in North Wales. The green slate from the local quarry being particularly sought after. Although Michael had inherited the slate fortune, it was not one that could be sustained. Extraction was labour intensive and, in the post-war years, no longer economic. Already parts of the estate had been sold off. But in 1949, although changing times threatened the Welsh slate industry, these problems were still in the future.

Michael, tall, ramrod straight and handsome, with a distinctive stutter, was the godson of Queen Mary, Consort of George V, and therefore close to, and enamoured of, the Royal Family. He was also a generous, if eccentric, host who strove to re-create the glory days of entertaining at Vaynol, occasionally amusing himself by serving dinner to his neighbours in reverse order, starting with coffee and liqueurs and ending with soup. A brilliant raconteur with a mischievous sense of humour, his particular penchant was to dress up as his godmother, complete with strings of pearls and toque hat, and visit country houses in order to alarm the occupants with an unexpected royal visit. This apparition sometimes appeared in the company of David Herbert, attired as a lady-in-waiting. Michael was capable of witty, pitiless accounts of the appearance and activities of acquaintances and high society. In a letter to Cecil Beaton he describes the guests at Princess Elizabeth's wedding to Prince Philip: 'Queen Mary ... shimmering in the iciest of ice blue, nodding away like a contented potentate, so ancient that she scarce held together; [Queen] Juliana positively crawled in what looked like sea-food, which clung to her hat.' Queen Mary gave the bride, 'a tiara of vast diamonds, and bracelets to match, all from her own collection so that she now is left with only 48 tiaras'. After Queen Mary's death there was concerned talk of the dispersion of her hats – 'My old darling's toques'. Cecil Beaton has some, the Victoria and Albert Museum has others, but some are missing – causing a certain amount of distress.

In contrast to his humour Michael could be waspish and resentful, sulkily harbouring grudges that were not easily dissolved. He had been married before, in 1935, to Joan Marjoribanks, the marriage being annulled rather acrimoniously a year later, so he had been single for over ten years when he finally persuaded Caroline to become his wife. It is not quite clear why she agreed, installed as she was in London with Audry and her own independent life there. After her father's death she had bought a neighbouring house to the one she rented in Chelsea. 56 Paultons Square would now, with her companion Audry Carten, always be her London home. Perhaps it was David Herbert, close to both Michael and Caroline, who encouraged her to take her place as a married woman in society. She had lost both her parents, and Plas Newydd was now home to her brother and his growing family, and this may have left a vacuum. There was no doubt such a move would increase Caroline's security and allow her to become mistress of her own large house. Above all, Michael was relentless in his persuasion for, although his tendencies were homosexual, he was utterly fascinated by Caroline.

They were married in a register office in July of 1949 when Caroline was thirty-six and, whatever the private arrangement between them, Vaynol once again became famous for its hospitality. Over the years, animated weekend house parties included the Queen, the Queen Mother, Princess Margaret and Lord Snowdon (Michael's godson), together with politicians and show business personalities. At the investiture of the Prince of Wales at Caernarvon Castle in 1969, the house played host to eighteen members of royalty. Vaynol was welcoming and full of life and invitations were eagerly accepted.

Five months after their marriage, and at Caroline's instigation, the couple adopted a baby boy, whom they called Charles, after Caroline's father. Caroline was a gentle and loving mother but, in the manner of the day, Charley saw his parents only occasionally, busy as they were with their own lives and frequent entertaining. Michael was a cool and reluctant father. Almost inevitably, as the years wore on, the couple's lives drifted further apart, although they never officially separated. Perhaps Michael felt the child only added to the obstacles that already existed between himself and Caroline, for he became increasingly resentful of them both and, as Charley Duff remembers, 'I think once that started to happen neither of us could really do much right.'

There was a small studio in Caroline's garden at Paultons Square and she had written to offer it to Peggy in time of need. But Polly, not welcoming the thought of Peggy becoming, yet again, part of her life, quickly moved in there and firmly made it her own. Dressed, as usual, in her 'sailor outfits' and Basque beret, she settled down. She had more than done her bit and now had ample time to read her books – and took to smoking a comforting pipe. Sharing the studio with a companion of similar years, she was a ready and competent baby-sitter when needed and, much loved by those around her, she slid into a calm old age.

In the early years of her marriage Caroline continued to rent out the Castello to summer tenants, staying in it herself with her own friends from time to time in order to keep an eye on its upkeep, find out who was doing what with her grapes and olives, and see whether the harvests might be making any money to help support the estate. She came to understand what every Provençal farmer knows: 'There is no such thing as a good olive harvest until it rests in your wallet'.

As with the house in London, this was her other life and it seems Michael was not one of the Opio visitors.

Chapter 33 🌿
ADIEU

Expatriates now returned increasingly to the south of France, to move lightly clad through the warm, scented air, sail the waters of the Mediterranean and try to forget the Cold War and the new enemy – the Soviet Union. An enemy that had, at least, drawn together most of the governments of the western world into a group bonded by foreboding.

Normal social life was returning, although Peggy did not always approve of the visitors to the hill: 'I wish the Castello did not have to be a *Maison de Rapport*, often requiring a red lamp over the door'. At the end of 1948 she began a tradition of giving a Christmas tea to all the children of the village, as well as continuing Elisabeth's interrupted practice of seeing that each child had a small present of his or her own. On these occasions Monsieur Michel, the Mayor of Opio, told the children and their parents that 'not only is she our beloved *bienfaitrice* but now we all consider her to be our *Deuxième Maman*'. Which is how Peggy got her title of *Maman Noel*. As well as the Christmas treats, every afternoon of the school term she took, or sent, a supply of milk to the village school. By those villagers who remember these events, she is always referred to with respect and affection – if with slight awe.

To see in the year of 1949, she gave a large New Year buffet dinner for her friends declaring, 'I'm now completely ruined, financial and nerve strain, but this wild extravagance comes only once a year – it isn't every day a poor man kills a pig.'

As the currency regulations were relaxed, so the house market began to revive. Polly's Bastide was the first to be sold. She had decided to cut her ties with Provence. Peggy was saddened: 'How deeply Polly's going – the last link of the old chain of memories, has stabbed my heart. Though for her I am thankful – nothing for her here save loneliness and memories.' After one or two unsuccessful negotiations the Bastide was suddenly bought by John Fortescue's niece Joyce Carew and her husband Peter. Perhaps Peggy's powers of persuasion had worked once more. It had been on Carew land at Manaton in North Devon that she had first parked her caravan on her flight from Many Waters in 1942. The Carews kept the Bastide for only two years, but it was an important time to be there.

She was less alone. Now friends old and new began to drop into Fort Escu regularly. Although her friendship with Caroline, always rather one-sided, seems to have faded into the background after her marriage to Michael Duff, there were others to fill its place. Renée Goldspink, from her new home in Peymeinade, was always on hand. Other frequent visitors were Lord and Lady Darnley of Cobham Hall in Kent, who owned Les Puits at nearby Roquefort-les-Pins; Colonel Paul St Aubyn, whose family owned St Michael's Mount in Cornwall, and the Duke and Duchess of Leinster whose home was the Domaine de Pigranel near Valbonne. And now Joyce and Peter Carew were, for part of the year, neighbours in the Bastide. A lively afternoon party for the men of the British Mediterranean Fleet, anchored off the coast, greatly enlivened springtime of 1950, Peggy choosing to entertain the ratings rather than the officers.

The days were often busy. Thérèse Vallée, her housekeeper, continued to run the house energetically, if rather eccentrically, and was fearless in dealing with any awkward villagers who crossed her path. But Peggy's two operations of 1947 and her exhausting lifestyle over the years had taken their toll, and her weary body, which had struggled for so long, now found it increasingly hard to cope. The slightest cold blew up into a fever, then bronchitis, and this would become a recurring problem irrespective of the season. Penicillin inhalations in Grasse became the prescription, if not the cure. She became anaemic and more fragile, changing her doctor from one in Antibes to one in Grasse. Car tyres were still so scarce that her Antibes-based doctor on his last visit had suffered three punctures to his old worn-out tyres on the long drive up into the hills. This made the poor man many hours late – too hazardous an arrangement. And now a lawyer took over the handling of the other houses.

But she always rallied. No newborn child in the village went without a pretty layette. Her niece, Jean Beech, her brother Guy's daughter, came to stay, to help out and improve her French. Peggy, wanting Jean to have a good time, took the Grey Pigeon from its garage and drove her, as she reported in a letter to Caroline, to 'cocktail parties, lunches, teas and dinners. To attend those orgies which Elisabeth, Poll and I always avoided!' But Jean quickly learnt the knack of driving in France, was given leave to use the gardener's Peugeot *camionette* and was able to enjoy herself thoroughly until her return home.

Yet another attack of bronchitis badly affected Peggy's over-strained heart, now deemed to be 'enormous'. For a while she was forbidden to climb staircases or hills and prescribed rest and '*beaucoup de chaise longue*'. Obliged to vacate her house for tenants in early summer, she went again to Luchon in the Pyrenees for a cure from their natural sulphurous springs. She had been there once before with her brother, but this time would travel quite alone. On the journey she caught a chill and on her arrival immediately fell ill. In her last book, a gentle potboiler entitled *Laughter in Provence,* she wrote an evocative chapter about the phantasmagoria of a high fever that engulfed her in her hotel bed. While outside her ground floor window the great boulevard of Luchon erupted into the Feast of Whitsuntide, complete with galloping cavalry horses and hunting horns, those she loved, long gone, floated in and out of her fevered mind. It was far from being an unhappy experience.

Over Christmas of 1950 Peggy was again very ill although, as always, the presents for the village children were wrapped and ready under the decorated tree in the dining-room-hallway. By New Year, rallying a little, she was able to follow the Provençal custom of remembering loved ones: for those who have died, a candle is placed on a window sill and lit at midnight. As the church bells of Opio and Chateauneuf rang out the New Year over the valleys below, Peggy lit two candles on her bedroom windowsill: a large one in the centre for Elisabeth, a small one at the side for Dominie, her little dog at rest in the grounds of far away Many Waters.

In early 1951 when 'the mimosa was a gold glory against the dark cypress hedge' outside her bedroom window and the tops of the sur-rounding mountains were capped with snow, her frailty increased. But in the early spring came a present: Eskdale Fishburn, his wife Bunting and their two little boys Dale and Dudley rented the Castello. The fam-ily enchanted her. They came when her garden was unfurling its tapestry of spring flowers, along with the first appearance of her roses. The sound of mating toads, croaking their ardent songs throughout the day and night, began to fill the valleys and plains of Provence, and this gave rise to much discussion and notes on the varieties and their habits: 'Bunting, you MUST have noticed that all males get restive in the Spring!!!' There is a toad that climbs the outside steps to her bedroom door at night: 'Something to be able still, at 63, to attract even toads'.

She was prone again with congestion of the lungs and the Fishburns visited, bringing conversation and flowers and were given in return big bunches of the Czar violets. There was much talk of beauty, male and female, and which men's faces most troubled her sensitive skin when kissed. She nostalgically remembered her husband John's satin-smooth chin, 'each bristle clipped with tiny scissors before shaving'. In spite of her weakness, those months of springtime were relatively happy ones. The Fishburn family brought freshness and cheerfulness, her friends came and went and she had her small staff to care for her.

On 4 March, Palm Sunday, she sent a *bon voyage* letter to the Fishburns at the Castello in the beautiful strong, flowing hand which never changed:

> I hate the idea of your going for I fear I'll never see you again and
> I loved you both at once. Don't pity my loneliness:
> > And this one life, exempt from public haunt,
> > Finds tongues in trees, books in the running brooks,
> > Sermons in stones, and good in everything.
> That's me! But I can '*faire la bombe*' [go on a spree] now and then.

Several weeks later, while preparing herself for the day ahead in her bathroom, Peggy collapsed and died very suddenly. The gallant efforts to be cheerful and amusing were over. Joyce Carew came swiftly from the Bastide and took charge. As she was a member of the family, formalities were quickly dealt with and Peggy was lain in her own small chapel. The following day the funeral service was taken in her garden. As the spring sunshine shone on the profusion of flowers which covered the coffin, filled her terraces and tumbled over the drystone walls, the Mayor gave a sincere and moving address, which, Joyce Carew said, 'almost finished me off'.

He began his speech by referring to Peggy as 'our distinguished guest' (for even after twenty years an expatriate is always an expatriate in Provence). But there were many words of real affection and gratitude for the devoted and untiring work she had undertaken for the children of Provence:

> On her return amongst us we have been able to appreciate she

who, by her good works, found in our misfortune the chance to reveal her generous spirit. We have seen her go from door to door bringing comfort to all. Our children have benefited from her generosity and her good works were not limited to her own community. We see her still, with her car loaded with clothes and food to distribute to children all over the countryside.

Fate has not allowed us to see her honoured, as she who heaped so many kindnesses on us should have been. For it was at the moment when the government of the Republic was about to give her a much merited decoration, that death took from us the one who loved us and whom we loved so well. Madame Fortescue, as we called you in Opio, sleep in peace in the little cemetery you have chosen, opposite the home that you loved so much. Your memory will remain for us a model of generosity and devotion. *Au nom des enfants, au nom de la population, au nom de tous vos amis: Adieu'*

Francis Navella, Elisabeth and Peggy's loved and respected mason, who had looked after their houses for many years and carved Elisabeth's rough hewn headstone, would now carve Peggy's. She had always asked, when she died, that she should be taken to her grave in his familiar small truck and her wish was respected. As the cortège left her courtyard it was greeted by crowds of village children carrying posies of flowers. Led by Joyce Carew and the Mayor and followed by her household, Renée Goldspink, a cluster of other friends and almost every inhabitant of Opio, the procession descended the rue de la Fontaine, through the Quartier St Peyre, crossed the valley floor and climbed the other hill of Opio. Here, in the village cemetery, she was lain to rest on the terrace below Elisabeth.

On her headstone is engraved her badge of honour – the *Croix de Lorraine.* And underneath:

'Maman Noel' of Domaine Fort Escu, Opio
Wife of John Fortescue. Historian of the British Army. 1951
St. Matthew 25:40

The extract from the New Testament reads: 'And the King shall answer and say unto them: Verily I say unto you. In as much as ye have done it unto one of the least of these my brethren ye have done it unto me.'

Chapter 34 🎋

A New Era

Peggy's brother Guy (now Canon) Beech, left his flock and hurried to Opio, arriving the day after the funeral. It was a desperate task to decide what to do with a house which no one in the family could afford to take on. Her niece Fay, who had been close to her, was now in Kenya with her surgeon husband and children, and the rest of the family were settled in their own homes in what was still post-war Britain. It was impossible to distribute all Peggy's possessions as she would have wished, and the difficult decision was made to sell the house along with the furniture. Her flowing tea gowns were packed and sent back to England. The precious pieces of Waterford glass – heirlooms from Peggy's mother – were left to Fay. These had graced Admiral's House in Hampstead, the softly lit alcove shelves in The Domaine at Magagnosc and again at Fort Escu, spent the war hidden in Grasse, and would miraculously survive further transportation to Kenya before returning to rest unbroken in a cottage in an English village.

Much had to be destroyed, more than anyone can now remember, certainly many papers and letters, including personal correspondence, burnt in the garden – where Peggy had once burnt Elisabeth's papers. Much was given away. Helped by Joyce Carew, Guy Beech did his best in very difficult circumstances.

Peggy's housekeeper, Thérèse Vallée, found other employment, and the spaniel, Gamine, went to a home in Grasse. Fort Escu was put on the market with an asking price of £7,000, which included the land and furniture. No sooner had the house been advertised than a Captain Vivian Lloyd rang up and announced, 'I'm buying at once, please tell me where to send the money.' It was bought sight unseen. He was right to be quick. Owing to Peggy's fame as a popular writer, many others enquired about viewing Fort Escu – much annoyed that they were already too late. Captain Lloyd had invented a light tank between the wars – the Cardon Lloyd. He was a fine yachtsman and scarcely lived at Fort Escu, preferring to sail the Mediterranean, and sold the property three years later. This time the buyer was a French musician and fan of Peggy's books. But although the house itself was more or less maintained the chapel was not, and the contents and fabric became neglected. All this changed when a Swiss couple became the new owners in the 1970s and, with much expense and great care, improved the house and sensitively restored the chapel and its contents as Peggy would have wished.

San Peyre had meanwhile been let to long-term tenants, an English colonel and his wife, who failed to understand the traditional arrangements with the local people on the harvesting of the grapes and olives, and this caused much bad feeling among the villagers. News of the problem reached Plas Newydd, causing distress to Henry Anglesey, for his father Charley had been much liked in Opio. Soon after this the house, land and the garage built into the hillside on the hairpin bend below, were put on the market. There was no alternative, as punitive death duties after Charley's death forced the sale. It was bought in March 1952 by a Parisienne, whose daughter and her husband own it still. It is beautifully cared for.

In the year following Peggy's death, the Carews sold the Bastide. They may have felt there was no point in continuing to live there now that Peggy had gone, along with the fact that Colonel Carew was constantly unwell, suffering from gout. The purchasers were two redoubtable Scottish ladies called Miss Sharp and Miss Middleton or, alternatively, Rolls and Bentley – as they had one of each. Sociable, eccentric and strong advocates of the whisky of their homeland, they sold after four years. After two more occupants (Peter Wilson, a Chairman of Sotheby's Auction House, followed by a member of the Reckitt dye family) the Bastide was bought by its present French owners, who have had it for many years, spend much time there and have preserved its rustic charm.

Once the decision was made to sell the Castello, it took several years for Caroline to find a buyer. The old house needed much restoration and must have been a daunting prospect to take on. But in the year Grace Kelly was enchanting everyone at the Cannes Film Festival, two suddenly appeared: Sir Alexander Korda, the film producer (now estranged from Merle Oberon), and an American, Dr Dallas Pratt. Caroline chose Dr Pratt, as Korda had made it known he would use the house for entertaining at the Film Festival and it would become, in many ways, a corporate villa, whereas Dr Pratt undertook to make it a home. In addition he was an American and captivated by the story of Elisabeth – and that is, perhaps, what clinched it.

A New York psychiatrist of great family wealth, Dallas Pratt had passed a rather lonely international childhood. His socialite, much-married mother had owned the Casa Estella on the Cap d'Antibes, so he was no stranger to the Riviera. He spent the summers in Opio and fulfilled his promise of caring for the Castello as Caroline had wished. His partner, John Judkyn, was British and a Quaker, as Elisabeth's family had been. An antiquarian, he and Dr Pratt kept the house in the simple style that suited it best, preserving what was left of Elisabeth's country furniture, basic decoration and books – these last happily having been spurned by Diane van Dommelen.

At this time the two men were also in the process of founding and equipping the American Museum in Britain, at Bath in Somerset, travelling far and wide across the United States to gather up the heritage pieces that were being rejected in post-war America and searching out additions to Dr Pratt's superb collection of antique maps. He grew to love the Castello, appreciating the toads, nightingales and the olive terraces along which the shepherd still passed with his goats and sheep. He felt this had been Elisabeth's creation and he tried to find out what he could about her, talking to the villagers, contacting people in America and making notes to try to fit the jigsaw of her life together. He fitted well into the village, although his role was not that of the bountiful *Mademoiselle du Castello* as Elisabeth's had been, for this was a new era. It was Dr Pratt who, exploring the attics, found Gouveneur Paulding's diaries of his complicated love affairs, written over thirty years before.

As Elisabeth had signed the contract to buy the Castello on a November day in 1921 so, almost thirty-four years later in September of 1955 Caroline signed the house over to Dr Pratt. The 'golden thread' was truly broken. When she returned to England Caroline went into the nursery to see her son Charley, now five years old. 'I wish,' she said, 'you could have seen it all'.

Chapter 35 🦋

AFTERWORD

Although Polly had been older than her other friends on the hill in the 'golden days' of the 1930s, she outlived them all, dying in 1963 in Caroline's garden studio at Paultons Square at eighty-seven years of age. She had tried to have a quiet life and, although fate had sometimes decided otherwise, in the main this had been permitted.

As the years passed, Caroline's partner, Audry Carten, became increasingly unwell and although Caroline always ensured she was cared for, Audry was no longer able to be an active companion. Distancing herself further from Vaynol and Michael Duff, Caroline began to travel, visiting her cousin David Herbert in his house near Tangier in the village of Jamaa el Mokra, on the Nouvelle Montagne. Here David held a bohemian court and, in his other role as *doyen* of the British expatriate community, combined this with amateur dramatics, reading the lesson at the English church and judging local competitions and dog shows.

In Tangier, Caroline met Marguerite McBey, the striking American-born widow of the Scottish painter James McBey. An acclaimed watercolourist in her own right, Marguerite lived in the villa El Foulk on the Vieux Montagne to the west of the town. The two women travelled together, making far-ranging trips to India and East Africa. Marguerite lived to ninety-five, dying in 1999. One of her greatest sadnesses was Caroline's death, from cancer, in The London Clinic in 1976, at the age of sixty-two. Warm-natured and capricious, immensely attractive to others yet full of self-doubt, Caroline's 'moonlight beauty' encircles her memory.

Never reconciled with his adoptive father, Caroline's son Charley would live an independent life, becoming an actor, theatrical historian and lecturer. Michael Duff, busy with civic duties which included the positions of Mayor of Carnarvon and High Sheriff and Lord Lieutenant of Carnarvonshire and of Gwynedd, lived on alone in a Vaynol which became increasingly difficult to maintain. Run-down, reduced in size by the demolition of one wing and maintained by a small staff of faithful servants, the days of sparkling weekend house parties were over. At his death in 1980 the house and grounds were sold to a group of local businessman and Vaynol, as it had been, was no more. It now hosts concerts and festivals and there is a move afoot to restore and preserve the estate.

Renée Goldspink stayed on in Peymeinade for three more years after Peggy's death, then converted to Catholicism, sold her house there and spent the rest of her life in Rome.

In 1945, the matron Miss Williams and her second-in-command Nurse Gladman had closed a, now empty, Sunny Bank Hospital and returned to England for a well deserved rest, re-opening it again a year later. In its last years the hospital continued to care for members of the British and American communities. But, as times changed, the Sunny Bank Anglo-American Hospital drew slowly to the end of its era. Shortly after celebrating its 100th anniversary on 8 April 1997, it was razed to the ground. Here, in place of the building whose first nurses welcomed patients descending from horse-drawn carriages, which had stayed open through two world wars and cared for such as Winston Churchill and Somerset Maugham and had an extension paid for by the oil millionaire Nubar Gulbenkian, stands a small, modern block of flats. But a new Sunny Bank is well on its way to a sort of resurrection. On land bought at the village of Mouans-Sartoux, a little higher and to the west, a state-of-the-art retirement home will be built, bearing its name. It is already over-subscribed and many people look forward to its completion with the same feeling of confidence the little hospital inspired over its long history.

Elisabeth's coastguard cottages on the Pointe de Douane, at Cap Taillat, are still there, romantic ruins standing sideways to their small curved beach. But the room nearest the sea has been restored and is now a tiny art gallery, still with the sleeping platform and pegs for clothes used by Elisabeth and Peggy seventy years ago. The beach scene from the 1968 film *Chitty Chitty, Bang Bang* was shot at Cap Taillat. With the narrow cliff top road now private, the only access by land is along a narrow path by the sea from the town of Ramatuelle. Carved out over uneven rocks and skirting small bays in which, in summer, beautiful young bodies lie naked by the shimmering sea, it leads eventually to one of the places where Elisabeth was most at peace.

Under overhanging trees, in a quiet country churchyard in the shadow of Amberley Parish Church under the lee of the Sussex Downs, there is a corner that is forever America. Elisabeth's uncle Alfred Parrish and his wife Kate lie side by side, with their two daughters, Gladys Huntington and Cora, Countess Emo. But Elisabeth never visited her Parrish family at Amberley nor, it seems, did they ever set foot in Opio.

After various owners, Amy Paget's Château Garibondy at Mougins was bought in 1993 by Count Jean-François de Chambrun and his new wife Raine, Dowager Countess Spencer, the step-mother of Diana, Princess of Wales. The new Countess de Chambrun redecorated the Château before her divorce from the Count two years later.

The dashing resistant Isabel Pell died of a heart attack in 1952, toppling from her chair in a New York restaurant. She was fifty-one.

Many Waters in Sussex was tenanted until 2002 when the Stonehurst estate was sold. The land was split in two and the new owners of the valley pulled down Peggy's old cottage to make way for a dramatic modern house on the edge of the small lakes.

Peggy's grave at Opio is fondly tended by invisible hands. Admirers of her books still come from near and far to weed, plant and pay their tributes. In the grave next to Peggy is Joyce Carew's husband Peter, who died two years later while revisiting Opio, and Elisabeth lies on the terrace above her, so she is not alone. Four of Peggy's books were reprinted by Black Swan Publishers in the 1990s.

The ancient olive mill in the valley below the Quartier San Peyre, once owned by Monsieur Michel, Peggy's 'charming young mayor', is still run by his son, who was also Mayor of Opio for many years.

Dr Dallas Pratt kept the Castello until his own death in 1994. The house then remained unsold for a while, cared for by his estate manager. But it has been lucky, for now a new owner bestows on it all the love and respect this ancient building deserves.

Indeed, the houses on that steep hill have been fortunate. Although the surface may be a little smoother, the rue de la Fontaine is still unchanged. It runs quietly, in the pine-scented air, between the rough stone walls of the houses and the tree shaded grassland, until reaching the point above Peggy's Fort Escu where the panorama of the valleys and hills of Provence is presented like an unexpected gift.

Further Acknowledgements, Permissions and Sources

I am most grateful to the following for permission to reproduce copyright material:

Transaction Publishers, Rutgers. The State University, New Jersey – quotation from Professor Digby Baltzell's *Philadelphia Gentelmen*.

Groton School Archives. Mass. USA – references to letters and school records of Dillwyn and Louis Starr.

Harvard University Archives. Folders (UAIII 15.88.10). Louis Starr – 1903–1904. Dillwyn Parrish Starr – 1904–1908. Monroe Douglas Robinson – 1905–1909. Stewart Robinson – 1906–1909. UAV 874.249. War Records. Louis Starr. Ca. 1921.

From the Theodore Roosevelt Collection, Harvard College Library. Use is by permission of the Houghton Library, Harvard University. Shelfmarks: bMS Am 1785.8(292), bMS Am 1785 (1461), *87M–102 – Extracts from the letters of Corinne Roosevelt Robinson and Stewart Robinson.

By permission of the Houghton Library, Harvard University, and Miss Elizabeth Winthrop on behalf of the Alsop family – Hagedorn Interview with Corinne Alsop, Roosevelt R200.Hl2i.

Dr Betty Boyd Caroli – permission to draw on her biography *The Roosevelt Women.*

The Wallace Literary Agency, New York – reference to *I've Seen the Best of It–Memoirs*. Joseph Alsop with Adam Platt. W.W. Norton & Co. New York. 1992.

Hôpital de Val de Grace. Direction des Archives de Service de Sante des Armées. Carton 251. First World War.

The National Archives. Kew: War Record of 2nd Lieutenant D.P. Starr. 2nd Battalion Coldstream Guards. WO339/52796. PRO REF: 97409.

University of Pennsylvania Archives. Dr J. William White Papers – Quotations and references from Collection UPT 50 W585.

Ms Bay James, Literary executor for the James family – Letter from Henry James to Dr W. White.

Cambridge University Library – Information from the French War Emergency Fund Quarterly Bulletin. Series One: European War 1914–1919. Part 5. Auxillary Services. Reel 10. 26cm. Paris 1917–1919. WRB445

The Archives of the Foreign Ministry, Quai d'Orsay, Paris – Anne Morgan's CARD organisation, from the files of Prime Minister Tardieu.

By permission of the Pushkin Press as the publisher of the English version of *Venices* by Paul Morand – Account of a dinner party at Villa Malcontenta.

The Departmental Archives, Nice, France. Madame Simonetta Villefranque, archivist – French naturalisation certificate of Elisabeth Starr. 6 M 436 Archives Départementales – Contract of the foundation of the Clinic of St. Christophe.

Princeton University Library. Raymond Mortimer Collection. Manuscript Division, Department of Rare Books and Special Collections – Letter from Edward Sackville West. CO271, Box 3, Folders 25–26. Published with permission of the Princeton University Library.

Mr Bevis Hillier. *Young Betjeman* – Quotations on Penelope Chetwode's visit to Opio.

Quote by *Nancy Mitford* from *Young Betjeman* by Bevis Hillier (© Nancy Mitford) is reproduced by permission of PFD (www.pfd.co.uk) on behalf of Nancy Mitford.

The estate of Lady Betjeman – Details of Lady Betjeman's visit to Opio and quotation from her letter to John Betjeman.

The estate of Sir John Betjeman – Quotation of Sir John Betjeman's dedication to Elisabeth Starr.

Mr Jeremy Lewis. *Penguin Special. The Life and Times of Allen Lane* – Reference to John Holroyd Reece.

Clarissa, A Memoir by Clarissa Eden, edited by Cate Haste. Weidenfeld & Nicolson, a division of the Orion Publishing Group – Reference to Caroline Paget.

The Viscount Norwich – Quotations from *The Light of Common Day: Reminiscences* by Lady Diana Cooper and *The Duff Cooper Diaries 1915–1951.*

© The estate of Edith Olivier – Extract from her autobiography reproduced with kind permission of Johnson & Alcock Ltd.

E.H. Shepard Archives, Guildford University – Information and references from the E.H. Shepard diaries of May 1934

The National Archives, Kew. Report from F.C. Stone, British Consulate employee at Monaco, to Anthony Eden. FO369/2789. (K.8598).

Permission of A.P. Watt Ltd. on behalf of The Royal Literary Fund. © The estate of Somerset Maugham – Extracts from *Strictly Personal.*

By permission of Hodder & Stoughton Ltd. *The Fringes of Power* by John Colville – Information on Consul Dodds, drawn from page 368.

By permission of A.M. Heath & Co Ltd – Lines from *The Last Enemy* by Richard Hillary (Copyright © Richard Hillary, 1942); Ms Claire Hopkins, archivist. The Richard Hillary Archives, Trinity College, Oxford – Quotations and references from the Hillary papers and diaries.

Mr David Ross – Permission to draw on his biography *Richard Hillary: The Definitive Biography of a Battle of Britain Fighter Pilot.*

Mr Michael Burn – Permission to refer to his biography *Richard and Mary;*

Manuscript Room. British Library. Winifred Fortescue/Macmillan Correspondence. MSS 55064.

© The Literary Executors of the late Sir Cecil Beaton, 2007 – Quotations from *The Unexpurgated Beaton. Diaries.* Edited by Hugo Vickers.

Mrs Robin Ravilious – Permission to quote from Laurence Whistler's biography on Rex Whistler, *The Laughter and the Urn.*

Solo Syndication/Associated Newspapers – Extract from The Evening Standard of 1939.

Felix Rosenstiel's Widow & Son Ltd. – Quotation by Sir Alfred Munnings, on behalf of the Estate of Sir Alfred Munnings.

Sir Ludovic Kennedy through Rogers, Coleridge & White Ltd – Quotation and information from *On My Way to the Club.*

By permission of the Master and Fellows of St John's College, Cambridge – Quotations from the letters of Sir Michael Duff to Sir Cecil Beaton, held with the Cecil Beaton papers.

All my attempts at tracing the copyright owners of the following have been unsuccessful and I would appreciate any information which would enable me to do so:

The Liberation of the Riviera by Peter Leslie. J.M. Dent, an imprint of The Orion Publishing Group (London). 1980.

[*My Philadelphia Father*]. *The Happiest Millionaire* by Cordelia Drexel Biddle. As told to Kyle Crichton. Sphere Books. London. 1968.

Uncertain Tomorrows. Elsie Gladman. Excaliber. London. 1993.

The Champagne Campaign by Robert H. Adelman and Colonel George Walton. Little, Brown. 1973.

BIBLIOGRAPHY

Adleman, Robert H. and Colonel George Walton. *The Champagne Campaign*. Little, Brown. 1973.

Alsop, Joseph with Adam Platt. *I've Seen the Best of It–Memoirs*. W.W. Norton & Co. 1992.

Anglesey, George Charles Henry Victor Paget, 7th Marquis of Anglesey. *One-leg: the Life and Letters of Henry William Paget First Marquess of Anglesey K.G. 1768–1854*. J.Cape. 1961.

Old Ardinians and Staff. *Ardingly I Remember*. Ardingly College. 1995

Balsan, Consuelo Vanderbilt. *The Glitter and the Gold*. William Heinemann. 1953.

Baltzell, E. Digby (Edward Digby). *Philadelphia Gentlemen: The making of a national upper class*. University of Pennsylvania Press. 1979.

Beaton, Cecil. *The Unexpurgated Diaries*. Editor Hugo Vickers. Weidenfeld & Nicolson. 1961.

Betjeman, John. *Letters. Edited by Candida Lycett Green*. Minerva. 1995.

Biddle, Cordelia Drexel. [*My Philadelphia Father.*] *The Happiest Millionaire*. As told to Kyle Crichton. Sphere Books. New York. 1968.

Borden, Mary. *The Forbidden Zone*. Heinemann. 1929.

Bresson, Jean. *La Fabuleuse Histoire de Cannes*. Editions du Rocher. Monaco. 1981.

Brian, Dennis. *Tallulah, Darling: A Biography of Tallulah Bankhead*. Sidgwick & Jackson. 1980.

Burrin, Philippe. *France Under the Germans*. The New Press. New York. 1996.

Chapman, Dick. *Dallas Pratt: A Patchwork Biography*. Mark Argent. Cambridge. 2004.

Churchill, Peter Morland. *Duel of Wits*. Hodder & Stoughton. 1953.

Clarke, Ida Clyde. *American Women and the World War*. D. Appleton & Co. London. 1918.

Colville, John. *The Fringes of Power: Downing Street Diaries 1939–1955*. Hodder and Stoughton.1985.

Cooper, Diana. *The Light of Common Day: Reminiscences*. Rupert Hart-Davis. 1959.

Cooper, Duff. *The Duff Cooper Diaries 1915–1951*. Edited by John Julius Norwich. Weidenfeld & Nicolson. 2005.

Cushing, Harvey Williams. *From a Surgeon's Journal – 1915–1918*. Little, Brown & Co. Boston. 1936.

Davies, Amanda. *The Good Straight Englishwoman*. Orford Books. Suffolk. 2005.

De-la-Noy, Michael. *Eddy: The life of Edward Sackville-West*. Arcadia. London. 1988.

Diebolt, Evelyne and Jean-Pierre Laurant: *Anne Morgan,Une Américaine en Soissonnais*. Editeur AMSAM. France 1990.

Digiuni, Didier. *Cannes 1939–1945*. Alandis Editions. Nice. France. 2002.

Eden, Clarissa, *Clarissa Eden, A Memoir,* edited by Cate Haste. Weidenfeld & Nicolson. 2007.

Erlanger, Philippe. *La France Sans Etoile: Souvenirs de l'Avant-guerre et du Temps de l'Occupation*. Plon. Paris. 1974.

Faucigny-Lucinge, Jean-Louis de. *Un Gentilhomme Cosmopolite*. Perrin. Paris. 1990.

Fitzgerald, Penelope. *The Knox Brothers*. Flamingo. London 2002.

Fitzgerald, F. Scott. *Tender Is the Night: A Romance*. Harmondsworth. c1934.

Fortescue, John W. *Author and Curator*. William Blackwood & Sons. 1933.

Fortescue, Winifred.

————*Perfume from Provence*. William Blackwood and Sons. 1935.

————*Sunset House.* William Blackwood & Sons. 1937.

————*There's Rosemary ... There's Rue.* William Blackwood & Sons. 1939.

————*Trampled Lilies.* William Blackwood & Sons. London. 1941.

————*Mountain Madness.* William Blackwood & Sons. 1943.

————*Beauty For Ashes.* William Blackwood & Sons. 1949

————*Laughter in Provence.* William Blackwood & Sons. 1951

Friends of France. The Field Service of the American Ambulance Described by its Members. Houghton Mifflin Co. Boston & New York. 1916.

Gladman, Elsie. *Uncertain Tomorrows.* Excaliber. London. 1993.

Hillary, Richard. *The Last Enemy.* Macmillan & Co. 1942.

Hillier, Bevis. *Young Betjeman.* John Murray. 2003.

Hinshaw, William Wade, *Encyclopedia of American Quaker Genealogy.* Friends Book and Supply House Distributors. Richmond, Ind. 1936.

Kennedy, Ludovic. *On My Way to the Club: The Autobiography of Ludovic Kennedy.* Collins. 1989.

Landsberg, A. C. *Tumult and Order – Poems.* Elkin Mathews. London. 1923.

Lenthéric, Charles. *The Riviera, Ancient & Modern.* T. Fisher Unwin. London. 1895.

Leslie, Peter. *The Liberation of the Riviera: The Resistance to the Nazis in the South of France.* Dent. 1980.

Lewis, Jeremy. *Penguin Special. The Life and Times of Allen Lane.* Viking, an imprint of Penguin Books. 2005.

Long, Helen. *Safe Houses Are Dangerous.* Kimber. London. 1985.

Marbury, Elisabeth. *My Crystal Ball: Reminiscences etc.* Hurst & Blackett. London. 1924.

Maugham, W. Somerset. *Strictly Personal.* Doubleday, Doran & Co. New York. 1941.

Mitchell, Percy. *The American Relief Clearing House: Its Work in the Great War.* Herbert Clarke. Paris. 1922.

Morand, Paul. *Venices.* Translated by Euan Cameron. The Pushkin Press. London. 2007

Morgan, Charles. *Ode to France.* Macmillan & Co. 1942.

Mott, T. Bentley and Myron T. Herrick, *Friend of France: An Autobiographical Biography*, Doubleday. New York. 1929.

Nouailhat, Yves-Henri. *France et Etats-Unis. 1914–1917.* Publications de la Sorbonne. 1979.

Olivier, Edith., *Edith Olivier: From Her Journals 1924–1928.* Weidenfeld & Nicolson. 1989.

Olivier, Edith. *Without Knowing Mr Walkley: Personal Memories.* Faber and Faber. 1938.

Ousby, Ian. *Occupation.* John Murray. 1997.

Panicacci, Jean-Louis. *Les Alpes-Maritimes de 1939–1945: Un Departement dans la Tourmente.* Serre. Nice. 1989.

Paoli, Dominique. *Henriette, Duchesse de Vendôme.* Editions Racine. Paris. 2000.

Redé, Baron de. Alexis. *The Memoirs of the Baron de Redé.* Edited by Hugo Vickers. Dovecote Press. 2005.

Repplier, Agnes. J. *William White, M.D. A Biography.* Houghton Mifflin Co. Boston & New York. 1919.

Ridley, Jasper. *My Reminiscences of West Hoathly: 1923–1979.* West Hoathly Historical Society, Sussex.

Robinson, Corinne Roosevelt. *Collected Poems.* Charles Scribner's Sons. New York. 1921.

Robinson, Monroe Douglas. *A Little Boy's Friends*. Charles Scribner's Sons. New York. 1926.

Ross, David. *Richard Hillary: The Definitive Biography of a Battle of Britain Fighter Pilot*. Grub Street. 2000.

Starr, Louis. *Hygiene of the Nursery*. H. K. Lewis. London. 1889.

———— *The Adolescent Period: Its features and management*. H. K. Lewis. London. 1916.

————*The War Story of Dillwyn Parrish Starr*. G.P. Putnam's Sons. 1917.

Stevenson, William Yorke. *To the Front in a Flivver*. Houghton Mifflin & Co. New York. 1917.

Vagliano, Danae. *Hôtes de la Gestapo*.

Van Vorst, Marie. *War Letters of an American Woman*. John Lane. New York. 1916.

Weber, Eugen. *The Hollow Years: France in the 1930s*. Norton. New York. 1994.

Whistler, Laurence. *The Laughter and the Urn: the Life of Rex Whistler*. Weidenfeld and Nicolson.1985.

Wilson, Roger Cowan. *Quaker Relief: An Account of the Relief Work of the Society of Friends, 1940–1948*. George Allen & Unwin. 1952.

Wilt, Alan. F. *The French Riviera Campaign of August 1944*. Southern Illinois University Press. 1981.

Wright, Adrian. Foreign Country. *The Life of L.P. Hartley*. Andre Deutsch. 1996.

INDEX